12/91

To Dad
with love
from
Sally, David,
Rebecca + Katie

ANDY LITTLE
IDAHO SHEEP KING

ANDY LITTLE
Idaho Sheep King

by
Louise Shadduck

The CAXTON PRINTERS, Ltd.
Caldwell, Idaho 83605
1990

Shadduck, Louise, 1915-
Andy Little: Idaho sheep king / by Louise Shadduck.
p. cm.
ISBN 0-87004-340-4.
1. Little, Andrew. 2. Sheep ranchers — Idaho — Biography.
I. Title.
SF375.32.L58S58 1990
338.7'6363'0092--dc20
[B] 90-1818
CIP

Printed, lithographed, and bound in the United States of America by
The CAXTON PRINTERS, Ltd.
Caldwell, Idaho
153146

Upon the 100th anniversary of Idaho,
my home both by birth and by choice,
this book is dedicated to the pioneer
men and women who devoted their lives
to the building of it.

CONTENTS

LIST OF ILLUSTRATIONS

ACKNOWLEDGMENTS

This book about Andy Little and his days in the Idaho sheep industry is more of putting into print the personal memories and anecdotes of many who lived and worked during that great building era of a pioneer western state, than it is of pure history. Any historical purist would tell you that is so.

As a young journalist in the forties, whenever a group of reporters would gather in Boise, I would invariably hear, "If only someone had been able to get Andy Little to talk about his life, what a story that would have made." As my life was enriched by coming to know members of Andy's family, I agreed that it was sad that no one had taken the time to record as much as possible of the building of that remarkable family.

Whether history or personal reflection, this, by the very nature of the passing of that generation (several of them have died during the research and writing process), is bound to be the last conversations about Andy and his time with many. Other elderly have urged me to "hurry with the book, so that I can read it."

There is no great detail on how Idaho's wool industry fit into the world economy, no statistical tables, nor grand panorama of sheep growing from the days of the first flockmaster, Cain, and his brother Abel, nor of Mary and Her Little Lamb, but primarily what I have heard in talking to hundreds who experienced that wool-growing life, or some aspects of it, when Andy was Idaho Sheep King.

Nor will the reader find any bewailing of the passing of the "lonely shepherd" and his sheepdog. There will always be shepherds and guard dogs. No one nor anything has done it better. The job and methods keep changing as the world changes. Pickups and four-wheel drives have replaced most of the horses, but not all. Towns and cities are closer to the ranges, and some are divided by major highways.

The second, third and now, even the fourth, generations are still working with sheep, in their own ways. But there will never again be anything quite like those days. Nor like those people. That is why I had to write the book.

Even so, it could not have been written without the help of several hundreds of people and institutions. Nearly eight years of going through shoeboxes filled with letters, bills, documents, pictures, scribbled notes, interviewing and transcribing. I soon learned that to write of Andy's life, many others must be brought into the story. Thus it became the recounting of an era from the memories of many. The record is as accurate as memories permit.

Most of those people are mentioned in the book. To them I am grateful. To any who are not properly thanked, my apologies. I also extend thanks to U.S. Senators Bob Dole, Jim McClure, Steve Symms and Congressman Larry Craig and their staffs; the Library of Congress; U.S. Forest Service; Tom Richards and Bob DeArmond for providing a winter office; Judy Hodge for transcribing notes and friend Bill Guthrie for editing them and adding cheer when the going got tough; E. Chilton Phoenix and Lloyd Howe for Union Pacific Railway statistics; Attorneys Joy Richards, John Ruebelmann, Heidi Fisher and Raymond C. Givens; Dorothy Kleineche, granddaughter of Bob Aikman, Sr.; Jennie Crawford, Margaret and Alex Struthers in Moffat, Scotland; Don Riley, for giving up a trip to St. Andrew's golf course to take pictures in Moffat; Merle Wells, Judy Austin, Guila Ford, John Yandell and Elizabeth Cox of Idaho Historical Society; Clarence Higer, George Yost, Eloise Anderson, John and Mary Shephard, Brian Reynolds, Ynez Durfee, Mrs. Tom Spofford, Mary Alice Glasby, Dick D'Easum, Carol McGregor Bettis, Dr. Evan M. Kackley; Stan Boyd and Tamara Schneider of Idaho Wool Growers; special thanks to Joy Beckman for making available her interviews with former sheep owners.

There are several without whose help and encouragement this book could not have been finished. From the very beginning Florence and the late Roy Murray and the late Myrn Little provided quiet spots in which to work, sleep, delicious food, and a car with driver to sheep camps and ranches. The chapter on the Basques was aided immensely by Idaho's longtime Secretary of State Pete Cenarrusa, who was always available for answering questions, getting in touch with knowledgeable Basques, and who contacted the president of the Basque Land in our behalf before a visit there; an especial thanks to Brad and Teresa Little for all of the advance research and continuing help; Mike Roach who unearthed material and provided transportation on many occasions; to Harry Bettis, who continued to pull items about his Grandfather out of memory; and to Andy's remaining son, David, and his wife, Geraldine Laidlaw Little, who stayed with the project from beginning to finish, providing information, ideas, finding pictures, telephoning other relatives, locating people to be interviewed and in every way being helpful. David drove the author along the original route his father walked from the Caldwell railway station to the Aikman ranch, providing information and stories along the way. All my effort would have been worth the friendship which has been built with that wonderful family.

Finally, the project is left in the hands of Publisher Gordon Gipson of Caxton Printers, Ltd., who has continued in the path of his remarkable father, James H. Gipson, who determined to make Caxton the foremost publisher of Pacific Northwest history. And succeeded. Gordon's assistant Bobbi Humphries has been most helpful. His brother, Jim, a longtime friend, keeps an eye on the project for old times sake. To all of them, my appreciation and affection.

Louise Shadduck
Lyondale Landing
on Lake Coeur d'Alene

INTRODUCTION

By Bob Dole of Kansas
U.S. Senate Republican leader;
ranking Republican member,
Committee on Agriculture,
Nutrition and Forestry

Hundreds who read Louise Shadduck's book on Andy Little and his life with the livestock and land of Idaho, will have thrilled along with those of us privileged to be in the chambers of the U.S. House of Representatives at a joint session last November when the Polish Patriot Lech Walesa, the shipyard worker from Gdansk, opened his inspiring speech with the words, "We the people . . ." I was deeply moved by what this one individual with an idea, a dream, a desire for freedom for his country, did in lighting the spark that flamed into the battle for freedom still going on in Europe.

We must always remember what a single individual, seized by an idea and an ideal, can do. In an entirely different area, yet with an idea of what he could do in American agriculture was Andy Little. Because of the freedom in which he could operate, Andy Little became one of the greatest American sheepmen of the twentieth century. He brought about modern large-scale ranching, updated management, and systematic breeding.

He also was a lover of freedom and equality. He treated the sheepherders like the good men they were, promoted from the ranks, and showed equal favor to a man's ability, loyalty and hard work, without regard to skin color nor the language he had spoken in the Old World. This book is about sheep and wool forming an important block in the building of American agriculture. It is also about building strong families. And of the western state in which all this flourished—Idaho.

My hometown of Russell, Kansas, appears to be akin to Emmett,

Idaho, and thousands of other small American towns from whence come the sustaining traits of friendliness, helpfulness and the building of extended families, to include employers, employees, friends and neighbors. I say that the farmer's existence now depends upon "faith, hope and parity."

I have known and become friends with a number of Idahoans, including sheep and woolgrowers. All of them have a strength of character and integrity that I am convinced is alive today throughout our land.

Idaho's Centennial Year is a good time to bring out a book which puts us in touch with the several generations to whom this one is closely knit. "We the people . . ." need to be reminded of what went into Idaho, to Kansas, and indeed, into the entire United States, and rededicate ourselves to the ideas and ideals that served our forebears so well.

Senator Bob Dole of Kansas
United States Senate
Washington, D.C.
January 27, 1990

ANDY LITTLE
IDAHO SHEEP KING

C H A P T E R O N E

BAPTIZED IN WILLOW CREEK

DRESSED IN A THICK, DARK WOOL TWEED SUIT, YOUNG ANDY LITTLE stepped down on the dust-blown train platform in Caldwell, Idaho. His senses could have told him this wasn't Scotland, without knowing where he was. The crisp smell of heather had turned to flat clay in his nostrils. The sun was brighter, clouds higher, wind stronger.

Andrew Little was twenty-four years old when he arrived in Caldwell on that unseasonably hot day in 1894. He was well-built with broad shoulders, about five feet nine inches tall, with light-brown to sandy hair and piercingly bright blue eyes.

He shouldered his duffle and walked back toward the baggage car where his dogs Katie and Jim had been kept on the long ride from New York. Steam exhaust swirled dust across the boards and his feet. The wooden station in this small southwestern Idaho town looked as if it was being slowly baked.

Try as he might, he couldn't chase images of green grain and purple heather from his mind, or the month-old scene of his parents bidding him good-bye from the door of the family home near Moffat, in the heart of Scotland's Border Country.

His clear quick eyes were the thing most people remembered about him. They twinkled when he was happy, teasing when he joked, and intense when he thought or studied. He was a fine-looking young man. He already had a full moustache. His complexion was ruddy.

Of the sixty-three million souls then living in the United States, only the couple to whom he had been given letters of introduction, and a few relatives in Idaho, even knew his name. In the years to come thousands of people throughout the country and, certainly, much of Idaho would know, or know of, Andy Little. But that was yet years away. On this Saturday afternoon, after a journey halfway around the world, he was eager to get his dogs, find his directions, and be on his way to the Aikman ranch.

Still marvelling at the different look of the land, Andy was glad to see leafy green trees and shrubs near the station. Peering beyond the trees he saw the sagebrush stretching to the mountains, and wondered if he had done the right thing in coming to the United States. Here he sought his future, his fortune, and a chance to try what he'd dreamed of while herding sheep on his father's lands.

His parents — Andrew senior and Janet Dalgleish Little — had raised their children well. They knew he was prepared for a better life in America. During the years of his youth Andy had herded the family's bands of sheep over the heather-clad hills from Moffat to the trade center of Glasgow.

The Border collies he trained had made many such trips with him. It warmed his heart to know they were with him still. Those dogs had helped him to get the sheep to the Glasgow market when he left on the final drive.

"Son," his father had said, "you are to take the dogs and the money from the sale of this band, and pay for your passage to Idaho. Other men who have gone from here seem to have met with success in that faraway place. When you get to Caldwell, look up a merchant by the name of Charlie Doane. He will give you directions to the Aikman sheep ranch somewhere near the small town of Emmett. You will find a herding job there."

Andy learned that getting the sheep to Glasgow was a small part of the immense journey. He felt wealthy, knowing that the proceeds from the sale, and the dogs were his. The feeling did not last long.

His fortune was suddenly depleted when he paid his passage to New York. Nearly all that was left was paid out for tickets for himself and the dogs from New York to Caldwell. Now, as he felt in his pocket to be sure the money was there, he counted once again the two remaining dollars.

When he walked from the car which had been his home for five days and nights, he felt no loss nor regret. From it he had seen vast country with changing scenery, many small towns and a few large cities, but it had been a dirty, dusty ride after they left Chicago. He was happy to be out in fresh air, and anxious to be on his way to the Aikman ranch.

The station master approached: "Are you new here, son?"

"Aye. From Scotland. And I need to get my dogs. I also have a letter for Mr. Charles Doane. He is to give me proper directions to my next stop."

"Charlie Doane? Why, he's a merchant," the station master replied. "Let me take you to him."

The station master liked what he saw in the young Scot: courtesy, deference, respect. He helped Andy reclaim his sheepdogs. Then he asked Andy to wait while he finished his reports on arriving and departing passengers and cargo. Then he would take Andy to see Charlie Doane, to get the information he needed to find the Aikman ranch. The ranch was a little more than half the distance from Caldwell to Emmett, where Andy would make his home for much of his life.

Andy had decided that Robert Aikman was well known indeed when a buyer at the Glasgow market told him to look up Aikman, and offered a letter of introduction to Charlie Doane. Both Aikman and Doane had helped Scots find work in the new land. The Glasgow buyer had known Andy from previous visits, and was impressed with the quality of the animals which came from the Little farm, and with the way Andy handled them. So, he volunteered the letter to Doane, and assured Andy that "Scotch Bob" as he was known in Idaho because of his brogue would be pleased to have this sturdy young man as one of his helpers. He had not sealed the letter, and Andy read it time and again on his long voyage by steamship and train.

As Andy waited for the station master to complete his records, he released the dogs from their box-cages. Long cooped-up during the train journey from New York and Omaha, they were all over him at once, barking, jumping onto his knees as he knelt to pet them, and licking his face. Although he wouldn't admit it, he almost felt like licking their faces back. He was as joyful to be with them as they were to look upon his familiar ruddy features. While he had learned not to make a pet of a dog expected to herd the sheep, he had also been taught as a boy that a herder without a good dog might just as well plan to go into some other type of work.

The station master approached, his face in smiles as he viewed the happy reunion scene. Seeing the smile, Andy felt it was acceptable to ask if he might take the dogs with them on the walk to Doane's store. It was. The four of them started the short walk.

As they left, so did the train. It was continuing to Portland, Oregon, and Andy watched it pull away. He could not know that within a few years he would be shipping hundreds of thousands of pounds of wool each year from his own flocks, and eventually one million pounds in a single year, aboard that very line. At this point, he was happy to wave a good-bye sign to the departing train.

Andy was excited at finally approaching the man who was to direct him to his new home. He was beginning to realize that his woolen suit was more clothing than he needed on such a warm day. As soon as he was on his way he planned to shuck the coat. He wished he could do it as they entered Doane's grocery.

While gold and silver had marked the beginning of Idaho and a prime mover in its rapid growth, by the time Andy arrived it was primarily an agricultural state. Twenty-one million of its fifty-three million acres were plowed for the growing of crops. Seven million acres were devoted to grazing land for the sheep and cattle. Two-thirds of Idaho's residents were involved in farming and related work. Sheep raising was coming into its own and the young man seeking directions was to be a giant figure in its growth. For the moment, however, he was bent on moving toward his destination.

Andy carried the letter to Charlie Doane, a merchant and grocer. The letter expressed the certainty that the Scot would be reliable and hard working. In addition, Doane's Scottish friend wrote that Andy "got along well with people, as well as the sheep." He knew that both would be important to Aikman on his large spread. The letter asked Doane to be kind enough to direct Andy to the stagecoach that would take him and his dogs to Emmett, from which he was sure Andy could find his way to the ranch.

Charlie Doane was genuinely happy to see Andy, and told people that he "liked the cut of the young man." Of late, he had been helping an increasing number of young Scots to find their way in the land new to them. But he frowned when Andy said he wanted to leave immediately for the Aikman and asked directions.

"I'm sorry, lad, but the Emmett stage has already gone. There is no stage now until Monday. Nothing runs on Sunday."

When told that the stagecoach fare was three dollars, Andy knew he was a dollar short. Nor did he have money for food or lodging that night.

"How far to walk?"

"About twenty miles if you take the Willow Creek route. Also the way of the creek is cooler on a day like today."

Reckoning he could hike the twenty miles before deep dark and that it would provide exercise which the dogs sorely needed, he asked Dunning to draw him a rough map and said, "I'll walk."

With admiration in his glance and a shake of the head, Doane wished him well. Once again, two men and the dogs walked to the station. Andy took off his heavy jacket, rolled it into a bundle, stowed in his duffel bag, shook the hand of the station master, whistled to the dogs and walked out of Caldwell.

It was less than a mile from the station to the rim of the Bench overlooking the thousands of acres making up the Boise valley. He paused for a few minutes, amazed at the five and six feet heights of the silver-blue sage that covered the scene. He wondered for a moment if ever he were to see the clear creeks, rivers and freshets which were so much a part of Scotland. Little did he then realize that one day, not too far in the future, his own sheep would be grazing over much of the land below him.

The road from Caldwell turned south and Andy, as directed by the map, walked east to Willow Creek, which he was to follow almost to the Aikman. With the creek he passed just west of the village of Middleton and along the banks, enjoying the trees and brush making up the wooded passageway. The path had been chosen many times before by those who enjoyed the birds, an occasional beaver, the sunshine and the rain.

Much as he enjoyed the greenery, he was disappointed at the

muddiness of the creek. He had thought he would see the clear, cool water, boiling over the great rocks as he had in Scotland.

Many years later, when he described this walk to his children, he would tell of the difference between the "clear streams of Scotland and the mud of Willow Creek." By the time he told the story, of course, he had found many clear Idaho streams. But Willow Creek, the first he saw, was to leave an indelible mark.

As he rounded a bend he heard a man shouting at his sheep and his one dog. Both were having a bad time in getting across the turbid waters. Unseasonably warm weather had melted the snow in the mountains. As the dog would run to one side, the sheep on the other side would turn back.

Andy gave a quiet command, "Katie, Jim, bring them by." Both dogs went at their task with a leap. This they liked. This is what they had been born and trained to do.

Andy waded after his dogs. "You do whatever has to be done to move sheep," he always said. The dark water softened the hard leather shoes, filled his woolen socks with native mud and soaked his woolen pants. Bright clay, still yellow with minerals, waiting for life to make it rich, dirtied Andy's clothes, while the water soaked his skin.

In a matter of minutes the sheep were on the other side of the creek and the herder, an older man, thanked Andy. He also offered to buy his dogs. Andy thinking of the meager two dollars in his pocket and not knowing when he was to receive more finally agreed to sell one, but could not let the other go. He decided to sell Katie.

A good herder was never without a dog. If possible, he owned two. As he saw Katie remain with the sheep and a stranger, he felt that perhaps he had been possessed by the dog. Already he knew he would get another dog as soon as possible.

As he walked across the valley, he found that Willow Creek traversed the basin which also carries a part of the Boise River. The creek itself flows through miles of sagebrush, bordered by thick willows. The basin is laced by ridges, mesas and few people.

Walking along the creek was not so hard, with little underbrush. Later he learned that this had been a thoroughfare for the Indians.

Once in a great while, he would spy a deep hole in the turbid water that seemed to clear. Already it was obvious this valley did not receive anywhere near Scotland's rainfall, but it should be good sheep country.

Andy was intrigued with the strange mountain that changed appearance every few miles. At one point, he could have sworn it was the body of a reclining or sleeping woman. Later, he was to learn that it was named Squaw Butte for a variety of reasons. Across the valley was another mountain, not so high but coursed with wagon ruts and trails. Freezeout Hill. Both were to become landmarks in his life.

It was dusk by the time he crossed the valley and moved toward the Aikman ranch. The entire land was amazing to him. He had tarried longer than he had thought. He was not yet aware that parts of the middle Rockies, the Great Basin, the Columbia Plateau and the Northern Rockies were in Idaho. The Snake River Plain, over which he was walking, was stretched from Yellowstone Park country westward to Weiser, along the Snake River which formed the boundary between Idaho and Oregon.

He was to come to know most of that land intimately in the coming years, and to send hundreds of thousands of sheep grazing across its vast acreages. Squaw Butte is a plateau that breaks abruptly into a series of sharp ledges and canyons and it continued to fascinate him. He would stop and make a complete turn to view this expanse of land, hills, mountains and valleys. It intrigued him that there was seemingly no spot from which he could not see mountains if he made a complete turnaround.

Finally leaving Willow Creek, he followed rutted wagon tracks. The sage and the bitter brush were anything but stunted, indicating good soil if cared for. There was so much of it, stretching across the valley to the foothills. He wondered at the immensity of it.

Here he was, an immigrant youth, with but a dog and few dollars to his name. What could have been his thoughts? Was it possible that he even dreamed that one day much of that land he walked would belong to him? Did he envision the many ranches which would belong to him dotting the lands here and beyond this horizon?

Of one thing we can be sure. He knew that he would be in the sheep business. For if any young man knew how sheep were born, fed and grown, can be trained, herded and their needs for survival, that young man was Andy Little. It was not until years later that it would be widely said of him that no sheepman did a better job of training workers and instilling in them the desire to be the best they could at their tasks.

Soon he saw the soft light of a kerosene lamp through the window of the Aikman home. Eager as he was to see his new employers, in the falling darkness he turned once more to view the way he had walked.

It was not the wild, wet green beauty of Scotland. But it was sunny and pleasant with foothills that must be deep in grass. And surely fruit and grain would grow well. He had seen evidence that water had been taken by ditches to the land.

He straightened his shoulders, took off his cap, turned and whistled lightly to the collie and hurried toward the lighted window. The Aikmans were still at the kitchen table, just finishing their supper, when they heard him shout, "Halloo!"

Both Bob and Mim Aikman rushed to the door and had it open when he cried, "Is this the Aikman?"

"Yes it is. You have arrived."

"I am Andrew. Andrew Little and I have a letter for you from Scotland."

Mim Aikman hurried to prepare his supper, as she explained that they had not expected him until Monday. "Did you walk all the way from Caldwell?" Bob asked.

"That I did. And it was a good walk for the dog and me. It is a big country."

While Andy ate and told of his journey from Scotland, across the United States, and the walk from the train station, Mim fed the collie. Bob explained that Willow Creek had some fairly heavy floods and that this was one of the springs for it. Aikman also explained that the names of a couple of the mountains he had seen were Schaeffer and Squaw Buttes and of the foothills known simply as the Boise.

Later those foothills were to carry the name of the Highlands from Andy's Highland Livestock and Land company. To the right of Squaw Butte was land which turned out to be Andy's summer ranges, in the Payette River drainage.

To the left, Aikman said, was the head of Crane Creek and Big and Little Willow, both of which run into the Payette River. He said there were many arguments between those who lived along the Willow and those along the Crane Creek drainages: "There is a saying that 'Willow Creekers won't stand up for the Crane Creekers!' "

Noting that the young man was nodding, but attempting to stay awake, Bob decided he'd save the story of Squaw Butte for another evening. Mrs. Aikman showed him his room and provided a small rug for the collie in the corner of the room. "This is only until he realizes his home is here," she said. "Tomorrow he will find himself a spot outside."

Bob stood in the doorway and said, "Tomorrow is soon enough to talk of your herding. Tonight, you need to sleep."

Andy's dreams were of his long walk, of all that he saw, and this huge new land. And perhaps he dreamed of an empire, more land than a nobleman might own in his native Scotland, grazed by his sheep, peopled by his friends.

C H A P T E R   T W O

HERDING THE AIKMAN

UNLIKE SCOTLAND, WHERE SUNDAY WAS A DAY OF CHURCH attendance for Andy, most of the day was spent with Bob Aikman walking miles over the ranch, inspecting the buildings and learning the lay of the land. It was not that the Aikmans failed to bring their Scots Presbyterianism with them when they arrived in Idaho, but that they were miles away from any church.

Yet even Scottish tradition excuses the shepherd from church. In the old days, deceased shepherds were buried with a lock of wool tucked in their hands. The wool showed Saint Peter that this Christian was a shepherd, and his long watches over his flocks explained his many absences from Sunday services.

Despite the ready-made excuse, Andrew and his seven brothers and two sisters had a strict religious upbringing. There were prayers every morning and evening, and church, usually several services, each Sunday. The parents and the smallest children would ride in a trap, a light two-wheeled carriage, pulled by a pony or small horse. The older children walked the five miles from the farm to the Moffat church and back. No unnecessary work was done on Sunday.

Social life was non-existent. Occasionally a call would be made on neighbors. On market day the parents would go to the nearest town, either on foot, horseback, or pony and trap.

Andrew's maternal grandparents, John and Ann Beattie Dalgleish, had lived on a remote sheep farm in a quiet valley which had been tenanted by his forebears for countless generations. The farm was Potburn in the Enrick district, a few miles from Moffat Waters area where Andy was to be born and reared.

The entire district is a part of the old Border Land, and has been celebrated in song and legend as a part of the ballad lore of Scotland. It is a connecting link between the land of the great poet, Bobbie Burns, on the west, and the land of Sir Walter Scott and James Hogg, writer and poet, on the east. Each of this illustrious trio left his mark on many places in the area that today's visitors find much to visit and to learn.

The district contains some of the most sheer and sublime hill scenery in Scotland's Southern Uplands. Ranges of hills on three sides are generally rounded and pierced by glens and ravines. The hills vary in color from vivid green to a dusky brown. The dales or hollows are lengthy and parallel the course south. Annan is the central stream, with Moffat but 300 yards from its east bank. The nearest of Moffat Waters is only two miles away. The streams unite two-and-one half miles below Moffat retaining the name of Annan, which discharges into Solway Firth about twenty-six miles south of Moffat.

Andy's thoughts of Sundays not only included the family farm at Sailfoot near Moffat, where members of the Little family had lived for generations. He thought also of his mother, Janet Dalgliesh, going to Sailfoot as a bride. She had cold water in the house, but no other labor savers. She and his father, Andrew Sr., had eleven children, one of whom died in infancy.

There were always two full-time, living-in maids, who would go home for a weekend once every six months. That visit was to take their wages to their parents. Any spare time, of which there was precious little, was spent in knitting or sewing for the children or for themselves.

Periodically a dressmaker appeared at the farm and would stay for a week, or longer, and make clothing as required for the family. Twice a year dances were held for all the workers in the valley. Other than those events, life was a repetition of that lived by each of them in their younger days.

Seven of the eight sons were to emigrate to the United States because their father could not afford to put them on farms in the Uplands. Now, Andy was being shown about the Aikman by a man who was to play a pivotal position in his life.

It had to be a Godsend for the young man to be put onto the

Andy's grandfather was William Little of Moffat, Scotland, one of a long line of sheepmen. His cane could be used as a shepherd's crook.

ranch of Robert Aikman Sr. There was much to learn from the canny Scot who had been born in 1865 at Melrose, near the birthplace of Sir Walter Scott, the same general area as Andy's home.

Although his formal schooling ceased at age twelve, he continued to read, study and learn and Scott's writings were among his favorites. Robert was from a large family with a small income and his formal schooling ceased when he hired out as a shepherd boy. His father, James, was also a shepherd, who lived and died in Scotland.

Workers and friends remember "Scotch Bob," as he came to be known through his burr and rolling Rs, and his reaction to anyone complaining about hard work and small pay. "Aye, and I well remember my first thirty shillings. That would make about $7.50 in American money then. It was my pay for a full half years's work."

As his children were growing, he pointed out to them, and later to Andy, that life at that point, seemed to offer little prospect but toil and poverty. But he was determined that he would not return to the family home and be an added burden in crowding a house already filled with ten children. So he continued to follow the sheep until, in 1882, he had saved enough money to emigrate to North America.

Aikman's first location was in Canada. He remained there but six months, working in a boiler factory. Soon realizing that this was not the work he had left Scotland to do, he made his way across the border and thence to California. There he soon found a sheep ranch and began to work. It took but little time for the ranch owner to note his diligence in work and his knowledge in handling equipment, dogs and sheep. Thinking if Aikman was that good in what he was doing, that he could well handle greater responsibility, the owner sent Aikman to Nevada to purchase a band of sheep and to herd them in that general area.

Catastrophe struck soon after. A lesser young man would have given up when half the herd was lost after eating poisonous weeds. Not Bob Aikman. He moved the remaining sheep to grazing land near Succor Creek which runs between Idaho and Oregon.

Again, putting into practice the self-denial, hard work and painstaking care he had learned as a boy in Scotland, he managed to save enough money to buy into the business. He was connected with that operation for four years, during which he became acquainted with a few Idaho sheepmen and their methods of operation, their living places, and grazing areas. They were helpful in showing and teaching Aikman until he felt confident enough to sell his interests.

He then purchased the Willow Creek or "Scotch Bob" ranch northeast of Emmett and north of Boise, which has now been known for many years simply as The Aikman. The ranch was headquarters for his eminently successful and extensive sheep business for the next sixteen years. So shrewd and successful was he that he rapidly accumulated much wealth.

"Scotch Bob" and "Mim" were no spring lambs when they met and wed, but theirs was a solid and good marriage. To them was born one son, Robert Jr., and one daughter, Agnes.

Aikman related much of this to Andy as they walked and looked over the ranch that Sunday. It was into this successful atmosphere and activity that young Andrew Little began his American sheep career. Aikman took a warm and keen interest in this ambitious young Scot. Doubtless he saw much of himself in the youth's desire to succeed and willingness to work long and hard hours to become so.

Aikman told Andy that his first job would be herding sheep on the range, further up on Willow Creek, away from the ranch. He had learned herding well in Scotland and knew his responsibilities to the sheep in his care. He lived in the camp, as did the camptender or foreman. The boss would tell the camptender where to place the camp, and Andy kept his sheep in the vicinity, herding on all sides of the camp, to keep the grass abundant.

He knew that the sheep required tranquility, lots of grass and water. Through good herding, he provided all three. Within three or four days, the camptender would show up again and pack up and move the entire camp. The packs would be loaded on mules and moved to greener pastures. Perhaps five miles, perhaps less, always depending upon the quality and quantity of the graze.

The camps are set out year after year in much the same way, often in the same spot as the year before. Camp is nearly always located on a mountain or hillside from which the shepherd can watch his flock or band of sheep in the valley below. Also, a good spring of water is required. A good tender is capable of handling three camps at one time.

Residents of Moffat are still reminded of the importance of the wool and sheep industry. In the center of Main Street is a bronze statue of a curly-horned and long-wooled ram atop huge boulders from the surrounding hillsides.

Pen Basin, with mountains all around it, was said to be one of the best grazing ranges in Idaho. Andy liked taking the sheep to Pen Basin. As the sheep munched the thick, green and nutritious grass, he had time to think of the future. He thought that soon he might become camptender, or even the riding boss.

The riding boss can be responsible for as many as six bands at one time. That was a fine job. He helped the camptender count the sheep every two or three moves. This was done to be sure they were keeping together, safe from the marauding coyotes, and so that none are lost. He had several "markers" for each band. "Markers" are those sheep with black spots, sometimes called "Pinto" sheep.

In those days when he herded for The Aikman, there would be 1200 ewes to each band. In his early days of herding, each ewe ordinarily produced one lamb. Later, as he developed his flocks, establishing better breeding and feeding methods, the good ewes produced twins. Some even reached a stage of fertility where triplet lambs were not unusual. Sheepmen keep those ewes which produce more than one lamb. As they "mouth them out" in the fall of the year, inspecting their teeth to see if they can still chew the grass well enough to be kept another year, there is joy in camp for each twin or triplet mother with teeth strong enough to be kept for another year.

It has been said that the Basque sheepherders could communicate with the sheep. So it was with Andy. He understood the needs of the sheep as well, he understood the causes for which they were created. Some saw only animals that munched, trampled and eroded grasslands. But Andy saw a complete factory, producing lamb, mutton, tallow, blankets and woolen clothing to keep a million bodies fed and warm.

He also sensed that there was history and money to be made in the sheep business in this new state of Idaho. Gradually, he came to know that he wanted to be a part of it. No one knows if and when his dreams encompassed just how great a part he was to become. But everyone who knew him also knew of his drive and ambition, and that he had the intelligence to put all together in a way that worked.

The money was to become important, but Andy knew early on that there was something more important. The land. He thought of what was to be done with the land in aiding the rush toward civilization of the valley and Idaho. The land and its various types, location and use was of prime meaning to him.

Yet, he had no desire to see the Emmett valley grow great in population. He liked the small village and the people who lived there. He thought of living there eventually.

Andy had not drawn any of the money that he earned. He had no need for it. He was clothed and fed. He would save his money.

Along with the shepherding and work in the camps, Aikman seemed to find more and more for him to do around the main ranch. He remarked to Mim that Andy was adept at whatever he asked him to do. He felt that one day he could manage a ranch of his own.

Before the end of his first year as a shepherd, Bob Aikman stopped Andy one day in the ranch yard and told him that he had enough salary due to buy one-half a band of sheep. "You can have the salary, if you want, or I will give you a half-band of sheep. If you take the sheep, I will sell the other half on a note and you will have your first full band."

Aikman went on to explain that Andy could take the note for the second half, and go down to Dow Dunning's bank in Caldwell and borrow sufficient funding on the note. Andy mentally calculated that he would need a herder for those 2000 sheep.

There should be a camptender. And there would certainly be equipment, salt, hay and groceries to buy. He thought it would take some time before he could pay back the note. "I'll think about it," he told Aikman.

He decided to saddle his horse and ride down to Caldwell and talk to Dunning. He thought some of taking the money due him and making a trip back to Scotland to see his mother, brothers and sisters who were still there. Still, it would be a grand thing to own his own band.

His mind kept running over and over again all the possibilities of either move. Stay or go. Go or stay. Even as he rode his horse towards Caldwell, he didn't realize how thoroughly he had been immersed on that first day in Idaho as he waded in to help the shepherd get his sheep across the flooding creek.

In the waters of Willow Creek, he had been baptized into that hardy breed known as the American Westerner. The future would likely be rugged, tough, and full of problems. Yet he had known little but that thus far.

Without realizing it, he had pledged his course without a verbal vow, and there was no turning back. As he tied his horse in front of the bank, one of the places where just last spring he had gone to meet the manager, he hoped that the correct decision would flash across his mind in so definite a way that he would have no doubts, no regrets.

While herding through the meadows and over the hills, he had a vision of what it could mean to be a sheepman on his own. He thought, "It would not be for only me, but for a wife and the family I someday will have." But, now, he was indecisive. It was a giant step.

He thrust his hands into his coat pockets, drew out a pouch of tobacco and filled his briar pipe. As he drew on the pipe and exhaled the smoke, he paced back and forth in front of the bank. He was thinking very hard on what he was to do.

Soon the clerks and tellers noticed the young man pacing in front of the bank. They called the manager and asked, "Who is he and what is he thinking of doing? Do you suppose he has a pistol in his pocket? Does he plan to rob the bank? Should we call the Sheriff?"

No intuition, no brilliant thought came to Andy's mind.

"Well, in I go. They likely won't take a chance on a lad who has so little. If so, back to Scotland I go. By any chance they loan me the money, I'll be in my own business. Dow Dunning helped me once and he may again."

He knocked the dottle out of his pipe and placed it back in his pocket, straightened his shoulders, thrust open the door and marched up to the first teller, shoved the sheet of paper in front of him, and blurted, "I'd like a loan on this note. Mr. Dunning knows me."

The teller said, "Thank God. We are relieved. We have been

watching you and thought for sure you were planning to rob the bank."

This incident became one of Andy's favorite stories on himself and he told it often. Today when a group of old time sheepmen and women get together, the story of Andy being taken for a prospective bank robber still comes into the conversation.

On the day of his greatest glory, not Bonnie Prince Charlie could have been happier, ridden his horse harder nor made grander plans than did Andrew James Bell Little, Jr., as he rode from Caldwell back to the Aikman. He had the loan. Often while he herded the band he had thought of what he would do with the money when his account for the year was settled.

It was then Andy decided he liked the plan whereby a rancher settled up with his men once a year. The owner deducted funds advanced for personal purchases and paid the remainder of the year's salary in money or sheep. Food, necessary clothing and herding equipment were provided by the owner. This was accepted practice.

But Scotch Bob Aikman had done Andy much better. He settled Andy's accounts before the year was over, and he had given him a note on the remainder for a full band of sheep. While herding and working about the ranch he had thought of returning home to see his mother and the rest of the family. And there had been no opportunity in Idaho to meet any young women his age, but he knew one or two in Scotland. No one special, but one of them might become so, given time enough to become better acquainted.

Then, at other times, he had also thought how cheap it was to buy good land in Idaho. He thought how good it would be, once his account was settled, to buy a bit of land. "And sheep, too," he thought. "I could start my own band."

Now he had the sheep. And he would have the land. Bob Aikman's generosity and the banker's trust had changed the course of his life. He would stay in Idaho. And he would raise sheep.

C H A P T E R   T H R E E

"A PLUS FOR THE WORLD"

"SHE WAS A PLUS FOR THE WORLD." THAT'S THE WAY BOB CRUICKSHANK of Ontario on the Oregon border adjoining Idaho, describes Adis Little, his aunt, nearly a quarter of a century after her death. That his aunt had made a definite imprint upon his life was evident as he spoke forcefully, yet lovingly, of the woman who had helped him get a college education: "She was the banker when I got my first car . . . Always there when needed."

Adis Little was five feet five inches tall and remained a trim 135 pounds most of her adult life. She was a handsome woman with classic features, deep brown eyes and black hair. So erect was her carriage that many later described her as taller than she was. Dignified in demeanor, she had a keen sense of humor which made her a popular woman.

Agnes McMillan Sproat, nicknamed Adis, was born in Scotland to Robert and Elizabeth McMillan Sproat. Other children included Robert Jr., Hugh, David, Rex, Jean (Cruickshank), Betty (Hitt), and Mary (Campbell), the latter remaining in Scotland when others came to the United States.

Elizabeth's brothers, John and Thomas McMillan, also came to Idaho in the 1880s and were early-day movers and shakers and builders in southwest Idaho. The daughter of a third brother, Anthony, was Mary, called "Mim." She married Robert Aikman and they established the Aikman ranch on Willow Creek near Pearl. It was this ranch where Andy found his first home and job in Idaho. The Aikmans had one son, Robert, who married Dorothy Bevington. Their daughter, Agnes, married James Spofford.

Soon after his arrival in Idaho, Andy came to know Hugh Sproat, who was working with his uncle Tom McMillan on a sheep ranch on Dry Creek. Later McMillan found another Creek so much like it, that he called it "Ditto." When Tom's brothers and sisters arrived from Scotland, he bought a second ranch on Ditto Creek and later purchased the Slater Creek ranch, so all would have a place to live and work.

Andy and Hugh became friends. When Andy went back to Scotland in 1901, following the death of his father, to be with his mother, Bob Aikman asked him to visit the Sproat family at Lennox Plunton dairy farm in Kirkcudbrightshire, about fifty miles from Moffat. Andy did this immediately after visiting his own mother.

As he approached Plunton dairy farm where he noticed the Ayrshire or Galloway cattle, he also noted an attractive, dark brown-haired girl turning hay. He paused for a few minutes to admire her deftness with the fork and seemingly effortless lifting of forks full of hay and tossing them onto the mows. She was not too tall, but must have been very strong. She had the lovely and clear skin that seems to be a part of the nature of Scotswomen. Andy suddenly realized he was staring as she turned and gave him a smile.

The day Andy rode up to the farm, sister Mary was ill and Adis had taken her place in the field. Andy halted and watched the lovely young woman pitching hay with a strength that was impressive. He was so impressed that he returned to Plunton Farm the following weekend.

It being such a distance, his mother felt that there must be an unusual attraction. There was. On his second visit, by the time he was told that Adis was only working in the hay because Mary was not feeling well, he was in love.

She told him that ordinarily Mary was what was called "the outside girl" and "I work in." Jean McMillan Cruickshank, an accomplished pianist and the musician of the family, explained that each family member had a specialty. Adis' sister, Mary, worked outdoors and Adis was a trained cook.

It made no difference to Andy. Adis felt the same way about him. Andy told of how he had been able to acquire his bands of sheep and many acres of land in a short time. When it was time for him to return to Idaho, they had "an understanding."

For the rest of their life together, they both joked of their first meeting. Adis would tease Andy about thinking he was going to get a field hand only to find he'd married a cook and housekeeper. Andy chuckled as he watched her deftness with any kind of work—indoors or out.

Jean Cruickshank also remembered that when Andy visited the Sproat home in Scotland he told of all the wonders of America, the freedoms for everyone, the opportunities to become wealthy if one were only willing to work. A servant girl was listening and finally said, "Oh, the lees [lies]!"

It was in 1903, according to Jean Cruickshank, that the Robert Sproats took six of their children, Robert, David, Rex, Betty, Jean and Adis and sailed on a Cedric Steamship Line vessel from Liverpool, England, for America. Mary had married a Campbell and remained in Scotland.

Jean remembered celebrating her seventh birthday on June 7 aboard the ship, with her brother, David, observing his fourteenth the preceding day. She remembered a sailor picking her up and holding her over the rail to watch the ocean roll. "I remember of feeling that he would not let me drop, but my mother was very worried until he put me back down on the deck again."

It was on June 10, 1903, that the ship docked in New York harbor. Andy Little was on the dock to meet them. The Sproats had taken rooms in a New York hotel and it was there that Adis and Andy were married by a Presbyterian minister.

Scots law requires that wedding banns must be read aloud from the pulpit for three successive Sundays before a marriage. In event anyone believed that the wedding should not take place, that view should be made known to the minister. The banns had been read in the church Borgue three miles from Moffat before the Sproats sailed for New York.

After the wedding, Andy took his bride to the popular Niagara Falls for their honeymoon. Later they joined the Sproats in New York and all took the train to Boise.

Jean said they took a large horse-drawn cab from the Union Pacific depot on the hill above Boise to the Aikman home at 12th and Jefferson streets, making too short a turn. A cousin, Agnes Aikman, came running out of the house and cried, "Ye've cut the wrong corner!"

The Aikman ranch where Andy and Adis went to make their home was several miles closer to Boise than the Sproat home on Ditto Creek. Jean said, "After we settled there, Father practically retired. He seemed to take no interest in the ranch and spent more and more time writing letters back to Scotland and less and less in working. We children did nearly all of the work."

Mrs. Sproat had died as a result of a wood tick bite and Robert took Betty and Jean back to Scotland. "After mother died, he didn't know what to do with us, so took us back to Scotland and put us in boarding school. David and Rex came over to visit and Betty went back with them. Father and I got caught with World War I starting, and remained there until it was over.

"In Scotland, I lived in a boarding school called Aberdour House in Dumfries. I had two teachers, one taught instruments and the other harmony and rudiments of music." Jean went on to explain that this was a branch of the Royal Academy of Music under the patronage of King Edward VII, Queen Alexandra and other members of the Royal family. The president of the Academy at the time was the Duke of Connaught and Strathearn.

A framed diploma on the wall of the Cruickshank home testified that Jean Sproat had successfully passed the examination in pianoforte playing, held in London in September of 1918 and had been elected by the directors a Licentiate of the Royal and National Institution, fully qualified as a teacher.

Upon their return to Idaho, Jean said she was impressed with the welcome. "Aunt Mim Aikman wanted to have us as dinner guests, so we got off the train at Mountain Home. We were met by Hugh and Ellen Sproat in a big seven-passenger Cadillac, and drove to the Aikmans in Boise for dinner. We knew we were back in the United States."

Jean made her home with Adis and Andy for several years and they encouraged her to give piano lessons from there. She laughed as she told of the fun they had together. "Hugh would come and visit and he and Adis would play the piano and sing lots of the old Scottish songs. Hugh would tromp on the loud peddle and sing to the top of his voice. He said that if it couldn't be good, at least it could be loud."

Jean took them up on their offer to give music lessons and had a number of pupils. Many Emmett residents today boast of having been a pupil of Jean Cruickshank. She gained the last name as a result of one of Andy's shearers, George Cruickshank, coming into the home more and more often. It was soon evident that he had eyes only for the diminutive music teacher and they were married. They had two children, Mary Adis, named for her beloved sister, and who later married Don Skippen; and one son, Robert, now of Ontario.

A photograph of twenty-six men in a shearing crew, including George, hung on the living room wall in the Cruickshank home. Andy, wearing the usual dark suit, white shirt, necktie, hat and clenching a pipe between his teeth, was in the center of his crew. Also on the wall was hand-painted plate showing an ancient fort and hayfield on the farm at Plunton.

Jean was small, but wiry and strong. She played a smashing game of tennis until she was seventy years of age. Then she turned to something she felt was less strenuous. She saddled and rode her horse often until she reached the age of eighty.

Idaho sheep ranch life was taking shape for Adis. She always kept a "coo" [cow] and sometimes two or three, and felt she couldn't live without chickens and a bountiful garden. It may have been in those early days that Andy began to dream of the magnificent home he would one day build for her and the children. It was already evident that she was creating an atmosphere of warmth and stability from which he could grow and extend his influence over the sheep industry.

Grace Jordan, wife of the late Idaho Governor and U.S. Senator Len Jordan, described Mrs. Little as having "a well-furnished mind." It was this attribute that made it possible for her to run the large home, care for and teach the children, plant and grow a sizable garden, frequently visit the sheep camps, travel with Andy, do a prodigious amount of knitting, and become the moving force behind the building of the Presbyterian church in Emmett.

All were Presbyterians, although they called their overseas

church The Church of Scotland. Andy's parents were known as "churchy people," he said. The family spoke with the broad Scots "Aye" and used the Scots dialect: "dinna ken," when not understanding something; "ain" for own and many other phrases from the old country, until becoming completely Americanized.

When Drew's wife, Myrn, asked her mother-in-law who had taught her to be such an adept knitter, Adis said that she had learned when still a small child in Scotland. "No one person taught me, because everyone taught me. I would take my yarn and needles and sit out on the stile, which was made of a couple of little ladder-steps over a stane (stone) fence, and when anyone would come along, I would ask if they could show me any new knitting stitches. Often they could and did. I was but five or six at the time, but I was completely fascinated with knitting and wanted to learn every stitch there was."

She seemed to have learned all of the stitches and put them to good use. Myrn said, "When I was to have my first baby, I asked how she knit such pretty little baby booties. She said, 'Oh, you do it this way,' picked up the needles and yarn, and clickety, click, click went the needles and she had a bootie done before I started.

"I said, 'I can't keep up with you,' but she just couldn't seem to knit slowly, and would say, 'Oh, Myrn, don't worry. You'll catch onto it soon enough.' "

Adis was a tireless knitter and could knit in the dark for the two hours that it took to see a movie at either the Ideal or Liberty theaters in Emmett (both owned by mortician Claude Bucknum) without dropping a stitch. She attended the movies often and everyone knew she was there by the needle-clicking. She looked only at the movie screen but there were no dropped stitches in her work. Florence Murray said, "Many an all-wool cap, scarf, knee bands or a section of a sweater were completed at the movies in Emmett."

During World Wars I and II, it is doubted that any other Idaho woman could match the bales of sweaters, socks, scarves and mittens that rolled off those needles, and sailed across the seas to the fighting fronts for American boys and men in the military service.

Florence Murray was in charge of knitting for the Red Cross

gifts of warm sweaters, socks, scarves, ski caps and helmets from Gem county to the servicemen during the Second World War. In her pickup duties, Florence remarked, "Every time I would collect, Mrs. Little had a gigantic stack of knitting to be shipped. She really could knit. And, boy, could she click those needles. She actually knit by the ton for those kids overseas."

Andy had learned to knit his own socks as a boy in Scotland and was proud of his ability. He would take yarn and needles along with him to the sheep camps and knit his own socks, mittens and caps.

He and Adis had a good-natured rivalry about their knitting abilities. He would often come into the room where she was knitting, pick up something she had finished, hold it to the light, scrutinizing carefully in the hope he could find a mistake about which he could tease her. At times when Adis had left her knitting to do another chore, Andy would come along, pick it up and start knitting where she had left off, and knit until her return. This contest for "the best Little knitter" went on all of their married life.

Both her daughters were the proud possessors of a silk bedspread fashioned by Adis. The oldest son, Andrew Jr., called Drew, learned to knit as a small boy simply by going to the Red Cross meetings with his mother. He liked knitting his own heavy wool socks. David also learned to knit. Jessie could knit, but didn't enjoy it. Knitting was not the only thing that Andy teased about. When Adis took daughters, Agnes and Jessie, on a trip to Scotland to attend the wedding of a cousin, Betty Parker, Andy solemnly warned the girls that they would never get a bath, and would be fed only kippers and oatmeal.

Evenings were a favored time for Adis to knit. Andy would work at the big roll-top desk in his study or read the *Congressional Record,* newly arrived from Washington, D.C., while she knit. At other times she preferred to sit in the library, listen to the radio and knit. The library adjoined Andy's study and workroom. When she used the library she was warmed by an old Sunburst heater and she kept the house at an even sixty-five degree heat. Myrn said that while others might be complaining of the chill, Adis would be bundled up in warm sweaters and unconcernedly knitting at a fast pace.

Occasionally, Adis and Andy would attend a dance. He didn't care much for dancing, but she enjoyed it. So he went.

But both Adis and Andy loved sports. She was particularly fond of baseball and she liked listening to the big league games on the radio as she knitted. She never missed hearing the World Series and even made her first bet on anything by betting a cup of tea on the outcome of the series with her friend Ruth Stone. David remembers his mother playing volleyball in the yard with her children.

Myrn felt that Adis was a perfectionist and because she could do so many things well, she could seem abrupt when she didn't mean to be. Myrn recalled that when she and Drew were married they moved into the large home with the family.

"I was trying to learn to cook and Mrs. Little was an excellent one, so I wanted to be as good at it as possible. She had studied cooking in Scotland and could make virtually anything. One day I got hold of a special cookbook which she had brought from Scotland. Walking by, she said, 'That book is not for beginners, you know.' "

But Myrn was an independent type in her own right, which accounted for her being able to take over and operate their holdings when Drew died at an early age. She did not care much for eating lamb, which was often the main course at the evening meal at the ranch. "I just longed for a good old beefsteak," she said.

"One day I gave in and went to a restaurant downtown and ordered a steak. Of course, some friend of the family passed by and hurried to tell Mrs. Little that I was downtown eating beef!"

Now, they eat more beef than lamb. Myrn said the only result of the "tattle-tale" was that she was teased a lot about her preference for beef when she was a member of Idaho's biggest sheep-raising family.

Katherine Hunt was among the many who recalled that, "No one ever made head cheese as tasty as that made by Mrs. Little." She was known as a superb cook and her beefsteak pie was a specialty. She made them with fancy roses of dough on the top crust.

"She could make something tasty out of any kind of food. When hogs were butchered, she made up seasoned sausage patties,

Agnes Sproat Little in what the well-dressed fisherwoman of the day wore. Adis, as she was better known, enjoyed fishing and was good at it.

stored them in a large wooden keg to which she added oil to preserve them. Lard was rendered from the hogs, with which she made her own soap.

"When they lived in the smaller white house that was later cut in two, and half of it moved to the Aikman ranch, Adis was able to handle most of the housework herself. But after the big house was built, it was necessary for her to have help," Katherine recollected.

Although she hired help, Mrs. Little planned, always supervised, and did much of the meal preparations. She enjoyed learning of new foods and recipes. Katherine recalled that when she returned from a trip to Chicago with Andy, she was enthusiastic about a lovely meal they had enjoyed as guests there. Each guest had been served a hollowed-out half of a fresh pineapple filled with other fresh fruits. It was made even more impressive by the fact that fresh pineapples had not yet been brought into Idaho.

Usually whatever members of the family were at the home ranch at mealtime ate in the kitchen's breakfast nook. When the entire family was there, and especially if there were guests, they were served at the long mahogany table in the dining room. Frequent polishings kept it in shining condition. Guests and family ate with the Georgian silver which Adis had brought from Scotland and the elegant French china she had purchased when she, Agnes and Jessie made a trip to Paris.

David said that his mother had some small success in getting the menfolk to dress for dinner. Andy always wore a suit with a vest, light shirt and a necktie, "regardless of how long he had worn it," David laughingly said. He would only get into what he considered his dress suit for special occasions. David also remembers his mother saying, "Dad enjoys it when he does dress up, but he doesn't do it often enough." He admitted that his mother was only partially successful in getting him and brother Robert into white shirts, ties and suits for those special occasions.

"One time, she had just finished inspecting me in my suit and as she turned to Robert, I scudded out the door and ran down to Mud Miller in the cook shack. I looked around and decided that the oven was the best place to hide. Mud wasn't as immaculate a housekeeper as Mother, and when she found me I didn't look too

This 1924 picture shows Adis at the entryway of the just-completed home. The jack o'lantern indicates it is Halloween.

spiffy. When I think of it now I realize that Mother just had one helluva battle getting Robert and me to look civilized."

The Littles are remembered by a number of guests as gracious host and hostess. They welcomed many into their home. Some for extended stays. One of their favorites, and they a favorite of his, was Idaho's best known U.S. Senator William E. Borah. The Senator kept an exhausting schedule when in Idaho, meeting with all types of groups, individuals and organizations in many sections. Borah appeared at the Little home one afternoon looking as though he would drop if he took another step. Mrs. Little insisted he go up the winding stairs and use her bedroom to nap until dinner.

Within a matter of minutes a constituent appeared at the door wanting to see the Senator. Adis said, "That won't be possible right now."

"Isn't he here?"

"Yes, he is."

"Well then, where is he?"

"Right now he is upstairs in my bed," was the firm reply and the would-be visitor turned on his heel and left.

When Senator Borah was the honored guest the entire family dressed for dinner. At such dinners, Ruby Frye wore a black uniform, white apron, collar and cuffs. David remembers the Senator giving Robert an autographed copy of a book, *The Life of Lincoln*, on one of his visits. Robert treasured it.

Although they entertained beautifully when they chose to do so, neither Andy nor Adis cared for the grand scale dinner. Usually the guests were a few family friends from the Emmett valley or the bankers and lawyers who represented them in financial and legal matters. Several remembered Andy as he prepared to carve at dinner. Rather than removing his suit coat and rolling up his shirtsleeves as seemed to be the custom in the valley, he practiced the habit of shoving his arms straight out in front of him to the extent that his shirt cuffs and lower coat sleeves clung just above his wrists. When he finished carving, he dropped his hands to his sides and shook them until coat and shirt fell into place.

Andy was not only hospitable in Emmett, but he felt free to tell any of his friends who were traveling to the British Isles to go visit

Adis enjoyed the dancing she had learned in Scotland. At the annual January 25 observance of "Robbie Burns' Birthday," she and Tommy "The Bagpiper" McLeod lead a country dance.

his mother in Scotland. His mother told Jennie Crawford, a niece, that one day she was having a sweep come in to clean the chimneys. Just as he arrived, a taxi drove up and one man got out while another remained in the cab.

"Is this Mrs. Little's home?" he asked.

"Yes, it is."

"Is it all right to bring our luggage in now?"

In surprise, she said, "What are you talking about?"

It turned out that the two were friends of Andy from Idaho and just the first of what was going to become several who had been told by Andy, "Go see my mother. She will be glad to put you up." The guests, who had given no advance warning of their arrival, stayed a fortnight.

Jennie Crawford, at her home on High Street in Moffat, was just as hospitable. When unknown visitors from Idaho arrived, they soon were friends and served tea from the table owned by Andy's grandfather, John Dalgleish.

Among the cookbooks and other culinary articles Adis brought to Idaho from Scotland, were two large wooden spatulas which were true tools of her kitchen work. Primarily she used them for taking moisture out of pats of freshly churned butter. Two smaller, corrugated, spatulas were used for making attractive rolls for the luncheons which she held for members of her Ladies Aid of the Presbyterian church. There were many tin boxes of various sizes and shapes to use a cookie cutters and a wooden butter mold. For the Scottish shortbread, with which she became renowned, were plain, old-fashioned tin rings of stars, half-moons, squares and rectangles.

Myrn reminisced about how easily Adis seemed to handle the house, the garden, the care of two or three cows which she kept at the home ranch, and the preparation and serving of three meals a day, plus tea in the afternoon. Despite the efficiency which she showed, Adis was timid about doing some things. "Why, she wouldn't even call Boise to reserve a hotel room," Myrn recalled.

"She was so competent that those of us who were less so felt a total loss both in the yard and the house. Let me tell you, she *was* competent. She kept those milk cows, cared for their feeding and watering, and took the cream to downtown Emmett to sell. A separate milk room with plenty of shelves for the milk buckets and pans was built for her.

"With her big wooden churn, she could whip cream into butter in no time at all. And when it came to preparing a hen for stew and dumplings, or fryers for the pan, she would grab those Rhode Island Reds and squeeze them along the neck, right where it ends beneath the ear, and with a quick karate pressure, they'd be gone. She would have them darned near plucked by the time she reached the house, where she cleaned and scalded them and plopped them into the stew pot.

"She would let the pheasants Grandad and the boys shot hang high before cooking. My, but they were good. She fixed them with a gravy sauce that would make your mouth water just to smell it bubbling. I get hungry even now, after all these years, just thinking about it," Myrn said. "Drew liked the head cheese and pickled tongue that his mother used to make so much, and was always talking about her cooking. I think all her family felt the same way."

A large and sturdy young woman by the name of Doris Dill came to the Little home as a cook. Yet Adis continued to do much of the preparation and cooking. She also hired a woman who helped with the washing, and another helped with ironing and the housework.

Myrn said that she had never known another woman the size of Adis who had such physical strength. It matched her strength of mind and character. Myrn explained that the old house had a leak into the basement. "Why, many a time I have seen her pick up that large washing tub heaping full of wet clothes and carry it upstairs from the basement to hang outside." A great, long mangle, so large that it looked as though it belonged in a laundry, and likely the first of its kind in the Emmett Valley, was bought by Adis and aided greatly in keeping clothing ready for her family and others who worked there.

To Geraldine Laidlaw Little, Adis was an ideal mother-in-law. "I would regularly go out once a week and have tea with her," Gerry said. "She, in turn, would stop by with eggs for us. She was always available in any emergency. Even if they didn't seem like emergencies to her.

"One night I called her when Jimmy, our firstborn, was a tiny baby and seemed to me to be very ill. I couldn't get a doctor and I was frantic. I called Adis and she came right over. She came in the door, picked up Jimmy, put him across her lap, belly down, lightly rubbing and stroking his back, all the while murmuring softly to him. In a few minutes he was just fine."

Katherine Hunt described Adis as "the backbone of the Presbyterian church." This isn't surprising considering the fact that the church has its roots in Scotland. Adis not only helped to organize a congregation in Emmett and spearheaded the building of the church, but "she kept it going."

Jessie became a bulwark in the Emmett church just as her mother had been. Katherine thought that she would be thrilled to see the modern church building which Jessie took such a role in getting built, and how involved the church is with many projects.

The church was an anchor in the life of Adis and she worked diligently to imbue the children with a strong belief in God. While all of them attended church with their mother, David recalls many Sundays when he and Robert were not enthusiastic about it.

Refreshing her memory for a moment, Katherine said, "There was once a woman preacher who came to hold a spot in the pulpit and Mrs. Little invited her to dinner. She prepared Andy for the visit. He rocked with laughter and said he had never heard of anything so ridiculous as a woman preacher. When she arrived, however, he was very gracious."

From the church membership, Adis had a number of friends. But there were two close friends, Ruth Stone, a professed atheist according to Katherine Hunt; and Mae Reynolds, wife of Dr. Reynolds, both of whom felt close enough that they would often stop by for tea without prior notice. Ruth, a Kilpatrick from Salt Lake City, Utah, and the wife of mining engineer Walter Stone, played lots of cribbage with Adis.

Jessie remembered Mrs. Stone well and said that, as a child, she had travelled with her parents, seven sisters, a nurse, a tutor and a maid to many of the world's interesting sights. That Ruth's father was an attorney for Standard Oil as well as for Brigham Young, leader of the Church of Jesus Christ of Latter Day Saints (Mormons).

The first formal portrait of the Little family (1913) includes Andy and Drew, Jessie leaning on her mother, Adis, and Agnes at the right. Insets are of Robert (left) and David (right) when in grade school.

The Kilpatrick family had been in the banking business and Ruth's mother, who continued to live in Salt Lake, held mortgages on many places and homes. One mortgage was on the Hartley place in Emmett and that is where the Stones settled. An engineer, Walter Stone, was in Mexico at the time of the 1911 revolution. Jessie said, "They barely got out of the country in time to take anything with them. They were looking for a place to settle, and decided on Emmett because of the mortgage her mother held there.

"First, they tried to operate an orchard and then to raise chickens. Neither was successful enough to make a living. Mrs. Stone had not been taught to be a cook nor a homemaker. I remember a dinner party they held. The table was beautiful with fine linen, china, crystal and silver. But when the guests were seated, they were served TV-type dinners!" Jessie reported.

That Adis enjoyed life, her family and friends, there was no doubt. She could be playful upon occasion. Katherine remembered the time that she and her mother, Agnes and Jessie and their mother, made a pleasure trip to Boise. The mothers went shopping in one direction and the girls in another, agreeing to meet at the Owyhee Hotel for lunch. The girls were seated in the dining room and their eyes widened in amazement when their mothers walked in.

There was a makeup woman in the cosmetics department of The Mode department store that day and the mothers had permitted her to make up their faces. Both were wearing, for the first time in their lives, bright red lipstick, mascara and eyebrow touch-up. Until then, the only makeup they had worn had been a light touch of powder to the nose.

Usually good natured, Adis could be provoked to anger. Two stories point to a patience pushed too far.

One occasion, thinking he was being of help, Andy took garden clippers to her beautiful rose bushes which had just begun to bud. She was furious and inquired why, when he rarely helped around the house, did he choose to do something he knew absolutely nothing about!

Jessie's wedding to Bob Naylor inspired Drew, Robert and Roy Murray to plan a kidnapping of Bob, just as they planned to leave on their honeymoon. By the time Mrs. Little got word of what was going to happen within a few minutes, she dashed from the house, confronted the trio and returned with blood on her dress from the bloody nose she had given Robert. Drew and Roy managed to get away and Jessie and Bob left without realizing there had even been a plot.

Everyone agreed that Adis was highly intelligent, and if she disagreed she could be critical of some of Andy's business moves. She kept neat and ordered books for the family business for a long time and also for the Presbyterian church. Myrn said, "I loved to watch her count the money for the church. It was methodical but quick."

Several members of the annual Cherry Blossom Festival picnic group which gathered at the backyard at the home of Roy and Florence Murray recall one memorable Festival with Adis. The Festival has been an enjoyable event for hundreds every year. There is an evening parade, led by a band.

Florence reviewed the particular event with this story: "One evening, we were a bit late and were still eating when we heard the band playing. This signalled the opening of the Festival and we didn't want to miss it. So, everyone grabbed their drinks and started for the house. Mrs. Little, who never imbibed, reached over, picked up a pitcher of bourbon, water and ice, which someone had carefully prepared, poured it all over the flowerbed, saying, 'They say iced tea is good for the plants.' "

If anyone knew what was good for the plants, it would be Adis. Both her vegetable and flower gardens were works of art. Myrn thought back to the vegetable garden and said, "I just loved to watch her get her new potatoes. She actually was excited about the new vegetables coming on."

She had a large fork, something on the order of a large meat fork, and with a glint in her eye that made her look like a kid taking candy out of a jar, scratched carefully into the side of a potato hill in order not to damage the smallest tubers. She would take out the perfect sized ones for dinner. She left those not yet grown and the larger ones to grow even more, to be used for bakers, for boiling or for winter storage. The dirt would be gently patted back into place. Someone remarked that she used that big fork so much that it seemed like an extension of her arm.

She also grew a lot of asparagus. Actually, she had everything one could want in a garden. A storehouse had been built next to the cookhouse. It had a dirt floor and large bins on each side. Into the bins went the bountiful garden supply of carrots, potatoes, parsnips, rutabagas and other vegetables that could outlast the winter. There was also a goodly supply of apples.

"And when it came to cooking vegetables, no one was her equal. As her sister, Jean Cruickshank, had gone to the Royal music school, Adis had taken a course in cooking. The school Adis attended specialized in meat dishes. Those puff pastry meat pies of hers melted in your mouth. And were lovely to look at. Her head cheese was absolutely out of this world. When we played bridge out at the home ranch, Jessie would get into the head cheese and it was great. Adis also made a blood pudding that was tasty." Florence said.

While Adis knew how to prepare Scotch haggis, the traditional national dish of Scotland and usually served, with great fanfare, on November 30, the feast day of Saint Andrew, the patron saint of Scotland, she rarely did. It was not a favorite of the family.

Her roast leg of lamb, however, was in demand. She cooked it at 325 degrees for about thirty minutes per pound and declared it done when the meat was barely pink. She cut off excess fat and sprinkled it liberally with one-fourth teaspoon of basil mixed with lemon juice. This gave a tangy flavor they liked.

She liked to serve red currant jelly with the lamb, despite the American custom of serving mint jelly. During the last hour of roasting, she brushed a glaze of one-half cup of currant jelly, the same amount of catsup and dry sherry, with a pinch of basil, heated together until blended.

All the outdoor work which kept her on a schedule, did not lessen Adis' managing of the large home. She kept the front halls and stairway highly polished and asked family members to use the backstairs to the second floor. One woman helped her on a daily schedule and two others came in once a week to help with the cleaning.

Myrn kept in her memory the fun times playing cards with Andy, Adis and Jessie when she and Drew were first married and living at the Little home. "Neither Andy nor I knew any of the rules of bridge, so we just played by good old instinct. Jessie and Adis were alike in knowing every card and remembering just how it had been played.

"One time, I remember, Andy won the game and Grandma said, 'But you don't do this and you don't do that,' and he would reply, 'I did all right, didn't I? I won.' Then she said, 'But, when I play this card you are supposed to play that card.'

" 'Well, I don't know why. I won, didn't I?' And she would have to admit that he had. He just played the way he wanted to and that was it."

Adis loved the drive to Cascade where the family would go in June and spend the summer. Early on they pitched tents and camped. She remarked about how much she enjoyed being able to hang the wash on the limbs of the pine and fir trees and how fresh the dried clothing smelled.

As they grew older, Agnes and Jessie didn't care much for the camping out. They would drive up from Emmett with supplies, stay all night, and then return the next day to the home ranch. Later, a small summer house was built for Adis at the Cascade ranch.

Two other summer activities she enjoyed were stream fishing and picking huckleberries. Idaho has a state flag, a state motto, a state bird, and even a state horse . . . the Appaloosa. If the citizens were ever to choose a state berry, surely it would be that extraordinary and succulent dark blue and tiny orb . . . the huckleberry.

Adis was a huckleberry aficionada. She was so enthusiastic about going to the high country for the berries, which take much effort to find and pick, and realizing the length of time that it took to fill a gallon can, she was adamant about saving them for pies, jelly and canning. She made the jelly right in camp, but most of the berries went into pint jars for later use. One pint would make one pie and she usually canned fifty to sixty pints, and sometimes as high as one hundred, a year.

Myrn chuckled as she said, "I never had a fresh huckleberry in my adult life." But Myrn caught the fever and found herself saving the berries to make into delicious dumplings. She often made them in the sheep camps and said that the tenders and herders pronounced them "Ummm."

Myrn's recipe is simple: Make dough with one teaspoonful of sugar and one teaspoon of baking powder to each cup of flour. Add enough moisture to hold together. Beat the tar out of it and drop into bubbling hot huckleberry syrup.

The strong character and firmness of purpose of Adis Little, and perhaps a bit of her shyness at not wanting to trouble others, were all shown when she suffered a stroke in 1949. She had joined Jessie and Bob Naylor, who were still living at the home ranch, as guests of Roy and Florence Murray at a dinner to honor Jessie's birthday. Later they all learned that Adis was suffering a paralytic stroke on her right side that evening but, "didn't let a peep out of her," according to Florence.

She was using her left hand to cut her meat, then took up the fork and ate with her left hand, holding her right hand in her lap. Only she knew that her right hand and arm were numb and becoming useless. By the time the dinner was over, the Naylors had difficulty getting her to the car and into it. Jessie explained that she had been feeling ill and spent most of the day in bed. But she insisted upon getting up and going to dinner.

The next day they took her to the hospital in Boise, where the doctor confirmed that she had suffered a stroke. She soon recovered enough to return home, but her right arm and hand did not function well. In spite of that, she went to the summer house near Cascade and let it be known that she planned to go huckleberrying just as soon as the berries were plentiful, lush and blue. She had Myrn take her and set her in the midst of the huckleberry patch and "she scooted around and picked more berries with one hand than the rest of us did with two," Myrn said.

On one occasion in the huckleberry patch she fell and broke her arm. Yet she objected when others wanted to take her to the doctor, saying, "But look, this is such a fruitful patch. I am going to stay right here until we get all these berries." If there had been a way to transplant huckleberry bushes to her garden, Florence and Myrn were sure she would have done it.

Gerry said that her mother-in-law seemed always to have an angel food cake on hand. She would use the yolks to make sponge cake, using any leftover yolks to prepare a boiled dressing, which was a type of forerunner to mayonnaise. She liked to serve cold consomme with a dollop of sour cream. At Gerry's weekly afternoon tea visit, she said they would have angel food cake, fruitcake or Scottish shortbread.

The white fruitcake was called The Sproat Cake and was from a family recipe which three of the Sproat sisters, Mrs. Houston T. Hitt, Mrs. George Cruickshank and Mrs. Little always used. Each would make the family recipe yielding more than eight pounds of cake at one baking. It was then wrapped in a brandy-soaked cloth and stored in a covered container. It was never cut without a very sharp knife capable of slicing thin slices.

Although afternoon tea was a ritual which she enjoyed, there was another perhaps more important. Her Rhode Island Red hens and rooster were fed everyday at four o'clock. Even though chicken-feeding time often coincided with the appearance of tea guests, the flock was fed first.

Marie Arrizabala had graduated from Emmett High School in 1940 and went to work in a beauty shop. It was there that she came to know Mrs. Little. Shortly thereafter World War II came along, the shop closed and she joined other in going to California to work in the war-related industry. When the war was over and Marie returned to Emmett, she went to work for Ida Hutchins in her beauty shop. Ida had been doing Mrs. Little's hair for several years.

Marie describes her with, "Mrs. Little was a jewel. A real honey. She knew everyone who worked in the shop and enjoyed talking to all of us. She may have been the richest lady in town, but she was as down to earth as an old shoe. She wore her hair pulled back and done in a bun. We all really liked her. She looked serious, but underneath that appearance she was full of the devil and liked to have a good time.

"She was so easy to deal with and there was never one ounce of pretense in that woman. She was so good to all the girls in the shop. Although she was always neat as a pin, she never got all dressed up to come in. She wore about what we would be wearing.

Whenever she took a trip with Andy she would bring back an apron or a lovely handkerchief for each of the girls. She is what I call a handsome woman. She worked just as hard for her church as she did on her home place."

In talking of her mother, Jessie said, "My father did very little of the training of his children. So, all our early training came from our mother, and she was a real taskmaster. While neither of our parents made any attempt to bring any of us up in the mold of another, we all had chores to do. We were expected to do them well and on time. We had to do our share and no one was exempt. It was 'direct route' training in making beds, sweeping floors, scrubbing, washing and all household chores. We also worked outdoors.

"We received our assignments from mother. Agnes would wash and I would dry the dishes. We took care of the chickens, the cows, and each of us had our own horse. And we took care of them. If we wanted pets we were absolutely duty bound to take care of them. Mother had a huge garden and we all hoed potatoes and weeded. Mother did have help, but a family of five children were kept busy because she could think of millions of things for us to do. She needed us because she not only cooked for us, but also for the haying crews."

Jessie gave her youthful version of crime and punishment in recalling that when she was four she and her sister, Agnes, ran away from home. They heard their mother calling them, but just kept going. Adis came hurrying after them, took them by the hands, a girl on each side, and led them home. Right through the house, out the back door and to the clothesline they went. Adis tied them to the clothesline and when it was time to eat, she brought out two plates and they ate while still in bondage. "We never ran away again," Jessie said.

In those early days when the children were young, Andy was gone most of the time, either to the sheep camps, to the office or the headquarters, and he rode horseback to get there. He had a big black horse and Jessie remembers his riding down Fourth street at the end of the day. "Agnes and I would have waited for a half-day just to see him, so we would then run down the road to meet him. He would pull his horse to a stop, get off, and lift, first Agnes and then me, onto the horse and walk the rest of the way home leading the horse with his little girls proudly sharing the saddle. If anyone spoiled us, my father did. We were his only recreation. He kept so busy.

"But if anyone spoiled David, Agnes and I did. He was the baby and we were in our teens. We camped out at West Mountain and felt we were 'raising David.' I laugh now when I think of how we would take both clothing and the baby to the hot spring and wash them simultaneously. But it didn't seem to hurt him," she said in a thoughtful tone. It was obvious that the bonding that took place between sister and little brother so many years ago had only grown stronger over the years.

Jessie was working at the office one morning when someone came in looking for Andy. She telephoned the home ranch and her mother answered. "Where is Dad?" Jessie asked. "He and Harry are playing hide-and-seek and, if you must know, right now he is under the dining room table," Adis responded.

Andy would be reading his newspaper in the evening and small grandson Harry Bettis would run up to him, put his hands on Grandpa's knees and scoot his head up under the paper. Andy would emit a guttural sound from his throat, and Harry would run screaming down the hall. In a few minutes the little boy would be back and the routine would be repeated. The third time Harry came back, he would plaintively say, "Grandpa, don't do that." Andy would then chuckle, pick him up and put him on his lap and snuggle him a bit.

Some time after gall bladder surgery, Adis demanded that the drain be removed from the incision. Her family was hesitant to have this done, but she insisted. The surgery was completed, but Adis Little died in Emmett on Monday, July 3, 1950, at the age of seventy. Service for her was conducted at the family home, the place she and Andy had built, on the following Wednesday afternoon. Rev. E.E. Dagley of the Emmett Presbyterian church officiated.

She was survived by all her children but Robert, and by all her siblings. Jean Cruickshank lived in Emmett, Betty Hitt was in nearby Boise and Mary Campbell had remained in Scotland when the family emigrated in 1903. Hugh, Rex, and David Sproat had all stayed close to home in Boise, but brother Robert had moved to Klamath Falls, Oregon.

C H A P T E R F O U R

THE BAND OF BROTHERS

ANDY CAME TO THE UNITED STATES, AND WAS FOLLOWED BY ALL BUT one of his eight brothers. They were part of the prolonged exodus of herders from the Scottish homeland. The movement had its roots back as far as 1747 when the inherited rights of the chiefs of the clans were abolished.

Until then vast areas of Scotland had been under the control of the clans and each of their chiefs, whose power came from the numbers of men they could rally. After the 1747 edict, the wealth of the chief became the symbol of his influence and stature. To increase his importance, the clan chief essentially became a landlord to the hundreds of Scots sheepherders.

Then came The Clearances: thousands of small farmers and crofters were forced from the valleys and glens that had been home to them and their families for generations. Many Scots still speak bitterly of The Clearances. Dispossessed, thousands of hard-working, ambitious, and sturdy young people began the movement to Canada, New Zealand, Australia, and the United States.

When one remembers that Scotland was born fighting, it is not difficult to see from whence the Little brothers' scrappiness came. The Scots had to fight their land to make it produce; they fought the English in a desperate try for independence; they fight one another to right wrongs, imagined or real. Despite their violent history, visiting with the Scots puts any thought of fighting out of mind, for they are also a warm and hospitable people.

The Scots brought so much to America. The diligence, the lyricism of Robert Burns and Sir Walter Scott, the song which has been adopted by Americans celebrating New Year's Eve: "Auld Lang Syne." Which of us hasn't felt a warming heartache as we hear "On the bonnie, bonnie banks of Loch Lomond?" All these have left us with visions of Scotland as completely tartan-and-heather clad with skirling bagpipes wailing "Scotland Forever."

And Scotland is the land of kilts and clans, of grouse moors and peat bogs, of the Loch Ness Monster, of border collies and terriers, of magnificent abbeys ruined by abuse and neglect after a millennium of dedication to God, misuse and neglect, of Bonnie Prince Charlie and Rob Roy, of Tam o'Shanter pursuing witches across the Auld Brig o'Doon, of the doomed Mary Queen of Scots, crowned at nine months at Stirling Castle; and it is more. Much more.

And the United States, and especially Idaho, have benefited greatly from the Robert Aikmans, the Andy Littles, the McLeods, the Laidlaws, the Sproats, the Campbells, the McMillans, and thousands of others coming to the State to establish permanent homes. Above all, the Scots are builders. Andy and his brothers were of that constructive and fertile stock.

Andrew Little was the American forerunner for his family. He was followed by his brothers James Dalgleish Little, John Dalgleish Little (who for a time was called, "Big Jock Little," finally giving way to the simple designation of Jock), Simon Dalgleish (called Sam), Robert, Walter Carruthers Little, and William were to follow. Margaret Little Waymire of Howe, Idaho, eldest child of Jim Little, remembers the story her father told of the brothers gathering together before Andy left for Idaho and agreeing to give to their brother David Forrest, called Forrest by the family, all of their interests in family holdings near Moffat in return for his staying with his mother and two sisters, Annie and Grace. Forrest agreed to the arrangement and remained a bachelor until late in life, after his mother had died.

Jim, who was ten years younger than Andy, always looked upon his older brother as a father figure, according to Margaret Waymire. It was natural since their father had died when Jim was but twelve. The father, Andrew Sr. was born in 1817, meeting their mother, Janet Dalgleish, who was not born until twenty-six years later, in the Dalgleish home when she was but a child. He was a friend of Janet's father, John. She was a pretty and winsome lass and he decided then and there that he would marry her when she became a young woman. Andrew Sr. was born in 1817 and Janet in 1843.

During the intervening years Andrew Sr. was often chided about not marrying. He would smile and say, "I'm waiting for Janet Dalgleish." And he did. They were married in 1865 when Janet was twenty-two and Andrew forty-six.

Jim was born at the home near Moffat on January 8, 1880. During the six years from age thirteen to nineteen he apprenticed to a drygoods store in Moffat.

When he arrived in Idaho in 1901 Jim was twenty and immediately went to work with the sheep for brother Andy. As "Scotch Bob" Aikman did with him, Andy gave Jim some land as part payment for his work. Imbued with the same strain of ambition and drive, Jim, along with Adis and Andy, three days after Christmas in 1905, signed a note for $7,500 with an interest rate of eight percent, to a widow, Hester A. Davis, for parcels of land making up three-fourths of a section in adjacent areas in what was then Blaine, Jefferson and Fremont counties in south-central Idaho.

As did his older brother, Jim knew the value of water. Along with the land was 120 inches of water from the Little Lost River that had been originally granted to F. Ireland in 1886. He also received a second water right of seventy inches of water from the Little Lost which had been decreed to H.R. Jones in 1891.

When the note was paid off, Jim then traded parcels of land originally received by him from Andy in exchange for work for the land Adis and Andy had in the Howe area. Jim established his own sheep ranch near Howe. That land remained for many years in the ownership of succeeding generations of Jim Little. As had become the custom with so many Scots and Irish immigrants, where there had been one ranch there were now two with Littles operating both of them.

At age thirty-seven, Jim bought his sheep outfit from Ed Ireland and paid for it with a single check in the amount of $100,000. Grace Little Anderson, widow of Judge Blaine Anderson, has kept the cancelled check as a memento of her father and of what, within a few years time, a brainy, hard-working immigrant youth could do in America.

When Jim and Andy had traded land, Jim loaded a band of sheep on the train from Emmett to Blackfoot. From there he trailed them at least fifty miles, as the crow flies, on to Howe and herded them on land now occupied by the National Reactor Testing Station.

Jim met and married Alice Roberta Mays, who had come from the family home in Ashgrove, Missouri, with her older brothers when the Carey Act opened up much of the western land to homesteading. Alice was an adventuresome lady who, upon her arrival in Idaho, decided to homestead her own little farm at Howe, where she and Jim were married.

Margaret Little Waymire was their first born. She was followed by James Dalgleish Jr., who died at age seven; Andrew, later to become a well-known sheep man in his own right; Forrest, who spent five years in the armed forces during World War II, much of that time in the South Pacific, and later went into ranching; Grace Little Anderson, now of Eagle; Helen Little Miller, who died along with her husband, David, in a tragic automobile accident near the ranch they were managing for her second cousin, Harry Bettis, in Long Valley; Calvin, a brilliant student at the University of Idaho, and who had been named by his Uncle Andy as an act of admiration for President Calvin Coolidge, died of an embolism at twenty-three; Jean Little Werry, and Jay D. Little.

In describing her father, Margaret Waymire, laughed and said, "He looked a lot like Andy but, of course, *I* thought he was better looking. He had those blue, blue eyes, sandy hair, but was taller and thinner than Andy. A noticeable feature was his moustache, except for which he was well-shaven.

"He was mostly all-business, but he did like a good joke. He was a man's man, and went to all the sheep conventions which were then attended primarily by men. In his work he was with men all the time. It was the mother's job in those days to raise the family."

Grace Little Anderson also remembers her father, Jim, as "a very serious, stern and strait-laced Scotsman, hard-working, ambitious and fair." She told of his being a member of the Draft Board in Butte county at the time their son, Forrest, became of the age to

James Dalgleish Little and wife, Alice, were photographed in 1920 with their oldest daughter, Margaret (age three). Margaret is now Mrs. Waymire of Howe.

enter the service. The father's wish, as he wouldn't think of attempting to get the son a deferment, was that Forrest would enter as soon as he was old enough, get his required years in and get out.

It was not to turn out that way. Forrest served in some of the fiercest fighting to regain South Pacific islands taken by the Japanese. He was to be gone for five long and cruel years.

Jim may have been serious and stern, but a loving father continued to pay the salary of Forrest, at the same rate as he did others on the ranch, all the years he was gone. The money went into Forrest's account in the bank. His father died in 1943 and when his estate was settled, Forrest's share had added to it the salary paid to him all those five years he served his country.

Grace also remembered that her father cherished a $20 gold piece that he had won on a punchboard in a local store. "During the depression years," she recalled, "money became so tight and hard to come by, that Dad carried that gold piece in his pocket all the time. He thought that he might have to spend it, but he never did. And we got along."

She brought to mind how much he liked oranges. He had told the children that if he and his brothers and sisters each received one orange at Christmas, they thought it a wonderful gift. Jim also told of the time that he and Andy had been buying groceries in Boise and were delighted to find the biggest oranges they had ever seen. As they rode back toward Emmett they thought and talked more and more of those oranges. At Dry Creek they could wait no longer to savor the luscious fruit. They stopped the car, reached in the sack and each took a bite into the golden globe. Lips puckered and eyes watered as they realized they had bitten into grapefruit!

Helen Miller remembered of Jim telling of one rainy season when he was herding sheep for Andy in Long Valley. "My bedroll never got dry during that entire summer," he said. Her husband, David, remarked that when his family first arrived in Idaho he believed that half the livestock people in the southern part of the state worked for Andy.

That belief likely brought about the legend that one Basque immigrant, when asked who was the president of the United States, said, "Andy Little."

The family partnership Jim had left his children was soon altered. The sisters sold their shares, Forrest purchased his own ranch in Montana, and Jay went into ranching north of the home property at Howe.

Oldest son, Andrew, took over the ranch in 1968 and operated it for the following twenty-five years. He finally sold the ranch to a Californian by the name of Hartman.

Usually there were 20,000 head of sheep at the winter ranch properties near Howe. They grazed in the lush, green Lost River mountains during the summer months. Summer headquarters was at Sawmill Canyon at the head of Lost River. From the grazing areas of Birch Creek and Little Lost, the rivers run to the Snake River desert plain where they sink out of sight to become a part of one of the great underground water reservoirs of Idaho.

Jim Little's son, Andrew, inspired the same sense of loyalty in his employees as did his father and the uncle for whom he was

Jim Little and his oldest son, Andrew Dalgleish Little, at the Little Lost River Ranch.

named. A lovely Basque woman, Ynes Ydarraga Durfee of Wendell, remembers that her father, Galo Ydarraga, served for at least a quarter of a century as what the Scots call the "head herd" for Andrew. The "head herd" was in charge of other herders with a great deal of responsibility for the successful day-to-day operations of the ranch and sheep in the grazing areas.

William Little loved beautiful horses and matched teams and became a successful drayman in Boise, hauling horse-drawn freight from the railway station to homes and businesses in the area.

John D. "Big Jock" and Robert remained bachelors and made their home at Ola on Squaw Creek northeast of Emmett, where they farmed.

Family members laugh as they tell the story of Andy's car being stuck in the mud and Jock driving by with his team of horses. He reined the horses to a stop and said, "Ah, Andy, are ye stuck?"

"Yes, I'm stuck!"

"It looks like you are stuck. Well, if I hear anyone asking about you, I'll tell them where you are." Whereupon he clucked to the horses, jangled the reins against their necks and drove on.

Grace, as do others of the second generation, recalls that the brothers shared a great sense of humor. When talking among themselves, they referred to their sisters-in-law as Mrs. Andy, Mrs. Sam, Mrs. Jim, Mrs. Walt.

Jim Little said that one Sunday morning when he and Andy were just lads they were walking back to the Selfoot farm from lengthy church services at Moffat. They met an outstanding fisherman coming from the river with the biggest string of fish either boy had ever seen. They stopped and talked to him and then walked on. They openly wondered if God perhaps didn't think it was just as well to fish on Sunday morning as to attend church. After all, they discussed, wasn't Peter a great fisherman? Weren't a number of the other apostles?

Their mother soon answered the questions they proposed to her upon their return home. The answer to all of them was, "No."

Jim suffered from heart problems and for the last six or seven

Another band of Scots brothers—and sisters—in Idaho: the Sproats. Adis was a Sproat. When sister Mary Campbell came from Scotland in 1937, a reunion was held. Brothers, left to right, are David, Bob, Hugh, and Rex. Seated are sisters Adis Little, Mary Campbell, Betty Hitt, and Jean Cruickshank.

years of his life was a semi-invalid. He died in August of 1943 at Idaho Falls, two years after the deaths of brothers, Andy in February and Walter in October of 1941.

The two brothers who had not yet to come to Idaho, Walter Carruthers and Simon Dalgleish Little (always known as Sam), arrived together in 1900. Both were born at the family home near Moffat: Sam on November 12, 1881, and Walter two years later. The father of the brothers, also an Andrew, was a sheepman in Scotland, before his sons and the Littles herded sheep in the New World.

When they arrived in Caldwell, they entered Wilson Petrie's grocery store and asked a chap by the name of Frank Moore, who was standing there, "Where is Emmett?" Moore took them out onto the sidewalk, pointed toward Emmett, gave them direction for finding the town, and wished them good luck. Just as Andy had done, they walked to the town and easily found brother Andy, for whom they both went to work.

Sam worked for Andy for three years during which he saved as much money as possible to begin a business of his own. He started his spread in 1903 with 1200 head of sheep and a farm of 150 acres near Middleton. He wintered his flocks in the Middleton area and they were taken to the summer range in Bear Valley. Mutton from Sam's sheep was sold in Omaha and Chicago. He also raised his hay on the ranch.

His widow recalled how difficult it was for him to go into the bank to borrow money with which to buy the farm. "Sam was always timid about asking for anything. He would hang back and I would push him forward. He let me make the decisions and never complained about what I decided to do."

He ran the sheep on government ranges and the hay raised on his farm went to winter feeding. Within a few years, Sam had 16,000 head of mixed sheep, raised for both wool and mutton. He marketed the sheep in Omaha and Chicago. He soon purchased a second farm, one of 500 acres, in Washington county.

In *A History of Idaho* of 1920, listing prominent Idahoans, it was reported, "Something of the volume of business that he has developed is indicated by the fact that his payroll amounts to about twenty thousand dollars and his feed and grocery bill close to fifty thousand dollars annually, all of which money is spent in Canyon county, thus contributing to the material development and prosperity of this section of the state."

The article went on to relate that "His brother Andrew, who had reached Idaho six years before S.D. Little, is the largest individual sheepman in the state, being interested in about one hundred thousand head, which he ranges over seven counties, and his income tax is one of the largest in the state."

Sam was a fun-loving, story-telling sheepman who liked to say that he took care of having fun, that his brother Walt took care of visiting, that Jim took care of working, and that Andy took care of business. Sam was given the name of Dalgleish for his mother's father, who had lived with the family in Scotland.

It was while he was herding sheep in the Thunder City area that Sam met his future wife. Sadie Alvey was born in St. John's, Kentucky, "down from Louisville," as she described it, on May 11, 1890. At age twelve, Sadie came with her mother to the Thunder Mountain mining area of south central Idaho. Minerva "Minnie" Alvey Armstrong accompanied the McCall family, for whom the town of McCall was named, on their move from the East. Minnie operated the Thunder City Hotel east of Cascade.

Desiring proper schooling for her only daughter, Minnie enrolled Sadie in St. Theresa's school in Boise. She graduated from there at eighteen, in 1908, rejoining her mother in Thunder City. St. Theresa's School for Girls remained a highly desirable school until it was closed many years later. Andy's daughter-in-law to be, Geraldine Laidlaw was one of three eighth-grade pupils at St. Margaret's Episcopal School. In the early '30s this and the high school were donated to Boise Junior College by Bishop Barnwell in behalf of the church. After one year of high school at BJC, Geraldine transferred to St. Theresa's, which also opened to boys who had attended St. Joseph's.

What happened when Sadie met Sam isn't what the romance novels tell us usually occurs when "boy meets girl." When asked if she were impressed when she first met him, Sadie threw her hands into the air and said, "Lands no! He was just a sheepherder and he

Simon Dalgleish Little was always known as Sam. He had a legion of friends and was fun-loving and story-telling. He and his brother, Walter, arrived in Idaho from Scotland in 1900 and both went into the sheep business. Sam's daughter, Betty, still lives in Caldwell with her husband, Les Summers.

was nine years older than I was. I hadn't figured out yet that I wasn't the smartest girl who lived. I had just gotten out of school and I went to California and met a guy. The first thing I knew, I was married. The next thing I knew, I was having a baby. The marriage didn't work out and I brought my baby son, Art Brown, back to Idaho."

Sadie went on with her story. "The day I met Sam, he was with some other sheepmen in the cafe at my mother's hotel and I picked up my skirts when I walked by so I wouldn't even touch any of those sheepherders. Sam looked at me, grinned, and snapped his fingers and called out, 'Waitress, waitress.' That made me so mad that I kicked him out of the cafe. He just laughed. Later I met him in the hotel lobby and we got to talking. The first thing I knew he was courting me.

"No one had more fun than Sam Little. We went to dances at Thunder City that lasted all night and he didn't miss a dance and was still going strong when the sun came up. When the Thunder City hotel burned down Sam and Walt were doing the Highland Fling.

"Sam had a shrill voice that carried all over town. He would write a check for ten dollars and then yell, 'Sadie, have you got change for a hundred?' "

Sadie said that she had opened a millinery shop and candy store one summer. "But it didn't last long. The saloon did all the business."

Sam and Sadie were married April 23, 1915. They were married for fifty years and had celebrated their Golden Wedding anniversary before the death of Sam.

They honeymooned at the sheep camp. His brother Walt and his wife, Ellen, were also living at the camp. Sadie recalled living in a tent for a few weeks before going south to Crane Creek for the shearing. Their firstborn was a daughter, Mary. Sadie described her as a sprightly child who was the joy of Sam's life. "He had also come to love Arthur as his own and Art felt the same way about him."

At age ten, Mary became extremely ill when peritonitis set in after an appendectomy. In early Western medical style, the doctor described a drink of whiskey to alleviate the pain.

"You asked what kind of man Andy Little was," Sadie said in remembering the fatal illness of her first daughter. "I'll tell you what kind of a man Andy was. The word was around that it would help Mary to have a drink of liquor. You would have thought that there would be some around, but there was no sign of any. Somehow, Andy got the word and here he appeared at our doorway the very next morning. He handed me a bottle and just said, 'It's for Mary.' It didn't do any good, but he tried. And *that's* the kind of man Andy Little was."

For a long time after Mary's death the usually frolicsome Sam became a quiet man. "Sam always liked kids. It was so hard on both of us when we lost little Mary." Sadie said that during many of the quiet times that followed the burial, Sam talked of his childhood, his brothers and sisters, parents and grandparents and of the sheep ranch in Scotland.

"Us boys slept in sort of a dormitory upstairs. We all talked about coming to America. It was sort of a dream and yet we really believed that we might be able to do it when we grew up. Our Grandpa Dalgleish lived with us. I was named for him as Simon Dalgleish Little. He was sort of crippled up and lame. He walked with a cane.

"We were Presbyterians who only missed church when there was an absolute necessity. We walked into town to the large Presbyterian church. If our father did not attend the services for what had to be a good reason, he would ask for a text of the sermon and conduct a questioning session just to be sure that we had been in attendance. And Grandpa was just as strict about his belief.

"Us boys liked to play cards and Grandpa made it plain that he would not stand for card-playing in the house. So we outfoxed him by one of us standing guard outside the door. As soon as the guard heard the click-click-click of Grandpa's cane bringing him nearer, he would quickly slip into the dorm and give us the sign. Cards disappeared as if by magic and we would all be talking or reading when Grandpa made his nightly check.

"I don't think he ever got wise. Sometimes, though, he'd have a peculiar look on his face. Always finding us so good must have been a mystery to him." Sam would chuckle and Sadie would tell some story of her days at the Academy in Boise.

Thus the days rolled on and together they were able to bear the grief of losing little Mary.

Sadie still smiled as she reminisced about taking Art and Mary to the sheep camp, riding horses up the beautiful and green Bear Valley to Landmark. They all liked to fish. "Sam could catch fish where there just plain weren't any. Everyone talked about it and wondered how he did it.

"Our daughter Betty learned to fish from him, because she just loved to fish. When just a little tyke, she would stand on the creek or river bank and pull one fish right out after the other."

Betty was born in 1919, just after they had moved from the ranch to Caldwell. It was also time for Art to begin school. Betty grew to young womanhood in Canyon county and married Leslie Summers of Caldwell. They are owners and operators of a stationery store.

The move came about when Sam and Sadie reluctantly came to the conclusion that the sheep business was not going to be a success for them. When it became necessary to sell the ranch, livestock and equipment, Andy bought the sheep and horses. "When we got rid of the sheep, we went into cattle."

Son, Art, decided early that he wanted to take the name of Little. He finished schools in Canyon county and went on to the University of Idaho. He died at age forty-nine.

When Sam arrived from the land of hills and heather to make his home in the land of hills and sagebrush, he brought with him the jokes and funny stories he would like to tell.

Sadie said that he was "probably telling a story," when he suffered a heart attack. He was rushed to a Caldwell hospital where he died.

It would not have been surprising if one of the brothers would come near dying in the Gamage Barber Shop. They all patronized the shop when they were in Emmett and were valued customers. Charlie Gamage and his son, John, operated the shop for many years. John said that there were usually four barbers at work and often a long line of customers waiting. He said that if Andy came in and there was a line, he would greet those he knew, pick up a newspaper or magazine, and read until his turn came.

Walter Carruthers Little arrived in Idaho in 1900 and worked for his brother Andy for seven years before going on his own. Walter had the electric blue eyes of the Little family. He married Ellen Allen in 1917. Their son, Walter Jr., and his son, Bill, now operate the ranch.

"No matter how busy he was, he never acted like he was in a hurry. We appreciated that," John said.

Like all his brothers, Sam was a rock-ribbed Republican. He had also been an active member of the Idaho Wool Growers Association and was asked by the U.S. National Forest Service to serve on an Idaho advisory board for many years.

Walter Carruthers Little also worked for Andy from the time he arrived with Sam in 1900 until 1907, when he went into the sheep business on his own. His son, Walter, describes his father as looking much like the other brothers with the piercing blue eyes, ruddy complexion and sandy hair. "The brothers all had about the same physical build. They were stocky men."

Ten years after going on his own, Walter married Ellen Allen, who had been born and reared in Emmett. The wedding took place on Christmas Eve at Emmett in 1917. Her father was a partner with John McNish in the McNish and Allen sawmill.

Walter and Ellen became the parents of two daughters and a son. Janet Little married Harris Falk of Boise, by whom she had three sons. Walter Edward was married to Evelyn Manis of Payette in November 1945. Their children are Robert, who now has three daughters and has remained on the family ranch; Ann Little of Boise; and Bill, a Boise attorney. Ann married Marvin Murphy of Lansing, Michigan. She studied dietetics at the University of Idaho, interned at New York's Montefiori Hospital, and served as a dietitian for the U.S. Army during World War II. She had no children. Both Janet and Ann are now deceased.

Florence Murray remembers Walter Little Sr. and how he loved to visit. "His Scottish brogue was so thick," she remembered, "that I could scarcely understand a thing he said. A young woman who worked for them in their home later said that for a long time she didn't realize that it was Scottish, as she thought he was speaking in a completely foreign tongue."

The Walter Little home in Emmett burned to the ground during the winter of 1929 and the family moved to Boise for a few years. The move was made back to Emmett. Walter Jr. took over the family ranch, located between Emmett and New Plymouth. He now has 2,000 ewes and runs 200 stock cows. He also keeps between four and five hundred Herefords, some Black Angus and some crossbreeds.

After Andy Little's brothers followed him from Scotland to Idaho they built farms and businesses. Then their children built farms and businesses in their turn. Like Scottish immigrants all over America, the Littles' hard work, thrift and honesty made their adopted home a better place.

CHAPTER FIVE

CLIPPED, DIPPED, AND SHIPPED

The Clipping

By Alex Struthers, Moffat, Scotland

There's not a day throughout the year
With this one can compare,
Look around and see the sight
It'll make you stand and stare.
Sheep pens full, perhaps a thousand,
Old hill ewes with gleaming eye,
A light wind blows from out the west
And up above a light blue sky.

The shearers are a worthy bunch
Who will hold you in their spell.
It's been a year since last time round
They have many tales to tell.
The catchers are the younger lads
Who have yet to make the grade,
Keen to watch the older hands
It's how to learn the clipping trade.

And then there are the winders
The ones who also pack the bags,
And constantly need reminding
To remove the clarts and clags.
If that cruddy stuff goes in
The price will surely fall,
A point sheep farmers sorely grudge
They just don't want to know at all.

The shearers then oil up the blades
And set to with a will,
Many hours of toil will pass
Before these shears are still.
Some ewes are easy done
And have a decent rise,
But some are just the opposite
Oh! the language and the sighs.

"Wale me out a decent one,"
Is an oft repeated phrase,
"This old Blank is so tight,
You'd think she's wearing stays."
Some fleeces full of brambles
And some are full of sand,
Blades don't like this stuff at all
And things get out of hand.

Then you get the odd old ewe
Determined to show fight,
Her horns are sharp as razors
And your jeans soon let in light.
Ripped they were from crutch to heel,
Oh! What a wondrous sight,
Exposed old Jim's anatomy,
The young lads roared delight.

His long johns now are shredded
And the colour you guessed wrong,
Brilliant pink from Pakistan,
He bought them for a song.
"A bit o' baler twine," he roars,
To spare his private parts,
By tying flying ends together
Those jeans look really smart.

The trouble was he tied too tight,
When o'er the next ewe he did bend,
The stitching to the rear gave way
And exposed Jim's ample end.
A quick reverse into the shed,
That old Jim will never wilt,
Grabbed an empty wool bag
And made himself a kilt.

Determined to come out on top
He grabbed the first ewe to the right.
The glowing red in that sheep's eye
Meant Jim was going to have a fight.
She kicked Jim on the ankle,
Then she twisted to the left,
Struck a horn into his armpit,
The worst ewe in the heft.

The fleece was only halfway off
When Jim yelled out in pain.
She'd bit him in the oxter
And took off like a plane.
Cleared the other two shearers
By two foot six or more,
Trailing fleece behind like bridal gown
And straight out through the door.

Bright red paint is what we use
So initials can be seen
On snow-white ewes just newly clipped
With a background of grass green.
But she knocked the paint pot flying
And it landed upside down,
You'll never need ten guesses,
'Twas right on her bloody crown.

A bright red sheep she then emerged
Out through the sheep pen gate,
Landed on a Volvo's bonnet,
Oh! What a cruel fate.
For in that instant she did pause
And looked round to the right,
The windscreen showed her image
Which she hit with all her might.

She landed in the driver's seat,
It really was quite smart,
Front feet through the steering wheel,
That ewe looked just the part.
And in case you did not know,
I feel I ought to tell,
That car belonged to dear old Jim
Who gave a mighty yell.

He's buying on hire-purchase
With five more years to pay,
What he called that poor old ewe
I would not care to say.
But one thing is for certain,
He has joined the privy elite,
The only Volvo car I know
With a red sheep-skin front seat.

There's a Blackface angel up on high
Who keeps looking down with glee,
When Jim starts herding sheep in Heaven
She's the first old ewe he'll see.
Why did he put her in the fridge?
I really cannot tell,
But because he lost his temper
She means to give him hell.

Aware of it or not, the shepherds and crew of Andy Little followed the admonition of old King Solomon of Biblical times to the Israelite sheep people: "Be diligent to know the state of thy flocks and look well to thy herds . . . the lambs are thy clothing . . ."

In little different words and with a Scotch burr, Andy's orders were those of Solomon. His crews took great care to guard the flocks against cuts during the clipping, against diseases and pests during the dipping, and to see that stops were made for feeding when they were finally shipped. He was as aware as Solomon that the sheep was the only animal since time began that both feeds and clothes mankind.

It is now about 150 years since the first sheep were brought into Idaho. As travelers ride along or fly over Idaho, they can see the indelible marks of our sheep industry. The tracks of millions of sheep making thousands of trails tramped into the high hills leading to higher mountains, and across mesas and plains where sheep trailed and grazed. That is as it should be, for much of Idaho's history is intermingled with the woolies, the collies and shepherds, the herders, the clippers, the dippers and the shippers.

The year for most begins on January 1; for those whose business is benefited, on July 1; for the sheepmen and shepherds the year begins with preparation of the bands for breeding. This takes place in late summer or early autumn. There are exceptions according to type of sheep and location.

For those who think sheepherding is a snap, they should consider the care and attention required just to get the year started. It isn't that easy, and things can go wrong. When the rams are put out too early the lambs may be born in the cold and snow; if spring is late in arriving and the ewes are not well-fed they will not have enough milk for their lambs; if the rams are put out too late, the lambs will be born late and unable to have the choicest spring grass that makes them grow.

Then there is the preparation of the ewes for breeding. The shepherd gathers his flocks and makes sure they are well-fed. Inspection is made for sore feet or eyes; dirty wool tags—dags or clarts—of the hindquarters are removed, and wool must be trimmed from around the udder.

Before the clipping, there must be sheep. A band of Little woolies stretch from here to haystacks.

The rams are also checked. Their hooves are trimmed and any excess wool underneath is sheared off to avoid a temperature so high that fertility is harmed. Period of gestation is about 145 days.

Crutching, as removal of fleece and any manure from the docked tail and around the udder and back legs is called, is done seven or eight weeks before lambing. Because of this process the shepherd watches the progress of the birth process without undue disturbance of the ewe, which does not want to move when she has settled on her birthing place.

Once the lamb has arrived, the mother licks and cleans the lamb, nudging it into a standing position and then toward her udder for its first feeding. The distinctive sounds of hungry lambs bleating for food is music to the ears of the sheepmen.

Jim Yates, who spent his boyhood at Parma, Idaho, near where Andy's sheep were brought down from the mountains each au-

Johnny Basabe at the gate at the Aikman Ranch is working with Bob Schweitzenberger, in white jersey, as two herders sort the ewes from the lambs.

tumn, said, "As I recall, the lambs started arriving in February and March, and the bleating of thousands of ewes and lambs could be heard for miles around. It was a part of our life."

When a lamb is stillborn or dies shortly after birth, herders look for a healthy newborn which has been rejected by the ewe, sometimes in the case of twin lambs, or an unusually puny one. Having found a reject, he quickly skins the dead lamb and pulls that fleece over the body of the unwanted one, and carries it to the ewe. It is only by the smell that the mother knows the newborn. The ewe smells the fleece of her own, lets out a bleat and moves around for the lamb to suckle.

In the early days, Andy's sheep were clipped or sheared with handshears and a clipping stool as they did in Scotland. The sheep were laid on their backs on the slatted stool which had four inches between each slat for the dirt to fall through. There was a deduction, of course, from the buyer if the wool was dirty.

While some wouldn't admit it, the early-day clipping became a social occasion. The best clippers among the shepherds would go from one sheep farm or ranch to another and clip for as many days as necessary to get the job done. Some would take a fiddle along to entertain in the evening, others were "sheep poets" who would entertain while they clipped. Always there was good food with the cook or sheepowner's wife securing extra help for that time.

In Scotland, they referred to the "yoking" at shearing time. That was when any bystander got "yoked in" to helping. Shearing usually starts in early spring when the weather begins to warm. Andy and his family in the sheep business had shearing sheds with corrals on the side. High wooden frames held long wool bags where the tromper worked to fill the bags to capacity. The packers held hanks of tie cord to bind the fleeces when tossed to the tromper. The tie was made of a heavy paper so that it would dissolve when the fleece was washed.

Before the advent of the electrical shears, each shearer sharpened his shears on a whetstone, leaving the points dull so that there would not be nicks in sheep nor fleece. A good shearer operates quickly, quietly and carefully to take the fleece off in a single piece.

This shearing scene of April 20, 1949, is inside the shed at the Highland where a twenty-man crew turned out 3,000 shorn sheep in a day. The shearer in the center is placing the ewe properly before grabbing the shears.

Bob and Jessie Little Naylor watch the fleeces drop off the sheep at a rapid clip at the Aikman.

High wooden frames hold long wool bags. The man on the top of the wool bag is making a final tromp to completely pack fleeces tied with cords made of paper which dissolves when the fleeces are washed.

A small part of the clip from the Aikman is compacted so tightly that wool is popping out of several bags.

In more modern days, the sheep is set on its backside with shearer's knees holding the animal steady. The sheep's right foreleg is placed across the left side to tighten the skin and the first stroke goes completely down the left side. The next is parallel and the third starts shearing on the right side. When the middle of the belly is reached, the skin is pulled toward the brisket and fleece is sheared right across the belly. Shearing of the legs goes as far as the dock with strokes from left to right.

When the fleece was off the sheep the shearer tossed it into the tie box, from which the packer retrieved it, tied it and tossed the cinched fleece to the second packer or the tromper, who dropped it into the sack and stomped it firm. When he was at the top of the sack and it was full, it was tied and ready for piling onto the wool wagon or truck. Some of the Little's trompers from the 1942 shearing book were: Ross and Tony Tipton, J.J. and Royce Irby, and Charles Smith.

It is said that shearers have the softest hands of any occupation because of the lanolin, natural grease, in the wool. It is not unlikely that a tromper has the softest feet, even if the grease has to ooze through the shoes.

After the clipping comes the dipping. A 1935 crew at the Aikman prod the shorn sheep through the dipping vat to rid them of pests and parasites.

Now comes the branding with paint. The Stetson-wearing brander has just dipped his stamp into the paint in the old skillet and is applying it to the shorn sheep.

Little Billy Ackroyd ("little" was a term of real affection for the short man) was considered one of the best wool graders in the world. He was from Boston, but spent much time in Idaho, as he was hired by Andy to come out to Emmett each year and grade the wool before it was shipped. This saved time and money.

Billy would climb right up onto the platform where the fleeces were tossed before being tromped into the wool sack and grade it as it was being sacked. He would mark the sacks with a black ink mark, indicating the grade of wool. Two or three of the world's biggest woolen mills were located in Boston and sometimes Andy's wool sold right away. At other times Andy would hold it for awhile before selling.

The wool then goes to the warehouses for sale. Clips from sheep of Walter Little are shown in the foreground, followed by those from the Highland Land and Livestock Company.

The wool was graded fine, medium, or coarse. And then there were the "black and tags," which brought only half the price, and that was used for making army blankets and other heavy materials.

This pre-grading process saved opening up the bags when they arrived in the East and grading them there. In addition to the time and money saved, Billy enjoyed getting away from the city and always had a good time when he was in Emmett. He liked the Littles and they enjoyed him.

Jessie explained, "Grading the wool was just like the lumber mill grading the lumber. We got a better price for the best wool. The fine wool, which came from the Rambouillet, was used for suits and other clothing. The medium was used for the same thing in a less expensive grade and came from the Panama, the sheep that was produced by Gerry's dad, Jim Laidlaw. The Lincoln produced the coarse wool."

Bob Naylor is auctioning wool from the Big Springs Land and Livestock Ranch with the bidders appearing to be thinking deeply.

The Rambouillet was named for a town in France but was developed in the United States and Germany. The wool is of fair density, uniform shrinkage and long staple, which makes it ideal for those who like to spin by hand, as well as on the machines. It is a ıardy sheep and can survive little forage and tough weather condi-

e final step is shipping. Well-fed lambs are being herded into the Union Pacif-
reight cars for a journey to the stockyards in Omaha or Chicago.

Courtesy Union Pacific

tions. The Lincoln has long and coarse wool of a good quality, as well as a good meat conformation. The Panama is described elsewhere in this book.

The Targhee, a Columbia offshoot, was developed in the United States, also in Idaho. At the U.S. Sheep Experiment Station in Dubois, Idaho, where much research has been of help in advancing the industry throughout the world, ewes of the Corriedale and Lincoln-Rambouillet breeding were mated to outstanding Rambouillet rams. The offspring of these matings were inbred to produce the Targhee. They were named for the Targhee National Forest in which the flock grazes during the summer. They were developed under usual conditions on the sheep ranges and chosen for production. The ewes are said to be "good milkers" and they carry a fleece of an average eleven pounds.

An *Idaho Wool Growers* item of June 17, 1931: The Andy Little wool clip, approximately 800,000 pounds from 92,000 clips, sold one-half to private companies and one-half to the National Wool Marketing Corporation. Wool prices by private companies are ranging from thirteen and three-fourths cents to fifteen and three-eighths cents, with an average price of fourteen cents. Private companies took principally the fine and one-half blood wool stock.

Another shearing item of more than thirty years later appeared in the *Idaho Daily Statesman* in an article written by Denton Brewerton from Emmett, where he had observed the shearing of 10,000 fleeces in eight days. About 1250 sheep were sheared each day on the Aikman ranch, then operated by Jessie Little Naylor and her husband, Bob, president of the Highland Livestock and Land Company.

Brewerton wrote that during lambing the Highland purchased three million pounds of onions, which the sheep gobbled up. Naylor said, "This is the time during the sheep cycle when we want all the sheep families to smell alike, and they do when they eat onions. If a mother ewe has only one lamb, but could handle two, we give her twins and pass her lamb on to some other ewe. They know their own lambs only by smell, and with the onions none are the wiser. With a lamb being born every three minutes the ewes don't have time to do anything but care for the added arrivals, and they accept any lamb since they all have the same smell."

Though the story was printed in the *Statesman*, David Little says he was never aware of an onion-feeding program.

After the clipping comes the dipping and branding (painted). Sheepmen have long known that a parasitic infestation of any kind can lower the vitality and disease resistance of the animals. So, all sheep are treated for insects and external parasites through the dipping process.

There are a variety of dipping vats and equipment, with all meeting the same purpose, to rid the animals of pests. Some small ranchers used a portable, galvanized vat, which a number of owners may own cooperatively. The larger operators use a concrete reinforced vat or a wooden one made of heavy tank material, grooved and fitted to hold the dipping solution. The vats are ordinarily set into the ground to a depth of four feet, and extend another foot above ground.

A running board leads from vat to the draining pen and is placed with the lower end on the bottom of the vat and the upper just below the top, for the easy movement of the sheep.

Dipping was not as enjoyable a task as the shearing and no celebration was made of it. It was simply an essential part of making a living in the sheep industry and contributed to the comfort and well-being of the animals. High pressure sprayers have replaced this equipment on most ranches.

In addition to the shipping of the sheep and wool to the eastern markets, another type of shipping has grown in recent years. A number of Idaho stockmen ship animals to warmer climes during the cold winter months.

Both Pete and Louis Cenarrusa truck their sheep to Palo Verde Valley in California before winter sets in each autumn. The shipments also have included cattle for several years. The brothers figure that bigger and higher yielding lambs are the result of moving to the warmer winter territory. Several other Idaho sheepmen are also hauling to Arizona and California winter pastures, citing cheaper feed and larger lambs as well as reduced labor costs.

Among others who ship sheep south for the winter are State

Senator John Peavey, also of Carey. Peavey comes from a line of sheep operators, including his grandfather, U.S. Senator John Thomas, and his daughter and John's mother, Mary Peavey Brooks. Peavey's Flat Top Sheep Company winters in the Mojave Valley of Arizona.

Admittedly, there are drawbacks as well as advantages, including problems that come with renting grazing land with enough feed to last the winter. A cost up to $50,000 can result if the sheep get into a farmer's lettuce or cauliflower field. Liability insurance is essential.

Raising sheep right, for their own health and safety, as well as for the greatest profit, is a year-round job. Andy Little was one of the first sheepmen to keep his crews on for the full year, just for those reasons. Andy's success is the proof of the system.

CHAPTER SIX

IT'S IN THE RULES

WHILE IT WAS NEVER DOUBTED THAT ANDY WANTED THINGS DONE AS well as possible, he was not a perfectionist. He well understood that all men were not as adept as some; that one was not as strong as another; nor that because one worker was quicker that they all should be. He was not what anyone would call finicky, but he was a stickler for the rules: rules that could be carried out by anyone who paid attention, rules that made it much easier to manage such a widespread operation as his grew to be.

Each new employee was given "The List." The List set the rules, set the times for doing the chores, and anything else that Andy thought would organize the gigantic job of keeping the ranches moving smoothly day after day.

Before the 6:30 a.m. breakfast, the horses were to be caught and fed grain. Dinner, which was a large meal, was served at 12:10 p.m. and supper came at 6:30 each evening. The list told the new worker that after each meal he was to take his plate and cutlery to the cookhouse for the cook to wash and dry.

There were usually about twenty shearers to be fed, along with the wranglers, branders, counters, sheepherders, and camp tenders. Two shifts for each meal was the rule rather than the exception. So, the cook had to be a good one and a willing worker.

Jim Harris, McCall grocer, recalled that Andy was a stickler for detail, but that he was not a Simon Legree. When the grocery lists went out to the purchaser, usually the camp tender was to buy only what was on the list. It did not take long for the grocery buyer to figure out that if he took a little less salt than was on the order, he could add a few eggs. Harris said that someone thought he was doing Andy a favor and told him what was going on.

Andy chuckled and said, "He'd hardly be human if he hadn't figured that out by now. Nor very smart. I like smart people working for me. As for me, what I don't know won't hurt me."

David Little remembered one of his dad's rules on the dogs was that all of the dogs on the ranches, in the camps and on the ranges had to be Little dogs. In each camp there would be a dog for each herder, the two or three camp tenders would always have a dog following, and there were always a few additional dogs on each ranch. Some of the dogs would be sent out with the sheep and would come back to the ranch to eat.

"A lot of herders would show up with their own dogs," David said, "but Dad wanted only dogs that had been trained by us. He was a stickler for rules and there were never any changes to that particular rule, and darned few others. We kids always had puppies for pets at home, but he made it plain that the sheepdogs were not pets. He liked his dogs, marvelled at how quickly the good ones could be trained, appreciated their value to his well-run operations, but he also knew that making a pet of one could ruin his ability to herd and guide the sheep.

"We earmarked the dogs," David went on, "as we did the sheep, with two tiny notches on the ear. Each year after the lambs were shipped there would be a surplus of working dogs and some could be sold. We never had trouble selling them as many people wanted one of our dogs because they had the reputation of being well-trained. It was one of Dad's rules that made them that way."

Andy never completely broke a rule, but he was willing to bend one when he felt the cause worthwhile. One year it rained for ten days and David remembers that the crews just sat around, becoming restless. Andy realized all the workers were good ones and decided to bend the rule of "No Poker Playing."

He explained it by saying, "This is a different type of a bunch of men. A little poker when it is raining so hard and so long isn't going to hurt them." Otherwise, there was a no-gambling rule on all the Little ranches.

"Up at the Butte ranch," David remembers, "the guys would

post a guard up in the top story of the bunkhouse to watch for Dad or anyone else who might be likely to tell him that his men were playing cards and betting. The guards would take turns and when Dad or any unknown could be seen riding toward the Butte, the alert sounded and cards and money immediately disappeared from view. When the visitor arrived he was greeted by a group of workmen appearing as though they actually enjoyed the quiet life."

Neither did he permit liquor nor women in any of the camps. Of unusual stamina himself, he knew that his workers would need both wits and strength about them to rise early, work hard and follow his rules.

Andy's men had to be up before 6:00, at breakfast by 6:30, and in the fields with the horses harnessed at 7:00. But Andy worked even harder and longer. In those early days he expected his workers to put in twelve hours each day. It was rare that he didn't put in fourteen to sixteen hours a day. While he was still alive, his strength of mind, character, and body became part of the Idaho legend.

He was what some friends called a "high-caliber" operator. Strength and diligence built his herds and ranches until he had as many as 400 employed at one time in the Little sheep outfits. He kept his men busy for twelve months out of each year and may have been Idaho's first sheepman to operate on an around-the-year basis. Once they became familiar with the rules and his methods of operation, the employees liked the system and many stayed with him for more than twenty years.

And how many in the various business and professional offices of our world must wish they had heeded Andy's rule, "Do not employ any near relatives, as this often leads to dissatisfaction?"

Other suggestions for the foremen included:

"Herewith hand you list of groceries which I furnish for ranch use. I aim to furnish all that the average family would consider necessary and proper. If there is anything more which you feel is necessary, kindly take the matter up with me and I will see about adding it to the list.

"Fresh meats (beef or mutton) will be furnished during haying time.

"Fruits should be canned in season, and make requisition for any fruit jars needed. Please report the number of Empty and Full jars of fruit at the first of each month.

"Be sure to inform all employees of the wages to be paid before they start work. Keep strict account of their time and they must have a time check or order from the Foreman before settlement at this office.

"Give special care and attention to Livestock. Horses should be fed, cared for and harnessed before breakfast, and should be properly cared for at night. Horses must not be neglected in order to rush off to town at night. Barns should be cleaned every day.

"Keep all farm machinery repaired and do not put same away in a wrecked condition. Do not leave Machinery and tools scattered about the Farm, but when through with a particular piece of work, bring them in and put away in the machine shed or tool shed where they will be protected from the elements and ready for the next job.

"Loss of small tools caused by carelessness should be charged up to the account of the person losing same.

"Neither loan nor borrow tools or machinery, except from my own ranches, and then see that the same are returned in as good condition as when borrowed. When loaning tools or machinery to my other ranchmen, always take a receipt for same.

"Kindly see that doors and gates around the place are kept closed and do not leave the ranch without someone in charge.

"Tool sheds, Blacksmith shop and such buildings should be kept locked and employees not allowed to go into such buildings at will. Attach keys to a small block of wood and keep them hung up in the house.

"Cows should be properly fed and milked at regular time. Feed calves with a bucket and do not let them suck the cow.

"Any surplus of Cream and Eggs may be turned to the office. Also any surplus in garden produce or fruits. When ordering supplies for ranches, be sure to make a *complete* list. Make a written request for household goods or cooking equipment to me. Do not ask the truck driver. Do not overdraw your butter account at the creamery.

"We have in the past had a good deal of loss in stacking hay too wet. To test hay for stacking, turn over a shock of the heavy hay, usually on the lower ground, take a handful from the center of the shock and twist it in the hands; if it cracks and breaks, it is ready to stack, and if it shows moisture and is wiry, it is too wet. Special care should be given to the third crop as we have a good deal of trouble and loss in stacking it too wet."

The "Supply List for Ranches" was attached to the letter for each foreman, and by that time in his career, Andy named three companies at the top of his letterhead. They were the A.L. Little Sheep and Land Company, Highland Livestock and Land Company, and Andrew Little Ranches.

The alphabetical list of supplies included: Allspice, Bacon, Baking Powder (Calumet or KC), Beans (Red), Beans (String), Beans (White), Beef (during haying), Butter (where have no cow), Candles, Chili Powder, Chocolate, Chore Girls, Cinnamon, Cloves, Coal-Oil, Cocoa, Coconut, Codfish, Coffee, Corn, Cornmeal, Corn Beef Hash, Corn Starch, Flour, Fruits, Dry (Apples, Figs, Prunes, Peaches, Raisins), Germetta, Crackers, Ginger, Cracked Wheat, Cereal, Honey, Lard, Lemon Flavoring, Macaroni/spaghetti, Matches, Mazola, Milk (where no cow), Mustard, Mutton, Molasses, Nutmeg, Oatmeal, Onions, Peas, Pepper, Potatoes, Rice, Sage, Salt, Soap (Laundry), Soap (hand), Soda, Sugar (white), Sugar (brown), Sugar (powdered), Spaghetti and Meat Balls, Syrup, Tea, Tomatoes, Toothpicks, Vanilla flavoring, Vinegar, Yeast, Fly poison and spray, Jar Lids and rubbers, Lye and Cleanser.

It is obvious that the pantries on the Little ranches were well supplied and the employees well fed.

From time-to-time when Andy felt a reminder or an additional instruction was needed, he would send out a special "Instruction for the Ranches."

One of these opened with, "Morning bell to be rung at 5:45 in the morning and followed by breakfast forty-five minutes later." The noon bell was expected to be rung at 12 o'clock straight up and followed by Dinner to be served ten minutes later. Supper was to be served each evening at 6:30 p.m.

Other instructions were that work should start promptly at

seven o'clock each morning and at one o'clock in the afternoon. Andy advised his workers, "When you are working at a distance, leave the field in time to be in the yard at twelve o'clock noon and at six o'clock p.m."

The rules proceeded with, "Give first care and attention to Livestock." A reminder seemed to be needed to those who were eager to get away from the ranch and into the nearest town and its bright lights: "Horses will be fed, cared for and harnessed before breakfast, and will be properly cared for at night. Horses must not be neglected in order to rush off to town at night.

"KEEP ALL DOORS AND GATES AROUND THE PLACE CLOSED.

"Employees must have a time check or order from the Foreman before settlement at office. Be sure that time and wages are correct before accepting time."

There were also "Special Instructions," a single sheet of paper, tacked to the kitchen wall in every lambing camp. These instructions specified that dinner would be served from 12:10 p.m. and supper from 6:30 in the evening.

But the first instruction was to put a stop to the giving away of lambs. Andy had good reason for the warning. Herders often were tempted to gift some youngster with a cute little "bummer" lamb whose mother was not interested in caring for it. A bummer made a nice gift in exchange for a roast leg of lamb from a friend or relative.

Instructions read:

> No lambs will be given away with season. Giving lambs away will be considered stealing them.
>
> Positively no cars kept or allowed around the camps, unless on business.
>
> Feed Drop Band three times a day. Feed hay mornings, noons and nights where possible.
>
> Wagons will go around after Feeding in the morning and clean up all litter and dead sheep will be hauled off and buried, and hides moved to the proper place.
>
> Night herders will commence work before day men leave the sheep, and stay until the day men come on in

the morning, and bring your lanterns in and clean and fill same before quitting for the day.

Ewes not fit to raise lambs will be turned in with the lambs, and not put back into the Drop Band.

Hay haulers will feed, clean and harness their teams before breakfast.

Ewes with twin lambs should be fed one-half pound of grain twice a day, morning and night. Ewes with single lambs should be fed one-half pound of grain once a day, in the morning. Do not cut sacks when feeding grain. No grain is to be fed to the stacks, and not scatter same by the way. Do not open more than one butt in stack at one time.

Breaking up equipment by carelessness will be charged up to person so doing.

Keep dogs and everything else from disturbing sheep as much as possible.

In cases where sheep are infected with foot rot, put them through the Vitriol dip every 7 to 10 days, and be careful each time to take out all showing signs of lameness, and properly trim infected hoofs and stand them in a tank for 10 minutes.

Do not leave the outfit without a full statement of time worked, and signed by the Camp Boss.

(Signed) ANDREW LITTLE

Camp Bosses will keep a record of all workmen's time, noting when they start work, and when given them an order for any wages they want to draw and a full report of time and a signed order when they quit work.

Andy also had carefully written INSTRUCTIONS TO IRRIGATORS that were handed to those who were to do the watering. They were:

In irrigating new ground, hay or grain, use small heads of water in corrugations. Do not allow water to come together in the corrugations.

Sometimes run part way through, then change to a new place for two days to keep from washing the ground.

All water should be set at night after supper. Set properly so as not to waste. Then finish off during the day. See that the ground is all wet and do not waste water. That is, waste as little as possible.

Have plenty of manure or straw at the head to keep from washing corrugates and ditches.

Do not cut corrugates. **POSITIVELY DO NOT WASH AND SCAR THE GROUND.**

Do not leave any pools or leaks about the turnout places or along the ditch.

Do not make sets on new ground after supper.

(Signed) Andrew Little

Old-time workers for Andy said that any man who wanted to do a real job, could simply read the instructions and know what he was supposed to do. "Why, hell, a guy could run his own outfit and make money if he just followed Andy's rules and regulations," one herder said.

C H A P T E R S E V E N

AN INSTINCT TO HERD

IT WOULD MAKE ONLY A LITTLE LESS SENSE TO ATTEMPT TO RUN A SHEEP business without dogs than it would without sheep. And Andy Little was one of the most sensible of sheepmen. The fact that he brought two Border Collies with him from Scotland when he came to Idaho in 1894, was the beginning of that proof.

Accustomed to herding in the unfenced hills of Scotland, he knew that the dogs could keep him from losing animals in deep valleys, ravines and in thick brush when herding to and in Idaho high country. To be caught in deep snow without a trained herd dog would be devastating. One dog would be worth four men in such a case.

Andy taught his herders and children never to make pets of the dogs that were to work with the sheep. "Once they are petted," he would say, "that takes away from the discipline they need for herding." He had arrived with the two dogs, selling one before he reached the Aikman ranch for his first job, and at the peak of his operations, he owned about a thousand dogs spread out through the various ranches and home place.

Once, after visiting a number of small sheep operations looking for sheep to buy, he said, "You know, I've got more sheepdogs than most of those guys have sheep." He had from one to three herding dogs for a band of a thousand sheep, with a number of additional dogs at the ranches.

Jessie Little Naylor and her husband, Bob, had their herders carry supplies by pack string. They found that a band of 2,200 sheep could be handled by each man with the able assistance of three or four trained Scottish Border Collies and Australian shepherd dogs. The Naylor ranch alone had sixty trained dogs, representing a small fortune in dogdom. The other Littles had been taught equally well the value of dog help.

Andy maintained that the sheep dogs were the unacknowledged administrators of the wool industry. While he did not want pets made of his dogs, he treated them with care and respect. That good shepherd had trained his dogs to know that they were working together in herding. This feeling for the dogs was passed on to his children.

The dogs did everything . . . they herded, guarded, protected, and they obeyed the commands of the herder. Andy had imported a pedigreed pair of collies from Scotland for breeding purposes and trained them to sheep ranch conditions, which were new to them. While proud of the pedigreed pair, he said, "Good sheep dogs need not be of fancy blood, but it helps to make a dog a bit better. The more sheep turned out on the range the more important the dogs become. One or two dogs can be of great help to the herder. Three good dogs are as many as any of them need.

"I think that when a herder wants more than four dogs, what he is doing is operating a dog pound. He isn't a sheepherder then. He is a dog herder."

He knew that when too many dogs got together they would get to "wrangling among themselves and neglect the sheep." His family heard him say on many occasions, "One dog or one boy, good. Two dogs or two boys, better. Three dogs or three boys, less than none at all."

Known as "Old Tweed" because he lived for nearly twenty years, the first pedigreed Border collie that Andy had shipped from Scotland was a black and white male. He was so well liked that for years after his demise, herders and family members were naming new pups Tweed. Just as another import, Jim, was to do for much of his life, Tweed rode around in the car with Andy. But when Andy was driving a team and the buggy, Tweed would run alongside rather than ride. Andy thought it a good idea, as Tweed had learned that if he ran to the Emmett butcher shop and lay in front of the door whenever he had a chance, the butcher would feed him meat scraps. He became a fat dog and needed exercise.

Later another Kate-and-Jim pair of pedigreed collies was imported to replace the originals who came with Andy to Idaho. Jim turned out to be a lazy dog, but Andy loved him. He rode in the back seat of Andy's car and knew nothing about herding.

Kate was a hard worker. Andy would boast, "Kate can practically move an entire band of sheep all by herself." Jessie said that when he purchased the dogs and had them shipped to Emmett, he had planned to raise their pups. After one litter, the plan didn't pan out. Not only was the second Jim lazy about herding sheep, but he was lazy about striking up a lasting romance with Kate.

In each band, Andy had eight to twelve black sheep which he used as markers. If one or two of the markers were missing, he would just bet that others were also gone. If there were *any* out, Katie would be sent for them and could often hold them at a clump of bushes or trees until the herder came along. If they were out 100 to 150 sheep, the camp tender would have to go and find them. He was depended upon to keep track of the bands. He had maps and routes outlined to where all the camps were located.

David tells of marauding dogs and the gruesome slaughter they can perform in a short time. At such an onrush even the best of the sheep dogs are helpless, almost as though paralyzed, he said.

"One cold winter night, I think it was in 1938, I heard the bell on the lead sheep, which meant they were stampeding, and I ran into the house and got Drew. He grabbed his old seven-shot Winchester shotgun off the rack as we bolted out the door. By then we could hear the bells ringing wildly, the sheep bleating, and a blood-thirsty growling and barking of the dogs. Drew slipped through the fence headed for the corral and I ran to get the hired man.

"It was a cold, clear moonlight night and with the light that was shining on the snow it was easy to see. We saw a big bunch of marauding dogs rampaging on a sheep slaughter. With a firm grip on his old Winchester shotgun and his finger on the trigger, the hired man came running. Seven shots were fired and he and Drew got five of the dogs. But not before they had killed fourteen of our sheep and crippling nine others. The rest of the dogs high-tailed it out of there."

Although Andy brought a "Jim" and "Katie" with him from Scotland, "Old Tweed" was the first Scotch Collie herd dog that Andy imported from Scotland (late 1920s). "Tweed" died as an old dog, but many later dogs were given his name.

Two of the herd dogs at the alert and ready for the signal to move the sheep. These are two of the "Jim" and "Katie" names that were given dogs that came after the original pair.

The remainder of the sheep were driven to a corral where it was felt they would be safe. The very next night the marauding dogs were back, their lust for blood only whetted. They gnawed through the wooden fence and began the second slaughter. They were finally cornered and killed, but not before killing twenty-three sheep and maiming thirty-nine others. Less than a week before, dogs were blamed for the death of sixty sheep at the Highland camp in the foothills near Boise. One of the dogs killed was a German police and another a bulldog. The monetary loss was well over $1,000.

M.C. Claar, who was secretary of the Idaho Wool Growers Association at that time, reported that the damage to Andy's flocks was just a part of the ravaging of Idaho sheep by the dogs. T.C. Pearson of Caldwell had his flock raided by dogs three times, killing, among others, several head of purebred Hampshire ewes. Art Van-

A marauding dog bares his fangs over a sheep. Dead sheep from the slaughter are lying all over the yard. The Littles did everything they could to guard against killer dogs, yet such slaughters cost thousands of dollars.

Courtesy Idaho Wool Growers

Sicklin of Salmon, former Weiser stockman, had 135 sheep slaughtered by dogs.

"Bad as it is, it could have been worse," Andy told his boys. "We lost nearly 500 in that thick timber above Idaho City one year. The bear did it.

"Always be careful to pick a bedding-down spot for the sheep—especially when the lambs are on the ewes—where they can get away if a bear gets into the band. Not only higher ground will do it. There can be no thick patches of brush or even any downed timber that they can't jump over. If you don't find that kind of a spot, they will become terrified, bunch up together and as many will suffocate as are killed by the bear."

"It is difficult to determine the killer dog," Claar said. He may appear friendly and peaceful at home, and be a killer when he is in the fields. But most killer dogs are underfed by their owners and so are forced to find food wherever they can. "Once a dog starts killing, he continues for the fun of it. A coyote is different. It rarely kills more than two or three sheep at a time, but both dogs and bear will kill as many as he can," Claar went on. Both the bear and the coyote are a vicious enemy to the sheep and owners.

Bears are considered much worse than coyotes in killing. The bear will stampede the sheep into running over a cliff. Coyotes, with rare exception, will kill only one or two at a time. A coyote will grab onto the heel of a sheep with its sharp teeth, slip its paws onto the body and while holding it slit its throat with its teeth. Andy's bands had between 100 and 200 killed at one time by bear. This is because sheep have more of a herd instinct than most animals.

"Except," he would say, "for the purebreds and they don't know the meaning of herd."

A number of years later, about 1977, Phil Soulen of Weiser, lost 130 sheep, grazing just outside the city limits of Payette, to a pack of hungry dogs. As the bears were wont to do, the dogs had bunched the sheep into a sugar beet field and then drove them over the bank into a pit where they could be more easily slaughtered.

So the Littles were not the only ones to lose sheep to dogs, bear, and coyotes. So disliked were the coyotes that the name was often used by all involved with the woolies to describe any despicable character. Anyone in the business for any length of time with more than a few sheep could expect to lose a number of them to the marauders. Though there were killer dogs, most of them were friend to sheep and man.

Bob Naylor was both a sheepman and a camera bug, taking hundreds of pictures at the various events on the ranches. One time while the crew was working with registered Suffolk sheep, Bob crouched down to get a picture of a Suffolk as it came out of the chute.

Drew's dog, the current Katie, seeing the running sheep, roared by at the same time and was joined by Allen Wilson's imported dog, Jim. Bob and camera landed end-over-teakettle.

Andy was in his car nearby with Tweed, his number one collie. Tweed had been trained to herd just a few sheep at a time and saw that singleton come out of the chute. He decided that it was his place to be down on the ground with his kinsmen who were making life mighty uncomfortable for Bob. Andy grabbed his cane to encourage Tweed to remain in the car. The wave of the cane looked like a "sick 'em" to Tweed and just as Naylor got to his feet, Tweed swept him off them again.

Despite the misreading of the signal by Tweed, Andy claimed that his herd dogs were so well-trained and good at their work that they could put a sheep into the back seat of his car.

The Little children liked Tweed, who wasn't very effective in herding a band but was invaluable in finding a lost ewe or lamb. One day they were playing in the yard and shaking an old gunnysack at him to grab with his teeth. Andy drove in and watched what was going on for just a minute.

As he got out he said, "This is the best way to ruin a good sheepdog. Dogs are like human beings. If they learn to play, they forget to work. Sheepdogs are working dogs, so don't play with them."

Both David and Jay Sissler, who worked for him, liked horses and racing them. They were racing in a relay when Jay fell and broke his leg while changing horses. George Cruickshank arrived just about the time Jay fell and they immediately got him into the car and to the hospital. While Jay had his leg held firmly in the cast and unable to work, he acquired a couple of fine collie pups. He did an excellent job of training.

Before long the collies were obeying his commands to move sheep to the left, and then to the right around an old tire he had placed as a marker in his corral. Soon after that, the dogs were performing smoothly in herding flocks into the corral.

A sheepdog trial can be, and usually is, a strenuous test of both dog and master. There is a run of 300 yards to find three sheep in a holding pen. The sheep are released from the pen as the dog arrives. It is his job to take them back to hesitate at his master's feet, then drive them through the gate and into another pen.

Judges observe carefully both dog and master and each is deducted points for mistakes in the job each is to perform. If the sheep run out of line, do not go into the pen immediately, the dog loses points. If the handler overacts in giving the dog commands, other points are deducted. So they must work as a team in a smooth way that displays the intelligence of both.

Over the next several years Jay Sissler built an enviable reputation as a trial dog trainer and owner, appearing with his dogs at many shows.

Idaho's Gem State Kennel Club usually held trials in early May at the White City Park in Boise. One year Andy Little entered two pedigreed Scotch collies, which he had imported from the south of Scotland the previous September. They then had been trained to the new conditions of the sheep business in Idaho.

Collies had competed in the trials before, but never the sheep dog, born and bred in the tradition of the flock. Andy had said he could take "one, or almost a dozen" to the trials, as the female had just produced seven puppies. He explained that good sheep dogs need not be of fancy stock, but that when the blood is of a pedigreed strain the chances are much better that the dog will turn out better than the common cur.

Though Andy called his mixed-breeds "curs," he wasn't quite accurate. The cur is of unknown ancestry; Andy knew what his dogs were. What Andy preferred was the first-generation cross of purebreds of different lines. He believed the offspring showed a great deal of hybrid strength and energy. Actually, the hybrid is most often more healthy and hardy than either parent breed.

Purebred or mutt, when the puppy is six to eight weeks of age, training begins. The basis for most of it is reward. The reward is to be given immediately after the action, and the pup forms a connection between the action and approval. Basics consist of the commands: "come, sit, stay, heel, come by on left, and come back on right," or vice versa.

The Border collie is an attentive watchdog and unusual sheepherder. Its strength sustained over long periods of time, quick response to commands, alertness and its sharing in the life of the lonely shepherd make it the best beloved of all the sheepdogs.

It was in 1938 that Jim and Katie were entered in the trials by Andy. Jim and Katie were the names chosen by the Littles who raised a large number of their herding dogs from the second and third generation parents. Old Tweed had died near his twentieth year. After some time had elapsed, Andy decided to keep Jim.

He gave Katie to Drew. But Katie had taken a liking to David and the feeling was reciprocated. Drew had no objection and Katie traveled often in the front seat of David's truck and would rest her head in his lap as they drove along.

Some of the dogs from Scotland had been trained to herd small flocks of sheep and were too high strung for the huge bands which the Littles managed. But not Katie. To Drew and David she was a priceless asset. It could never be said that dogs were not greatly appreciated on the Little ranches. Not only were they considered of great value, but when asked what the dogs do on a sheep ranch, all of the Littles had the same answer.

"Everything."

In 1938, David took a semester out from his studies at the University of Idaho to help on the ranches. Many years later, his sons were to do the same thing when they were needed. That year a number of sheep had been lost from the band, and David called Katie to the pickup to find them. The sheep were about three miles from the ranch. David turned the pickup around and slowly drove those three miles back with Katie herding the sheep right behind him.

Katie was about four years old and the Littles were puzzled and a little sad that they had not been able to breed her for producing pups as good as she was. She was prime for breeding, and though young, the Littles were concerned about replacing her in the event of her loss.

One day Katie was not to be found although they looked for her in every imaginable spot. Everyone on the ranch loved her and appreciated what a valuable dog she was. It was almost impossible to believe she could be lost and no matter where they went, the Littles kept an eye out in the hope of seeing Katie.

Sometime later George King had announced a sale of farm machinery at his ranch in the Grandview area. David drove down to the farm, which is now under the waters of the Strike Reservoir. The first thing he noticed were two black and white dogs, one of which had been kicked by a horse. The other looked so much like old Katie that David felt his heart throbbing. He had convinced himself that she was dead.

He looked at the dog and said, "Sit down." She sat. He said, "Come by on the right side." She did. Then he said, "Come back on the left side," and she did. Again, "Sit down," and she sat.

"Whose dog is this?" David asked. Some fellow he didn't know answered, "I found her out on Squaw Creek and she was looking for water and suffering from exhaustion." He went on to tell about what bad shape she was in when he found her. He took her home with him, and fed, watered and cared for her until she was built back up again.

"I was darned near in tears," David said, "and he could tell how glad I was to see her, so he said, 'Why don't you take her home with you, and if you ever get a pup from her, let me have it.'

"I put her in the truck with me and she just reached her head over and put her nose into my lap and the words just came out of my mouth aloud, 'My God, it *is* old Katie.' Whenever she rode in the car or truck with me, she had always set in the seat with her head in my lap. I had been sure she was dead and had hated to think that. And now, here she was alive. And she knew me.

"What had happened was that one day when we were moving Drew's cattle we just plain lost her. She probably was doing her job so well, that we just left her. And I didn't like to think that, either. We had looked everywhere for her whenever we could and finally felt sure she was dead. And here she was—alive."

Gerri added to the story with, "David came into the house and he had tears in his eyes as he told me, 'I found old Katie.'"

Andy Little and his kind may not have wanted their working dogs petted, but they gave them love, and got love back from them. The hundreds of dogs they raised and trained helped build the Little sheep empire, and the family never forgot it.

CHAPTER EIGHT

EMMETT – THE BLOOMING VALLEY

IDAHO IS A PLACE OF HIGH ALTITUDES AND LOW MULTITUDES. ITS RESIdents think of it as a young land, rugged and hardy. But it holds tight to its days as a part of the Old West. Its citizens still operate with an independence and individualism that make those who want to move more rapidly gnash their teeth in frustration. But few want to leave. Those who find it necessary to do so, seem to return at the slightest opportunity.

Those who stay work to improve life, but yet have the pioneer spirit of "We can do it together!" The high altitudes that stretch from the Canadian border to south-central Idaho feed roaring whitewater in the major rivers of the Clearwater and the Salmon, with hundreds of smaller ones cascading down the mountains. The southern part of the state is completely traversed by the mighty, but much more placid, Snake River, which rolls on to form a part of the borders between Idaho and her neighboring states of Oregon and Washington. It was that pioneer spirit that brought irrigation from the Snake and smaller rivers to the sagebrush lands of the south.

David Little said, "It was the kind of clear whitewater in the northern part of Idaho that Dad was expecting to see when he hit Willow Creek. He was disappointed when the overflowing creek was riled and muddy. The streams near his home in Scotland are usually like those up north."

Andy Little had known the value of water all his life. Moffat Waters was the second name for the valley in Scotland from which he had come. It was well-named, since water was part of its wealth.

When he arrived in Emmett, there was much talk of growing fruit trees in the valley. And within ten years those orchards were blooming, producing and shipping fruit. In their book, *Idaho: The Fruitful Land*, George Yost of Emmett and Dick d'Easum of Boise, wrote, "Fruitland . . . was in thriving condition by 1906 when it shipped twelve carloads of fruit on the Payette-Emmett branch of the railroad called the Punkin Vine. . . . The Idaho Orchards Company boosted Emmett to the catbird seat with an elaborate program about 1910. The company invited investors to buy acreage on the mesa where investment in orchards held promise of astonishing profit."

A brochure predicting that Emmett, then 2500 in population, would soon be 25,000 and a veritable Garden of Eden, was effective. Although it didn't reach the 25,000 population, land buyers came from Ohio, Iowa, and Colorado. The campaign contributed to the growth that brought the establishment of Gem County in 1915.

Gem County had been carved out of both Boise and Canyon Counties that year, with Emmett (known as Emmettsville until 1885, when the name was shortened) as the county seat. Payette County was born a couple of years later. Officials of both met to decide where the dividing line should be. At question was which one would get the dilapidated old Falk bridge, in need of extensive repair, spanning the Payette River. Andy Little was given credit for neatly tucking the bridge into Payette County when the agreement was signed.

Much of the early travel to the gold mines in Boise Basin was through Gem County and the attendant necessity for a series of road houses for the travelers was met. One of the early ones was at Picket Corral, a little over two miles below the present Black Canyon Dam. Its setting is a natural rock amphitheater with a corral of poles set in the ground and joined together with strips of cowhide. A well filled with fresh water, a dugout and a cabin for the guests made it a desirable stopping place. Many tales grew up about the Corral, including one that a gang of rustlers used it for harboring and branding stolen horses, until flushed out by the Vigilantes.

It was two decades after the first ranches appeared along the river banks that immigrants from the midwest plains begin to arrive and take over the sagebrush land between Emmett and Freezeout Hill. A part of the Snake River plain, nine-tenths of which is covered with lava flows, Emmett is blessed with an abundance of water. Ancient lake deposits are found along the edges of the plain and in the western end. Ground wells produce large quantities of water. Emmett has only twelve feet to reach the water table.

Adding its bit to the name of Gem County and Idaho, the Gem State, is the opal bed in the lava of Squaw Butte, about five miles northeast of Emmett. The lovely, flaming fire opals are considered prizes by those who find them. Pale blue water agates are also found nearer the town. Halfway to Boise, on Willow Creek, is a deposit of agatized and opalized wood of high quality. Farther up the creek is an area of nearly thirty acres containing opals in colors ranging from lightning red to a deep pink and white.

The town of Emmett lies in the ancient lake bed that is now a green valley northwest of Boise, the capitol city. It is situated at the edge of a mesa and is reached by an interesting road which traverses Freezeout Hill.

Farther to the north and a bit to the east is Squaw Butte rising 7,000 feet above the valley floor. It is a landmark from miles away. Airline pilots use it as a navigational reference, just as the immigrants of the 1800s used it to guide them on their way. It got its name from its profile, resembling that of a sleeping woman and about whom an Indian legend of massacre has grown. From miles away, across the low hills and deep valleys, the Butte could, indeed, be a sleeping earth mother.

The Payette river, which cuts through the town, helped to form the valley eons ago. Willow Creek is another watery visitor to the valley.

The town grew steadily from 1886 to 1916. The mercantile stores of E.K. Hayes and Company and Bilderback and Cartwright were doing well. Steve Dempsey's drugstore and Russell's hardware store served those needs of the town. Theodore Womack and Son had one blacksmith shop and Hardy Phillips and Jacob Hamm jointly owned a second. The Last Chance Ditch was built with teams of horses in 1890, providing a source of irrigation water for the farmers and ranchers.

Roy Murray said, "The first blacksmith shop I remember is the one on the east side of the canal, owned by Boise Riggs and Sam

McMillan. It was built right on the canal bank down by the bridge. From 1912 until 1916 they shoed horses for Andy Little."

"My dad's [David Murray] hotel also sat right on the river bank. It and the livery stable catered to the traffic of the freighters, miners and loggers. There were other livery stables and corrals, necessary for the freighting which was the only method of shipping until the Idaho Northern Railroad was built in 1902. Then Emmett was connected with the Oregon Short Line's mainline at Nampa.

"It seemed like John McNish owned about half the buildings in town. There were the McNish and Allen General Mercantile store right in town, and they owned the sawmill just west of town and below where Boise Cascade Corporation has its big mill now. John McNish was a great friend of Andy's, as he was of many.

"He was so respected that he acted as banker for many of the residents in the valley, although he was never bonded as such. And it was said that every farmer wanted a good reputation with McNish, so they paid up their accounts at the end of each year."

The Payette Lumber Company held timberland on the watersheds of the Payette and Weiser rivers and had a system of regulated log drives down the Payette. Lumbermen from other mills who wanted to join the combined drive could do so by paying a fee. Spring floods were capricious and ruined many a drive. By 1914, railway transportation had replaced the water route.

The Payette was associated with the Barber Lumber Company which had originated in Eau Claire, Wisconsin, and also in 1914 the two companies consolidated to become the Boise Payette (now Boise Cascade) Lumber Company. Ten years earlier the Payette had started leasing some of its lands to Andy Little for grazing purposes. This provided enough revenue that the practice was continued.

From nearly every home in Emmett it is possible to see another house, but none are jammed together. In recent years several of the handsome old homes have been bought and restored by young newcomers to the valley. It is quiet enough to hear the church bells on a Sunday morning. The citizens of Emmett live in a nice sort of privacy. There are meadows, pastures, orchards, hills, mountains,

Courtesy Idaho Historical Society

In the early 1900s, men and boys of Emmett line Main Street's wooden sidewalks in front of The Palace Restaurant, W.J. Rogers Livery and Feed Stable shared with "veterinary surgeon" W.D. Stevens, and the Hotel Emmett. Surreys, buggies, and a couple of stagecoaches line up for their drivers to display their well-fed and groomed horses.

rivers and the water that is backed up by the Black Canyon Dam, which is on the Payette river only three miles from town. It is a small lake 183 feet high and 1,039 feet wide. A diversion dam was completed in 1924, and it is a part of the Boise Project which has an irrigable area of more than 350,000 acres in southern Idaho and eastern Oregon.

Most of the residents own their own homes and indicate property boundaries by nodding toward a fence, an aging tree, a pile of rocks or the neighbor's lawn and saying, "Our property goes from here to there."

Spring is a particularly glorious time of year in the valley with blossoming cherry and apple trees, peach, prune and apricot attracting motorists to drive at least to the top of Freezeout Hill to view the blossoming panorama. Since a severe freeze in 1972, the fruit business isn't what it used to be, the people will tell you. Then they will go on to ask, "But what is?" For years there was an annual cherry blossom festival in Emmett with a late afternoon parade at which the governor of the state was often honored by riding in the first car down Main Street.

Summer is warm, often hot, and the patio and backyard picnics are a mode of life.

Autumn is another season of beauty when the leaves on the shrubs and trees along the river and creek banks turn into shades of red, orange, yellow and brown. By November the colors have turned to deeper browns and grays. Pheasants and grouse move into the fields to forage and incidentally provide flying targets for the hunters who come in droves to the valley. Deer are in the hills and higher mountains and are more easily spotted when winter snows begin to fall.

Emmett folk will tell you that their valley is the greatest place in the world to live and that many large ranches lie just over the hills in all directions. The lasting things of life are there, the water, the land, and a serenity that, to them, makes city life pall in comparison.

It was in the blooming valley of Emmett that Andrew Little decided to establish his permanent home. He had herded sheep on the mesa of Freezeout Hill and he liked the view of the valley from the hilltop. Nearly everyone does. He could stand and gaze out over those willows and bushes, the few evergreens there and the river running through the little town and think of the day he would have a home and family there.

There could be another reason: the name of the town itself. Roll these names around on your tongue and you won't spit them out. Rather, savor them. Galishiels, Peebles, Moffat and Glasgow. These were names familiar to Andrew Little.

Now, try Moffat and Emmett. Thousands of miles apart, yet in several ways alike. Both are in river-sectioned valleys. The hills on either side are about the same height. Many are tree-clad, or partially so. Both are fine sheep country. Moffat is built on a hillside and Emmett in a valley. Moffat has its High Street and Emmett its Main, both denoting the principal course through each town. These two villages which grew to be towns are the places wherein the character of Andrew Little was formed. To know the man was to know the towns and vice versa.

While Emmett was a frontier village when Andy arrived, it possessed little of the decay and dilapidation that often went with the speedily-built rural villages miles from a city. As the Western United States is wide, the Emmett streets were broad from the beginning. Wooden sidewalks fronted Main Street buildings.

Andy's friend and foreman, Allen Wilson, said, "You could hear every step you took on those sidewalks. Not only that, you could hear the guy in back of you, too. A fellow didn't know whether to stop and let him catch up with you or to cut and run."

With hills and mountains surrounding the village, two on the far outskirts, Squaw Butte to the northwest and Freezeout to the south, were to play a role in the life of the Little family and the grazing of the sheep and cattle they would own. Little Butte, where there would also be a ranch, located near the stopping place of Ola, was also the place of an Indian encampment and is now the ranching community of Sweet.

The first home of Andy and Adis was a large wooden two-story structure, a typical farmhouse, on Fourth Street. It was here that the Little children were born and grew to young manhood and womanhood. It was not until 1924 that they contracted to have built for them and the children the huge, solid concrete manor house at the very end of Fourth Street, but with land still adjoining the original ranch home.

Good schools, a modern hospital and convalescent homes along with the fine climate, lush fields, orchards, grains and gardens, timber stands and mills, the continuing livestock industry, and lakes make Gem County a place where many families make their homes unto the fourth and fifth generations.

CHAPTER NINE

THE FOREVER HOUSE

ANDY LITTLE'S HOUSE WAS BUILT IN HIS MIND DECADES BEFORE ground was broken for it. Twin inspirations for the reinforced-concrete edifice were the stone house of his childhood and the San Francisco earthquake nearly eighteen years previously.

A slip in the San Andreas fault on April 18, 1906, damaged property within a 270 mile section of the cut through Southern California. Buildings toppled in the city of San Francisco, but the real destruction was done by the fire. Most of the central business district and residential areas were incinerated. Hundreds died and the survivors camped on the sand dunes west of the cremated city. Property damage was estimated over $400 million 1906 dollars.

Andy determined to build a house that wouldn't burn or collapse. Later, Roscoe Rich said, "Andy was a builder; when he built something, he meant it to stay."

He built it out of solid concrete. Since the San Francisco quake Andy had read and listened to every comment and item concerning the thousands whose homes had been obliterated, and how reinforced concrete withstood shocks five times better than brick or stone.

Family members say that he often mentioned the catastrophe. And by 1923, when he was prepared to build the large dream home he had thought of for a number of years, he was determined that it would withstand any vagary of weather. By 1924, it was finished.

Aside from the fact that the house was of solid concrete, it was reinforced with all kinds of iron and steel scavenged from old equipment on the various ranches and from junk piles throughout the Valley. When the building was completed, Andy looked at it with great satisfaction and said, "No earthquake could ever take this down."

Carl Hummel of Boise, one of the architects, would stand and survey the building while it was in the building stages and remark to anyone nearby, "Do you know that thing is solid concrete? Not only that. It is reinforced with all that heavy metal. What a house!"

The Littles had six teams making round trips to the Payette River to haul the gravel used with mixing cement for the walls. David remembers riding his Shetland pony and following the dumpboards the one mile to the river. Dumpboards were made for the running gear of a wagon, with movable two-by-fours for the flooring. The boards would be moved to shake out the gravel for use in the cement mixture. That sand would then be sifted for the various grades of concrete.

No one who knew Andy was surprised when he started to build the big house, for the building took place in his mind long before the lumber, cement and other materials arrived on the site at the end of Fourth Street. For all of the early days after arriving from Scotland, when he worked for Bob Aikman, he was building his own sheep bands in his mind. Once the bands were acquired, his mind turned to the construction of barns, sheds and other necessities. It was only natural that he would, as soon as he could afford it, think of building a grand house for Agnes and the children.

And the new home filled one of his greater ambitions. While he wanted very much to leave Scotland and to do well in his new country, he thought often of the large stone house near Moffat in which he had lived as a boy and grown to manhood. It had provided warmth for them in the winter gales, and the family was there. When the decision to remain in Idaho became firm, and again when Adis agreed to be his wife, he began to think of a family home much like the one of his boyhood.

It is certain that Adis was proud of her new home, but she never bragged about it. On the contrary. When someone else made the remark that she must be overjoyed, her answer was, "I would rather have a cottage and a coo [cow]." She was wary of the Scottish social sin of being houseproud.

The new two-story house was built in the shape of an L. The long front covers the entry hall, the vestibule (as the Littles call the great hall) with a winding oak stairway leading to it from the second floor, and the doorway to the large living room at the end of which is a white marble fireplace. The mantle is of white-painted wood and intricately carved. The dining room adjoins the living room.

A hallway leads down the long part of the L. There is the library, where Adis sewed and knit and listened to the radio broadcasts of the World Series and other baseball games.

In the lower and shorter part of the L were the office, entry porch, the kitchen, and several storage rooms. There was an enclosed and large sleeping porch as well. Myrn related that, as he observed the new sleeping porch, "Grandad would say, 'We used to sleep in the house and go outside to the toilet. Now, we're going to the toilet inside and sleeping outside. Is that progress?' "

The oak stairway has a dark mahogany banister with painted round white wood posts. On the end of each step is a wood carving. While the walls are so smooth as to look like plaster, David remembers that his father hired a concrete craftsman who excelled in troweling the walls to the smoothness of marble. Now painted an off-white, the walls were a rosy brown color in the days of Adis and Andy. There were two colors of calcimine sold then, green and brown. In today's interior decorating scheme there are nearly fifty different shades of wall covering.

At the foot of the winding stairway was a huge grandfather clock of solid oak. It was brought back from a trip that Adis and her two daughters, Agnes and Jessie, made to Scotland in 1928. It is now in the home of the Little's oldest grandson, Harry Bettis. On the high wall up the first flight of steps is a twenty foot long, five foot wide tapestry in shades of red, white and blue. It has an Elizabethan motif of two maidens flanked by a unicorn and a lion, with rabbits and dogs at their feet. A bevy of birds with flowers is interwoven along the bottom.

The concrete finisher did a beautiful job above the small gold and black chandelier. Four teardrops and four bronze holders with golden globes reflect the design above. The scroll designs were continued above the lights in the entryway, the smaller hallway and on into the great hall.

In the living room is a splendid one-hundred percent woolen

rug of a beautiful chocolate-brown shade. After all these years, it appears new. The first electric phonograph to come into the Valley, with a fine collection of old Scottish records still in it, is also in the living room. Drew and a friend, Jack Hetherington—who was something of an electrical genius and it was said that it took a genius to operate—had a great time playing the phonograph. It is a multi-record player with mechanical arms that would reach up and get the next of twelve records which it could play at one sitting.

The twenty-or-more-foot dining room housed a solid mahogany table and chairs with ample seating for twelve people, and the possibility of seating sixteen when extended. The equally solid high buffet is six feet long and heavy enough to require eight legs. Dinners were served in the dining room when Senator Borah or other special guests—the wool buyers and graders, bankers—were there. Sunday family dinners and all holiday occasions such as Thanksgiving, Christmas and New Years found the family and relatives surrounding the table. Adis had the assistance of a cook and often a housemaid, but yet liked to prepare her own special dishes.

The second floor contains seven bedrooms and three baths. A large open area at the landing led to those rooms. A glass-front hardwood cabinet containing family mementos and photographs is in that area. Two rooms on the second floor were designed for servants quarters, but as time moved on, and it became difficult to find women to cook and do the housework as live-in employees, the rooms were sometimes used by the boys.

Craftsmen would have a fine time simply seeking out the many interesting touches built into the home. Someone did an outstanding job with the cornices, all perfectly mortised. All wood used inside was carefully mitered with not an uneven end in the entire house.

An eight-by-four-foot hallway is situated between the dining room and the great hallway. The telephone is located there and a large oil painting of an elk hangs on the wall. A smaller entryway stands between that hall and the kitchen. In that hall is a kitchenette where food could be kept warm until time for the serving in the dining room. A large breakfast nook was built into the kitchen, where many of the family's meals were served. From the window there, the mountains can be seen in the distance. Just outside is a magnificent Blue Spruce tree and a magnolia.

From the kitchen window one can look directly north to Squaw Butte. One door from the kitchen leads to another winding stairway that reaches the second floors. Another leads to a plant or flower room, several storage rooms and one bathroom. An enclosed breezeway just outside leads to a pantry, to a milk room that had been used as a mud room when the children were smaller, a laundry room, and another attractive entryway from the outdoors.

That entry (to the dining room) was an open, roofed porch. Referred to as the North Porch, that was where Adis spent her summer afternoons before the home was air-conditioned. Later the porch became Drew and Myrn's storeroom and their children's playroom when they took over the house.

The brown-shellacked wicker furniture which Adis had in the library was taken to the North Porch by Myrn and Drew. The wicker is still as tightly woven as the day it was purchased by Adis. "This is real wicker," Myrn said. "It is not the stuff we can buy now at the import store." The youth chair, not so high as our modern highchairs, and upon which the youngest of the Little children sat at meals, has also been moved to the North Porch.

There are six storerooms in the basement, which could be considered a third floor. Marking the era in which the grand house was built, are the hot-water radiators fed by lines running to the basement. A coal furnace heated the water and also ran it upstairs and all through the house. Andy bought lump coal directly from a mine and the furnace was fired up twice each day.

Drew had the coal-fired boiler removed when he and Myrn took over the house. He replaced it with a simpler, cleaner oil heater and tanks. But in the mid-80s winters it was costing Myrn an average of $68 a day to heat, about $2000 a month. She thought it would have been about one dollar a day at the time the senior Littles lived there.

Since the house was built so solidly of concrete throughout there was no insulation. As a result, winters could be very cold. Mrs. Little kept an electric Sunburst heater in the library where she

The building crew lunch at the Forever House in 1923. A specially-built dump board wagon permitted sand to be screened into containers for making cement. Note the long-handled wooden brake at the front wheel.

The beauty and majesty of the manor house is evident while ewes and lambs graze on the spacious lawn. Mrs. Little is near the porch. The house, in the estate of Drew and Myrn Little, is now empty but managed by daughter, Agnes Brailsford.

"Charley Bouquet" Marsh helped in the garden and around the house. He could often bag a few pheasants for the Little's evening dinner. The Little children talked of him for years.

liked to read and work. When winter's snow and wind brought extreme cold, she would add the necessary number of woolen sweaters or jackets to be comfortable.

"The first time I came to the Little house was as a guest of Drew at Thanksgiving. I was so cold that he loaned me some of his long underwear," Myrn commented.

Andy's office, between the library and large back porch, is where Andy kept records not at the Main Street office and commissary building. A washroom adjoins the office. It was here that he also entertained and talked with his employees and business friends. The large rolltop desk that he used is now in the possession of Carol McGregor Bettis in the red brick mansion on Boise's Warm Springs Avenue. Laura Moore Cunningham left that house to her great nephew, Harry Bettis.

An entire history is contained in a large glassed-in frame holding many postcard-size photographs. One shows large wool sacks with the A. Little cross brand on each one. Another shows unshorn sheep and lambs next to similar animals shorn and branded with a red or black paint. Some of the brands are of a diamond and those of another band are given the cross. They are then called "road-marked."

Other photos show the road to Squaw Butte, yearling sheep, pack mules, the castrated buck sheep known as the bellwether leading other sheep, the supply wagons taking commodities to the ranches, and wool wagons stacked high with sacks and pulled by six-horse teams. There is a smiling picture of the Butte ranch cook, China Louie and a group of sheepherders, some of them Basques, holding the musical instruments they played in The Sheepherders Band. Andy and his big black horse, Diamond, are also in one snapshot.

The Little home looks as self-contained as Mount Vernon, that masterpiece of architecture, building and organization designed by George Washington in Virginia. Though the houses are different, both have woven wooden fences, white woven picket types with the various gardens and buildings enough to care for an entire crew of people.

The nearby sheds are well-built and attractive. The old garage

Many picnics were enjoyed by the Littles and their friends. Left to right: (back row) Roy Murray, Edris and Albert Skinner, Florence Murray; (front) Jessie Little Naylor, Mrs. Ackroyd, Adis Little with ever-present knitting wool, Billy Ackroyd (grader from Boston). Andy Little is at end of the line.

The latest in motoring beauty and pleasure was the 1929 Packard Christmas gift to Adis from Andy, complete with rear-wheel chains.

which had been built near the former family home years ago has been moved to the big home. The chicken house has become a peacock run. There is the brick smokehouse where they smoked their hams and bacons. Hundreds of hogs were butchered at the home ranch. The shoulders, hams and bacons were put up in the smoke house and the family and workers ate the fresh chops and ribs.

Several small storehouse buildings, the bunkhouses, and Andy's old homestead cabin are on the grounds. A round stove made by, as it is blazoned on the front, the Detroit Stove Works, was used for heat in Andy's house, which was back of the bunk-

Andy enjoys a game of lawn croquet with Roy Murray at the Little home.

house when he purchased the ranch. In a small granary are hung clevises, wrecking bar, wire stretchers, wrenches, levels, hammers, squares, saws and all manner of tools used in operating the home place.

At the larger, two-story granary building there is a small bridge over the canal to the blacksmith shop. The shop looks as though it were waiting only for the smithy. The anvil is waiting with bellows hanging from the rafters, with an attachment to pull down when necessary to keep the fire hot. In addition, a whetstone for sharpening the scythes, an old Buick motor, and a two-handle draw knife await. Then come the cow and sheep barns, the corrals, another store shed, and the big horse barn. The dairy barn is a reminder that Adis always had to have a few "coos." There is a foot plough which she used in gardening. She also kept a few sheep on the home ranch. The five-pronged Jackson fork used to hoist hay up to the barn now hangs on the wall.

The top floors of the house were marked by a row of windows and wrought-iron enclosed porches with a red-tiled roof. It is a handsome edifice in a pastoral setting.

To this day many residents of towns in southern Idaho express a desire to "visit the Little mansion at Emmett sometime." Andy and Adis didn't think of their house as a mansion, but everybody else did.

C H A P T E R T E N

ARGY-BARGY AND KILKENNY CATS

THE SCOTS CALL IT "ARGY-BARGY." TO THE IRISH, IT IS "KILKENNY CATS." Among the British and Americans it is called controversy, dispute, and legal action.

Andy understood the language of all, for he was involved in a number of legal disputes during his adult life. He won some and lost some. None of them were major disputes, but all had a bearing on the sheep industry, the development of irrigation in the Emmett Valley, and the importance of water to the landowners of the valley.

Drew's widow, Myrn, said, "Grandad was a fair man, but if there was one thing that made him angry it was to feel someone was trying to take advantage of him. He had to work so darn hard to build up his home, the herds and the ranches, that he wanted everyone else to be willing to work hard too."

Others concluded that he was a litigious person or that he felt the courts were to be utilized by all who felt there were rights to redress.

Boise attorney John Ruebelmann, formerly of Emmett, feels that the case of Andrew Little and W.E. Harris as administrators of the estate of their friend John McNish, versus the Emmett Irrigation District in January 1928, denotes "an interesting episode in Gem County during the time of the development of irrigation in the valley."

The irrigation district, which was formed to bring water to the fruitful valley, issued warrants to raise financing to operate and maintain the irrigation system. Warrants were issued by the district to McNish for labor and materials furnished for construction and operation. One complaint involved warrants issued between August 11, 1913, and September 30, 1914, but not filed until May 25,

1925; the other involved warrants all issued February 21, 1914, and filed June 11, 1923.

It was found by the court that the district owned, operated and maintained the local irrigation system and that the warrants were issued in payment for ordinary expenses, work and services, materials and supplies furnished, and constituted a promise to pay "out of the moneys belonging to the Maintenance Fund."

The difficulty was that the district never made nor collected sufficient moneys to pay the warrants. Little and Harris, as administrators, sued the district and won at the trial level. However, the district appealed the case and the judgement was reversed on the basis that the action was brought too late.

The judgement concluded that "the so-called Maintenance Fund is not a special fund created by statute. The existence of the fund did not create, in other words, was not necessary to create the cause of action.

"While the board might give the fund a name for bookkeeping purposes, it did not thereby change its character as the proceeds of an annual assessment . . . nor could it change the character of the plaintiff's contract rights or claims against the general revenue of the district, and the right to have them paid within the time and in the manner provided by law."

Three of the most distinguished jurists to serve on Idaho's Supreme Court—Chief Justice William E. Lee of Moscow, Justice Raymond L. Givens of Boise, and Justice T. Bailey Lee of Burley—heard the case and concurred in the final decision. Chief Justice Lee was to go on to Washington, D.C., to serve as a member of the Interstate Commerce Commission. Two of Idaho's current attorneys, Raymond D. Givens, son of the justice, and Jess B. Hawley served as clerks to Lee while attending law school in the nation's capital.

A second case involving the Emmett Irrigation District took place when Andy bought two parcels of land through tax sale certificates. The owners were his brother John or "Jock," as he was better known, and Justin M. Burlingham, who was listed as the owner in possession of the lands. Jock Little held, by assignment from the Boise Title and Trust Company, a mortgage on the same property dated September 21, 1912, to secure a payment of $4,000.

The certificates which the Irrigation District sold to Andy described the land as being, "in the Emmett Irrigation District of Canyon County, Idaho," while Andy asked to quiet title on real estate in Gem County as he believed that the land was the south half of the southwest corner in section 13. The court ruled that there was a fatal variance between the certificates of sale and the tax deeds issued by the District. As such, they were not a sufficient description to base valid tax deeds and pass title. Andy appealed this May 17, 1921, adverse decision from the District to the Supreme Court and lost.

On June 8, 1938, Andy and Adis listed officially as Agnes Little were awarded an Idaho trial court judgement against the Bergdahl Oil Company and Axel and Edith Bergdahl. Thirteen years previous, the Littles had leased land to the Bergdahls and their corporation for the purpose of discovering and producing gas and oil. Andy sued to break the lease on a technicality. Adis had signed the lease on November 4, 1924, but did not appear before the notary public when the signature was notarized.

The court ruled in favor of the Littles, holding that the lease was not valid. The Bergdahls made no appearance at the trial, nor were represented by counsel. The decision quieted the title to the lands in question, located in Gem and Ada Counties. Although making no appearance at the court, the Bergdahls appealed the decision to the Idaho Supreme Court.

In the decision upholding the judgement of the trial court, Justices Alfred Budge, Raymond Givens, William M. Morgan and Sutphen concurred. Chief Justice James F. Ailshie deemed himself disqualified and did not participate in the decision. A request from the Bergdahls for a hearing was denied.

The wide-open, unfenced and generally unrestricted use of the public domain caused many an argy-bargy among the early day stockmen and frequently the argument would end before the courts. One such case occurred in May of 1913, when J.E. Chandler sued Andrew Little for permitting 4,000 of his sheep to graze on public land within two miles of the Chandler home.

The trial was held in Idaho's Seventh Judicial District, Canyon County, with Judge Edward L. Bryan presiding. The Judge ruled that Andy was to pay Chandler $100, deemed to be the value of the grass eaten by the sheep. Andy appealed the judgement to the Supreme Court. His attorneys E.J. Frawley and Scatterday and Van Duyn argued that the evidence was insufficient to sustain the verdict, that the rulings of the court, as to the admissibility of evidence, were erroneous and that error was committed in giving certain instructions, and in refusing to give others, to the jury.

In writing the opinion, Justice William M. Morgan cited Sections 1217 and 1218 from Idaho Revised Code:

> Sec. 1217. It is not lawful for any person owning or having charge of sheep to herd same or to permit them to be herded on the land or possessory claims of other persons or to herd the same or to permit them to graze within two miles of the dwelling house of the owner or owners of such . . . claim.
>
> Sec. 1218. The owner or the agents of such owner of sheep violating the provisions of the last section, on complaint of the party or parties injured before any justice of the peace for the precinct where either of the interested parties may reside, is liable to the party injured for all damages sustained; and if the trespass be repeated is liable to the party injured for the second and every subsequent offense in double the amount of damages sustained.

Chandler's attorneys, George F. Zimmerman and W.A. Stone, argued that Chandler, a farmer and stockman, had 160 head of horses and cattle, which were accustomed to range and pasture on about 1,000 acres of public domain and other unfenced land within a radius of two miles of his residence. Chandler charged that on May 24, 1913, Andy's "servants" and employees, as the herders were described in the courtroom, "brought two bands of sheep, of about 2,000 head each, upon the public range . . . and herded and permitted them to graze; one of the bands were so kept and pastured within two miles of . . . dwelling-house for about a week and the other for about half that length of time."

Chandler said that when the sheep were removed the grass was practically destroyed and the land was, for a considerable time thereafter, almost worthless for range. Andy's attorneys argued that since Chandler was not the owner of the grass growing upon the range within two miles of his home, but had a right only in common with others to pasture his horses and cattle upon it, the damage recoverable should be confined to the actual injury sustained during the time the sheep were herded there.

Justice Morgan wrote in the decision that "so many elements may enter into claims arising under the law regulating the use of the range that we will not attempt to lay down a general rule fixing the measure of damage in all cases, but will say that . . . it is the loss actually sustained as a direct result of the grazing, which, in reasonable probability, his [Chandler's] stock would have fed upon it had it not been so grazed off and destroyed."

Chief Justice Budge and Justice John C. Rice concurred in affirming the decision of the lower court.

Water: The word alone carries such significance in the agricultural and stock lands of southern Idaho that it was often involved in conflict of interests. Because many of the water users depend upon the same sources of supply, it became subject to regulation. For generations, Idaho irrigators, farmers and ranchers have fought to maintain state rights to water within its boundaries. Local and state action has far surpassed that of the federal government in developing water resources. In times more recent than that of Andy Little, research on problems of watersheds in agricultural lands, the production of crop and the caring for stock has been, and is continuing to be, helpful to Idahoans in the use and retention of water.

A constant stream always signified a good spot for a home ranch. Water on adjoining lands assuring a native hay supply made it even more desirable. Both of these advantages were looked for by Andy in the land he purchased over the years. "Don't monkey with my headgate!" was the slogan for at least one successful Idaho political campaign.

Charlie Morehouse felt that Andy and one of his employees, Clifton Sherman, had indeed been monkeying with his headgate. Morehouse brought an action to restrain Little and Sherman from interfering with the headgate placed in the banks of an irrigation ditch from which both Little and Morehouse were entitled to use the water from Big Willow Creek.

The water was conveyed through the Claiborn Canal. At the

lower end of the canal a joint headgate or dividing box was placed to divide the water equally. Morehouse charged that Little and/or Sherman had closed half of the headgate used by Morehouse with sand and gravel. The court found in favor of Morehouse and issued a restraining order against Little from interfering with the headgate unless and until the water in the Claiborn Canal measured seventy-five inches or less.

For twenty years Morehouse and Little had equally used the water from Big Willow down to the point where the headgate was placed. Little's answer was to allege affirmatively that Morehouse was entitled only to floodwaters for the irrigation of his land, and as soon as the floodwaters ceased to flow, that he was entitled to use of all the decreed water flowing in the canal. He said that he had, indeed, caused the half of the headgate to be filled as there was no water flowing in the canal to which he felt Morehouse was entitled. The original decision was handed down by the court on April 4, 1922.

A few months later, on July 17, Andy had the case reopened for the purpose of submitting more testimony. From this testimony it was shown that the headgate had been completely washed out as well as an embankment upon which it had been placed and that Andy had been taking water through a headgate placed in his own ditch. There had been no effort on the part of Morehouse to rebuild the headgate, and there had been no controversy between the two of them as to the division of the water.

The court found that, this being true, the cause of the action had been destroyed, and the injunction was abated.

Justice Alfred Budge wrote the decision and Chief Justice McCarthy, Justices William A. Lee and William E. Lee concurred.

Some of the cases in which Andy was involved were not appealed and it is virtually impossible to find the transcripts. In some of those cases no records are any longer on file.

Over and over again, individuals asked about Andy will mention his retentive memory, that is, "he could remember every little detail," or, "he never forgot a thing." Along with his fabled memory, he had a helper. He was never without his little green record book. A three-by-five-inch record book in which he daily made many notations. He kept them from the time he arrived in Idaho until he became ill. He would fill several of them each year. He kept separate books for a record on the sheep and on hay inventory.

In the hay inventory, he recorded the length, width and 'over' of the stacks. Andy figured 300 tons of hay to be used by each band of 1,000 sheep. That was considered fairly heavy feeding, but he wanted his animals in good weight.

Sometimes, while riding down the road with a driver, he would say, "Stop the car. I need to write something." The vehicle was stopped and from out of his shirt pocket came the little book and a pencil with which he made his notation. Soon he said, "Drive on," and another message was ready to aid him that evening in his office at home when he reviewed the happenings of the day.

David Little remembers a court action in 1938 in which a man, whose name he has forgotten, was on trial for stealing horses. David's father, Andy, was on the witness stand. When asked a question about where he was on a certain date and what he was doing there, Andy reached into his shirt pocket as he turned to the judge and asked, "May I refer to my diary, your honor?" The answer was, "You may refer, but you cannot read from it."

In the same case David remembered that it concerned an auction sale held by his brother Sam in 1924. Andy had purchased a driving team, a colt and a buggy from Sam's possessions. He gave all of them back to Sam with the agreement that Sam was to give the colt back to Andy when it was weaned. The judge asked for the date of sale. "Can you tell me the date?"

"Yes, I can, your honor," Andy said as he reached for the little book. Then, opening it, he grinned and said, "And I can tell you what the weather was like that day, too."

F.G. Renner and L.D. Love, writing on "Management of Water on Western Rangelands" for the 1955 *Yearbook of Agriculture*, pointed out that stockmen of the west have known the importance of water ever since they trailed the first herds across the "mile wide and inch deep" rivers of America's Great Plains.

No one knew any better than Andy Little that an enduring

stream on property meant a good place for a home, one where fruits and vegetables can be grown, a good supply of native hay, an opportunity to grow alfalfa as a crop, a daily supply of water for the sheep, and a chance to produce new range on areas now considered useless.

Andy's native intelligence told him much about water supplies, different uses, and the need for an effective drainage system. What he didn't know about stream banks and slopes, dikes and outlet ditches, he made it a point to learn from those who did. Andy went to court because he would not stand to be wronged, but also because he understood the value of land, water and the fundamental right to fair treatment.

CHAPTER ELEVEN

BASQUES: THE GOOD SHEPHERDS

ONE OF AMERICA'S MOST EXOTIC ETHNIC GROUPS, THE MYSTERIOUS Basques played a big part in building Andy Little's empire. They worked for him, worked with him and were his friends. Andy trusted the Basques, encouraged them to learn English and earn citizenship. Some of Idaho's most important Basque citizens got their first work experience, their first promotions and their education from the Scottish sheepman.

Inheritors of an ancient culture and speakers of one of the world's most unusual languages, Basques by the thousands came to Idaho from their native land in the western foothills of the Pyrenees Mountains, which form a part of the border between France and Spain. Some say that they originally came to search for gold during the rush in Idaho. That may be true for this was a period that coincided with the buildup in numbers of sheep and cattle in Idaho.

Unable to speak English and without knowledge of prospecting, Basques were willing and eager to take over the duties of sheepherders. However, Steve Mendiva, young Boise attorney, says that a number of Basques did, indeed, go into mining. There was a quite a contingent working at the old Morning Mine in Shoshone County.

The wool business was growing swiftly and there were many herding jobs. To determine if Andy helped the Basques, or did the Basques help Andy, is like the ancient question, "Which came first, the chicken or the egg?" The Littles are the first to say that Basque herders, managers, foremen and other employees helped build Andy's business as much as anyone.

Andy Little was not the only Idaho sheepman who early learned the value of the sturdy and dependable Basques. They composed much of the work force in most Idaho sheep outfits.

Many years ago, Betty Penson Ward, national award-winning writer for the *Idaho Daily Statesman*, wrote a delightfully entertaining column on Idaho's Basques: "Should you try to learn the Basque language, the first thing to do is put a large-size marble in your mouth. Then forget everything you ever knew about spelling. You'll run smack into an xt combination. Then into txa (almost like Greek but the x is silent). And there's zai (pronounced with a long i sound like Japanese) . . .

"You'll break your heart over those double consonant combinations, and even triple ones, as in the nickname of Antone Uranga, Urritubitxa (look out! there's that txa combo again.) . . . that is the name of the house in which Mr. Uranga was born in the little town of Ea, province of Viscaya, whence came many of the Boise Basques. A man is known more often by the name of the house he was born in, in the old country, than by his surname.

"In every telephone book in the Rocky Mountain states, there's a generous sprinkling of Basque names. There's Aldecoa, which means 'on the side;' Urruchua, 'gold nugget.' And Subisaretta, another of the real tongue-twisters, denotes 'under the old gate.'

"Who was the first Basque in Boise? The memory of the Basque, himself, is often in disagreement with that of his brother, even of his mother. But when oldsters try to recall early days in America they remember Mrs. Narcissa Gustel . . . born in Viscaya, but her husband, Joe, was Spanish . . . they had a florist shop at 224 East Idaho Street.

"Other old-timers look down their Roman noses. She may have been the first woman Basque . . . but first had come Annatola and Portua, who went on to Jordan Valley. There were the Azcuenagas who stayed."

Most Basques learned English language and American ways. And even without help such as Andy gave his best employees, many of them acquired sheep bands of their own. Others and many of the herders' children went into businesses and professions outside the sheep industry.

As word got back to the Basqueland of the Pyrenees that herding jobs were plentiful for men willing to work, more and more Basques arrived to make their mark on the state. Soon Idaho became known as the second home of the Basques.

When president of the Basqueland Jose Antonio Ardanza visited Boise on March 15 through 23, 1988, Pat Bieter remembers with pride Ardanza's description of Idaho as "the eighth Basque province." Bieter, married to Basque Eloise Garmendia, and father of their children, whom he describes as "a quarter Irish, a quarter German and half Basque," teaches courses in Basque History and Beginning Basque Language at Boise State University.

Even the non-Basques on hand to greet President Ardanza were proud of the designation of Idaho as a Basque province. State Senate President Jim Risch and Speaker of the House Tom Boyd signed a joint proclamation warmly welcoming him as "the first Basque president to visit Idaho, in recognition of the largest Basque population in North America." The proclamation pointed out that in 1786 the founders of the United States "looked to the laws of the ancient democratic republic of the Basques, then the oldest such republic in Europe, as a basis for writing the Constitution, as stated in the research paper of John Adams."

The proclamation was sent to President Ardanza, King Juan Carlos and the Prime Minister of Spain, and to the President of the United States. Secretary of State Pete Cenarrusa accompanied President and Mrs. Ardanza to Washington, D.C., where they met with President Ronald Reagan, and they discussed ways in which the United States could work with Euzkadi in furthering culture, educational, economic and governmental exchanges.

Basques of today are proud of the fact that they speak an ancient language which they and their ancestors kept alive despite pressure to conform in Europe and America. Someone described Euskara, the language that sets the Basques apart from both their French and Spanish countrymen, as sounding like a storm of marble-sized hail hitting a tin roof. Conversely, when one hears the Basque language in song for the first time, he is inclined to think he is hearing the angels sing.

Only Euskara, of Western Europe's living languages, does not belong to the Indo-European family. Linguists and philologists have made a study of the language for hundreds of years. During the Middle Ages, scholars traced Euskara back to Noah's grandson, Tubal, who settled the peninsula after the flood.

The studies continue and work is now going on in an attempt to determine the possibility that the language dates from the stone age. The Basque words for axe *(aitzor)* and stone *(aitz)* have made linguists curious to learn if Euskara may date from that time when stone was used in making tools. It is not unlikely, with the use of computers in such studies, that the mystery may one day be solved. In the meantime, those who are serious about learning to speak the language must be prepared for about 500 hours of study before they will be able to communicate with the Basques.

The first Basque to reach Idaho may have been Antoine Azcuenaga, arriving in Owyhee county in 1889 from Oregon's Jordan Valley. Later he went back to Jordan Valley, just across the line in Oregon, to set up a blacksmith shop. He came to the Boise Valley as a sheepman and merchant years later and died in Boise in 1950.

Steve Steigel, who once operated a small store in the Seven Devils mountain region of Idaho, often purchased groceries and supplies for a Basque herder in the region. The fellow would come in with a written list, usually asking for "aigs." Steve finally asked him, "Why don't you learn to speak English?"

The herder replied, "Ships don't spik Angliss!"

Others say that the sheepdogs and horses understand Basque as readily as English. So language is no problem to the herders. They were able to withstand the loneliness of life in the hills or on the plains with the sheep, and soon became known as the most dependable of workers. So well did the Basques succeed in fitting into the open lifestyle of Idaho, bias was never a problem.

Idaho's senior United States Senator Jim McClure tells of an employee of an agency in Washington, D.C., calling him to ask about the minority problems in Idaho. "We don't really have many minority groups," the senator replied.

"How about the Basques?"

"You be the one to tell the Basques they are a minority," Senator Jim chuckled.

Despite becoming such a proud part of Idaho's history, culture

Courtesy Pete Cenarrusa

Leaders in the Idaho House of Representatives present Speaker of the House Pete Cenarrusa with silver tea and coffee services, chafing dish, trays, and serving dishes at the completion of his first term as Speaker in 1963. Left to right: Ernest Allen (Canyon), Harold Snow (Latah), Pete Cenarrusa (Blaine), Charlie Winkler (Adams), Bill Lanting (Twin Falls), Herman McDevitt (Bannock), Tony Wessels (Lewis).

and work, the Basques have still preserved important features of their ancient culture. Idaho's non-Basques are delighted they did.

Among other Basque attributes, these immigrants and their offspring are obsessed with athletics. Because of the superb physical condition of their young people, some wag said that, "Twenty thousand years ago the Basques arrived in the Pyrenees with each man wearing a beret and clutching tightly to a prized pelota ball."

Pelota is something of a cross between handball and jai-alai, and such a fast game that only those in fine physical shape can play. "Pelota is more than a game with the Basques. It is an obsession," said one frequent observer of the activity.

At one time, Boise boasted three jai-alai/pelota courts. The biggest was 300 feet long, 60 feet wide and 30 feet high. With the speed of lightning, the pelota is banged against the wall by the two sides playing. Hundreds would play and even more would watch. Now that successive generations of Basques have turned to tennis, golf, baseball, basketball and football, the ball courts have been bulldozed to make room for other buildings.

The Basques, lithe and strong, are also adept at boxing and wrestling. Those who do not participate are cheering side-liners who like to watch all manner of sporting events.

Idaho Oinkari Dancers

Basques like music. They like singing. They like dancing. The Idaho Oinkari Basque Dancers are some of the most famous practitioners of those Basque arts. They are celebrated in Idaho and have become well-known in Basqueland as a result of several visits there.

Years ago the children and grandchildren of those who came to Idaho in the late 1800s and early 1900s returned to visit and learn of the land of their forefathers. It was on such a trip in 1960 that some Idaho Basques saw a traveling group of natives not only dancing but whooping and yelling as they sprang through the air from one dance position to another. So enthusiastic were the young Idahoans that they soon joined the Pyrenees dancers to be taught the steps.

Arriving back in Idaho they soon taught others of the race and the Oinkari group was formed. They borrowed the name of the dancers in the Basqueland for their own. *Oinkari,* pronounced Oh-in-kari, means "fleet of foot," or "fast-feet."

According to Steve Mendiva, the Oinkari dancers in Pamplona were disbanded because of the difficulties encountered when they carried the Basque flag during Franco's dictatorship.

Idaho's Oinkari dancers have appeared at hundreds of events in the inter-mountain West and were officially invited to appear at Idaho Day observances, and the World's Fairs in New York and Seattle. Their performances were greeted by cheering thousands of youth when they appeared at the Girl Scout Senior Roundup, the National Boy Scout Jamboree and the Boy Scout World Jamboree, the first to be held in the United States, at Farragut Park on the shores of Lake Pend Oreille in Northern Idaho. Called the Bounding Basques for their strenuous dances, the Oinkari Dancers fast, high-flying steps have, for nearly three decades, been accompanied by Jimmy Jausoro's accordion.

The familiar Basque colors of red, green, white and black were chosen by the dancers for their costumes. White shirts and slacks with bright green sashes, and a red or black beret (a part of every-day wear for many of the men in Basqueland) is worn by the boys. Girls wear full red skirts, trimmed with narrow black stripes along the bottom, black vests and aprons with red lacing over the white blouses, and white head scarves.

Smiles, yells and dancing feet announce the arrival of the Oinkari troupe. As the crowd goes wild with applause, the dancers shout a Basque greeting and leap into the air. The Oinkaris are at it again.

The dancers often give out with a blood-curdling yell as they enter for the performance. It may have come from an ancient war cry as the faraway and long-ago ancestors of the fleet feet met their enemies on the battlefield. So piercing, so horrifying and so memorable is the yell, that when the dancers performed for officials of the Girl Scouts of the U.S.A. at the headquarters in New York following an appearance at the World's Fair, Louise Wood, then the national director, smiled wanly and said, "We would like to have the Basques dance at the Roundup, but it must be on the final day."

"Why?" came the question.

"Because," now with a wider grin and twinkling eyes, she replied, "if it were on the first day, we could not stand to listen to those 15,000 girls yelling like Basque warriors for the rest of the Roundup!"

Ernest Hemingway lived many of the latter years of his life with his wife, Mary, at their home on the Wood River near Sun Valley, but he thought of Spain as his second home. Pamplona was a great favorite of his, because it was there that he enjoyed seeing the high-jumping dancers and the running of the bulls. In the Museum of Art in Bilbao, there hangs a gigantic oil painting of Hemingway and his Basque friend, Dunabeitia. They are relaxing on a wrought-iron bench, backs to sea and faces to the sun. A newspaper is beside Hemingway and he is holding reading glasses. The painting by Jose De Ucelay is entitled "Conversation piece, just leisure."

The Beloved Basque

One of the most durable of Idaho's Basque colony is the state's long-time Secretary of State Pete Cenarrusa. He is the son of parents who immigrated from Vizcaya (Biscay). Pete speaks both Basque and English fluently. A well-educated man, he is owner, with his son, Joe, of a sheep ranch at Carey in southcentral Idaho. Pete often serves as an advisor to other Basques.

Nearly forty years of his life have been devoted to state government service, first in the legislature for a period of nine consecutive terms and during which he was also elected Speaker of the House of Representatives, and then to the office of Secretary of State. He was first appointed Secretary of State on May 1, 1967 by then-Governor Don Samuelson, upon the unexpected death of Edson Deal of Nampa. Pete went on to be elected on his own in 1970 and has been reconfirmed every election since, being the top vote-getter in 1978, and near the top in all others.

It is not difficult to understand why Pete is listed in the rolls of the *International 100 Most Prestigious in the World of Basque Extraction*. People trust him, admire him, and they become more committed to causes which he espouses. They quickly sense the deep dedication to whatever program he plans to undertake, or to whatever he agrees to attempt for others.

There is no argument that he is Idaho's best known and most beloved Basque. Idahoans like his down-to-earth manner. His quiet dignity hides an ability to wage warfare in the legislative halls against injustice particularly when it involves his fellow Basques. There is a strength that makes him immovable when he feels his cause is right. The voters have given no sign that they will do anything but re-elect him so long as he wants to serve.

Pete was born at the village of Carey in the sheep county of Blaine (for many years now also the home of Sun Valley ski resort) on December 16, 1917. About ten years earlier his father had immigrated from an Euskadi village, whence came many other Basque sheepherders to Idaho. His father, Joseph Cenarrusa Beitia, dropped the common Basque name of Beitia soon after reaching Idaho. Joseph's brother, Cornelio, who also immigrated, soon did the same thing.

Pete describes the manner in which his father was chosen for his first job in Idaho in 1907. "A man by the name of Rossen came down to Boise from Muldoon [near Sun Valley] where he operated the ranch that was later owned by Gerry Little's parents, the James Laidlaws. Rossen was foreman of the sheep operation owned by State Senator Thomas C. Stanford of Carey.

"Rossen said, 'I need four men to work with the sheep. Line up.' My Dad lined up with a bunch of other men. Rossen took his time, looking them over with searching eyes, then pointed his finger and said, 'I'll take you and you and you and you.' My Dad was one of those 'yous.' And that is how he started in Idaho.

"Tom Stanford came to know and think a lot of my Dad and when he and Uncle Cornelio sought American citizenship, it was Stanford who vouched that they would be good Americans."

About seven years later, in 1914, Ramona Gardoqui came from the village of Guernica, known for its utter destruction by Axis aircraft aiding Franco's forces in the Spanish Civil War. Gardoqui came to the town of Shoshone, south of Muldoon, and it was there that she and Joe Cenarrusa met and married. Within two years they moved to Carey and purchased a range sheep operation with

George Harris. They developed that farm and range into one of the most successful sheep businesses in the area.

To Joseph and Ramona, now both deceased, were born five children, all of whom were taught to speak the Basque language right along with English. All of the family worked and had about 6,000 ewes. Pete says, "With 125 percent lambs that brought the total well over 12,000, including the rams."

After three years of herding, Cornelio went back to the Basque country. He later returned to Idaho when his brother went into business. He helped with the sheep for another three years and his son, Mike, now manages the Biskay Land and Livestock Company, a family corporation.

On the family ranch, Pete learned every facet of the wool and sheep industry, as did the sons of Andy Little. His parents were eager for him to have a fine education. After graduating from Bellevue High School he went on to graduate from the University of Idaho, which named him one of the Distinguished Alumni of the College of Agriculture at its May 13, 1989, commencement. This was just one more honor paid him by fellow Idahoans. He had been previously inducted into four Idaho Halls of Fame: Agriculture, Athletic, Republican and Basque.

After graduation from the University, he taught at several high schools, and added on-farm training for veterans following World War II. In 1942, Pete had enlisted in U.S. Naval Aviation, Marine fighter, and was commissioned a second lieutenant, dive bomber pilot, in 1943. He flew Navy Cougar jets, instructed naval aviation cadets, and retired a major. Pete returned to Carey after the war. He has now been a pilot for forty-five years, has over 15,000 hours of flying without an accident.

Pete is married to Freda Coates, the daughter of well-known Carey residents, Charles "Chuck" and Mrs. Coates.

Freda and Pete named their only son for his grandfather Cenarrusa. Young Joe followed in his father's footsteps inasmuch as he became an accomplished flyer and is a graduate of the University of Idaho. Joe is married and has two sons, Andrew (thirteen) and Tyler (eight), who often visit the family ranch at Carey.

A proud grandfather, Pete said, "They may become interested

enough to work in the business, but we want them to do whatever they feel is best for them.

"After all his years on the ranch, young Joe went into the business of feeding others. After he had set up the Biskay Land and Livestock, named, of course, for the Bay of Biscay in Basque country, he came to me and said, 'Dad, I've decided that the best way to sell lamb is hot and by the plate. I am going into the restaurant business.' "

Joe did just that. He and Bert Bender are now owners of the Red Robin Cafe in Boise, the Pine Tavern Restaurant in Bend, Oregon, and have their eyes on a third property. Lamb will be sold.

Pete's younger brother, Louis, and his son, Jim, are also in the sheep business in Carey.

Jim Yates Gets "Bummer"

Retired Boeing Company architect Jim Yates, now living at Lyondale Landing on Lake Coeur d'Alene, recalls Andy Little's operations near his boyhood home at Parma in southeastern Idaho. He especially remembers the Basques: "I'll never forget the Basque sheepherders living mostly in tents or canvas-covered wagons. I thought of how lonesome most of them must be in their nomadic lifestyle. Those huge bands of Andy Little's sheep would come down from the mountain ranges every fall. The Basques herded them into the lower Boise Valley to graze on the harvested fields. Bad weather and lack of forage would then send them to the winter feeding pens nearby.

"The sheep drives on the country roads passing our farm were always exciting to me as a boy, because we boys and our dogs always went out to keep the sheep away from the lawns and Mother's flower beds. Occasionally there would be bitter fights between the sheepdogs and our dogs.

"The Basques would appear at our ranch home after dark and we would invite them in to visit. Communication was difficult but we did our best to talk with them. They all burned sagebrush in their little tent campstoves and their clothing was permeated with the odor of burning sagebrush. That is an unforgettable smell. A little gift of wine almost guaranteed our friendship with the Basque shepherds for another year, and we wanted that."

Andy Little had a strict policy against giving away lambs, but the friendly Yates boys and their visits with the herders could change the policy once in awhile.

Jim says, "When the bands left in the spring, my brother and I would ask the sheepherders for any 'bum' lambs. These little lambs were the ones that had been abandoned by their ewe mothers or were not strong enough to keep up with the others. On occasion we were given one. Then we raised the 'bum' on bottles and eventually sold them for some extra spending money."

"Highland" Joe Arrieta

As solid as Sheep Mountain, built of sedimentary rock and basalt, is Joe Arrieta. A dark and handsome, sturdily built man, Joe was given the name of "Highland Joe" soon after he went to work for Jessie Little Naylor, owner and operator of the Highland Livestock and Land Company. Woe to anyone who switched the title to the Land and Livestock Company.

"The Livestock *always* comes first," Jessie had occasion to say many times in her life. Her nephew Brad is just as swift to pick up on any random alliteration of the title. His correction is with a wide grin and quoting Jessie. "Livestock pays the bills," Jessie would say. "The land is overhead."

Highland Joe arrived in Idaho from Viscaya, Spain, on December 28, 1958. Just sixteen days later he was at work for Jessie at the lambing camp at Notus, on a plain near the Snake River and southwest of Emmett. During those sixteen days, he stayed at a rooming house owned by his mother's cousin, Tomas Astorgue. Later Astorgue sold the building to Basil Aldecoa, one of Boise's most highly-respected citizens.

It was on a cold and bright afternoon in late February, 1989, that Joe was found working with the sheep at the Notus camp. He took an hour off work to reminisce about his coming from Spain, the many times he had gone back to visit, and always returning to America and Idaho and the sheep.

Joe said when he first arrived in 1958, he'd heard that Jessie, the Soulen family, and John Basabe were responsible for getting immigrant domestic help for work shortages. They had helped organize the Western Range Management Association to work with the U.S. Department of Labor in bringing domestic help.

Highland Joe put it this way: "In the mid-Fifties, as the Korean War started winding down and with the troops coming home, there was a surplus of labor. The Immigration Department got complaints that there were not enough jobs for the service people returning. So, the Department started sending our Basque herders back to Viscaya. When Jessie and some of the others found they couldn't get herders and other workers for the sheep ranches, they decided to form an association to again get the Basques to Idaho.

"Jessie got together with the Soulens, Harry and his son, Phil, and John Basabe. They worked out an agreement with the U.S. Department of Labor to secure what was called an H-2 status to bring in laborers if there was a shortage of domestic help. And there was a shortage, as few of the returning soldiers, sailors and marines wanted to herd sheep."

In telling of all the help that Jessie was to him and other workers for the various ranches, Highland Joe said, "She could do anything. I have never known of a problem that Jessie couldn't handle. She did all of us herders' taxes, got our money into the bank, and was very good to all of us.

"It seemed like Jessie was always in the office to take care of whatever needs or problems came up. But she did like to get out to the camps and on the range to see what was going on. She knew sheep, and she would be at that lambing camp at least once a week."

Brad interjected the comment, "The first shipment Jessie ever missed was when Teresa and I got married. She couldn't be at both, and we were pretty flattered that she chose us instead of the shipping!"

There was an average of six shippings a year, with two lambing camps at Big Bend near Adrian, across the border into Oregon, and Notus. In 1968 some sheep were sold off and those shipping points closed off. At one time the Littles had fifteen lambing camps, including the Highland, Apple Valley at Parma, north of Parma, the Upper and Lower Johnson ranches, the Upper Bench.

Highland Joe and Brad talked about shearing at the Butte ranch and at the Aikman, when the shearers average 100 sheep for each a day. It was not unusual to see 2,000 shorn sheep at the end of the day.

Originally, they had taken the motor from the Chevy pickup which Robert had been driving when it went into the river, and took it to the Aikman where it was used to generate the power for the clippers. Andy was one of the first sheepmen to use electric shears. The crews were not accustomed to them and much blood was seen until they learned.

"We started shearing in March and continued until mid-June. Shearing involved two crews of twenty men each, operating full time. It began at the Aikman and finished at the Butte. Ten shearers stood on each side of the shed," Joe said. "One time they sheared sixty bands in thirty days, never stopping until 60,000 had been sheared."

Who says that the life of a sheepman is a relaxed way of living?

After the shearing, one band was herded toward Boise and another toward the old mining camp of Pearl, then over the mountain to Black Canyon and toward Squaw Butte. Where the Littles once had sheep on top of the Butte, they now run cattle.

"Horses." Joe said, "When I came everything was done with horses. Andy had beautiful Belgians and there were five teams when I arrived."

Brad added that his Grandfather had a minimum of 500 horses for the total operation of herders, camptenders, the pack strings and farm operations. The largest horse barn was at the Van Deusen ranch.

What he didn't use, he sold. Surplus horses weren't a cash-flow item.

"Grandad would say, 'You can't eat horses,' and another of his axioms was, 'There are three things you lose money on: a threshing machine, a stud horse, and a sawmill.'

"Jessie was also good to the sheep and other animals. She always had a salt lick up at her cabin on the summer range, so that she could wake up at night and see the deer. One night, she said, she awakened at a noise and a deer was looking in the window at her."

Jessie had set up a fund for Joe's act-alike son, John, about twelve. John told us how to count to ten in Basque. Here is how: *bat* (one), *bi* (two), *iru* (three), *lau* (four), *bost* (five), *say* (six), *saspy* (seven), *sorrtsy* (eight), *bethedadsy* (nine) and *amarr* (ten).

Highland Joe went on to talk about some of the extraordinary Basques who had worked for the Littles. As in others' memories, at the top of Highland Joe's list was Canuto Otazua, or "Canno," who had started with Andy more than fifty years ago.

"Canno was probably the best in the sheep business. He knew everything about lambing, shearing, and shipping that there was to know. And he had done them all." One other he mentioned by name was Pablo Aramburu, as an all-around good man.

Basabe In-Training

The man industrialist J.R. "Jack" Simplot chose to be the first president of his J.R. Simplot Land and Livestock Company is a lively Basque with an olive complexion, twinkling brown eyes, and a touch of gray in his hair, of medium height and the build of a weight-lifter. John Basabe had great responsibility in handling one division of the empire built by Idaho's processed and frozen potato magnate. On the day that John Basabe talked about his early life with the Andy Little sheep companies he was at complete ease, no rush to be about other duties, and he enjoyed the mind-travel back to his youth.

To emphasize the feeling that the Littles had for sheep, he told of the time Jessie Little Naylor was taking a sick ram from one of the ranches to the veterinarian in Emmett. She was driving a brand new Chrysler sedan.

Noting the gas gauge was at "empty," she stopped at a station to gas up. The attendant glanced into the car's back window, looked inquiringly at her and asked, "Jessie, what are you doing with that sheep in the back seat of this nice new car?"

"Well, he paid for it, he should be riding in it," she retorted.

"And that was the general feeling among the Littles about the sheep they owned and for which they cared so well. That is why Andy became a legend in his own time," John said, "but the whole family was involved in it and that was their life. That is why they were so successful. They also taught a lot of the rest of us some things about work and loyalty that made big differences in our lives."

John's parents, the Gregorio Basabes, were from the Basque section of Spain. His father, who became George in Idaho, arrived in 1905 or 1906. He made two trips back to Spain, the first in 1915, when he married Andresa Urquisa, and again in 1918, to bring his wife to the United States. They settled in Emmett.

During the early years George worked for the Johnson Sheep Company, and was working for the Van Deusens when Andy Little bought that outfit. George was then camptender and riding boss for two bands of Little sheep. The work was all done on horseback, and he also took care of six to eight horses. "Even when the autos and pickups came along, Dad stayed with the horses," John remarked.

Describing the Emmett of his boyhood, John said, "It wasn't much of a town then. There was a working sawmill, lumber hauled right through town by horse teams, wooden sidewalks, and the police had no cars. They did all their work by foot patrol. If necessary, they rode a horse. Boise Riggs was the blacksmith and he shod lots of Andy Little's horses. Boise later became our sheriff. There were over a thousand people living in the area, and times were bad, with lots of people out of work. Many were coming in from Oklahoma and Missouri and some from Tennessee and Kentucky.

John said, "My brother George and I started to work for Andy when we were just kids, thirteen and eleven years old. I swept out the office where Jessie was the manager. I remember leaving school at the end of the afternoon and heading straight for Jessie's office. I learned a lot by just being there. The commissary was there, too, and lots of activity with people coming and going all the time. We put up the groceries by the carload, using paper sacks and ten pound tins. At that time we were supplying about thirty herders who were taking care of 12,000 ewes.

"We had a lot of kid fun, too. We played ball and went swimming in the canal, like the kids in Emmett had been doing for a long time. We would dive off the bridge that crossed over Main Street and came on down the river to Second Street, near the office.

"I remember that there were many teams and pack horses. Lots of them belonged to the Littles. The horses and mules were used in pack trains. Everything on the ranches was done by horses and wagons."

John Basabe was the only water boy working with the threshing crews. For each ranch he would take four or five of the one-gallon glass jugs, wrap them in burlap, fill them with water, and make the rounds of all the ranches up and down the Emmett bench. These ranches included the Black Canyon, Upper Bench ranch and then head due west to the McConnell ranch, the Liteuy, Worthman, Burns, Bane, Johnson, Hartley and Lower Bench ranches No. 1 and No. 2.

As Basabe grew older, he was trusted with running the wagons (they were the old iron-tired wheels then) and worked with twenty to thirty different horse teams.

"There were runaways going on all the time," he laughed. "Some of the horses were just being broken to drive and haul. They were frightened by the noise of the threshing machines in the fields. I became experienced enough that I broke a number of the horses to work with the wagons and crews.

"We hauled truckloads of wool owned by Andy," John said, "and ten-wheelers were the biggest in those days. Shearing was done at the Aikman, Van Deusen and Little ranches. Jessie kept weighted score, when they weigh the bags. The wool was shipped in numbered burlap bags. Then they were all hauled to the depot in Emmett, loaded on Union Pacific trains and generally shipped to Boston. Different times, different loads . . . for most of a week the shipping went on."

John and his brother learned a lot by working in the commissary and putting up groceries in bulk. "With the twenty-eight to thirty herders at the time, it made sense that the Littles would buy supplies by the truckload. On the floor above the office, we kept tents and pack saddles. The Littles made horse blankets. They would buy blankets and canvas to make them. Times were so tough and they did everything they could think of to keep the operations going.

"Lots of workers were dependent upon that family, and they

both knew it. The workers were glad to have jobs and the Littles felt a responsibility to keep them employed.

"In addition to the tough times," John recalled, "I remember one October when thousands of sheep were caught in an early blizzard in Pen Basin. I think Drew was in with the herders and camptender and the sheep. Many of the sheep died before they could be moved out. Feed was so scarce that the pack mules ate the saddle blankets. The only road out was by the way of Warm Lake and they cut down pine trees and pulled them behind the saddle horses to break a trail through the snow. Those people were resourceful and they were tough."

John used the word "tough" again in describing Drew, whom he said worked hard all of his life and was "one tough hombre," and also in mentioning Andy. He said that Andy was, "A fine, tough old gentleman. In the Depression days, when times were really tough, he fed all of his workers well. They had all the necessary staples.

"When he got tickled at something, he would turn aside in Scottish reticence, but couldn't keep from laughing. And he could take a joke.

"One time, my cousin Tony Basabe, who also worked for Andy as a foreman over a number of his bands, pulled into Smith's Ferry with Drew to spend the night. They were fooling around down in the dining area of the hotel, and when Tony finally went upstairs he sneaked over and jerked all the covers off Drew. Only it wasn't Drew. It was Andy. And he only laughed."

John Basabe collected a treasury of memories and tales about the Basque shepherds who worked the Little spreads. These hardy men contributed both to Andy's success and to the quality of and pleasure in life of that time.

Amazing Canno Otazua

Some of the most interesting characters who ever lived worked with those Little operations. In recalling several of them, John Basabe also headed the list with Canno Otasu.

"Canno was absolutely the best sheepherder to ever come out of Spain," he announced with an air that made one know it was an incontestable statement.

"He never came out of the hills. He stayed on the job and *never* lost one sheep. I mean *never*. He worked twenty-four hours a day and never missed a day of work in over thirty-five years. He had Jessie take care of all his money and kept it in a bank. When he needed anything, he would have Jessie get the money for him. He was such an amazing guy. And he loved animals so much, he didn't want people to touch them."

In a later conversation with Brad Little, he said that when Canno went back to Spain for the first time, he had Jessie wire his savings of $150,000 to $200,000 to a bank in Madrid. Jessie was immediately contacted by the Federal Bureau of Investigation because the agent in charge couldn't believe that a sheepherder could accumulate that much money, no matter how long he worked. Jessie would put his money into certificates of deposit and as they matured, with interest, she would reinvest for him.

Brad agreed with Basabe that Canno was absolutely amazing. "He knew every sheep that was missing. He knew how many the coyotes had killed. He knew how many were lost. He was unbelievable. When he was over seventy years old, he did all the irrigation at the Notus ranch and hand-shoveled all the corrugation," Brad said as he shook his head in wonder. Canno's nephew, Felix, is now an employee of Brad's.

Tony B.S. Arrubarena

Tony Arrubarena is a different story.

"He was a crazy, wild man and pulled so many pranks on people that it is a wonder he didn't get killed," John said. "He was always B.S.-ing people, and soon came to be known as 'Tony B.S.,' a title that stuck and when people talk about him today that is the name they use. Everyone knew Tony B.S., but darned few knew Tony Arrubarena."

On one occasion, Andy caught him red-handed in stealing a rooster. "What are you doing, Tony?" he demanded. Quickly Tony said, "I need an alarm clock to wake up in time to take care of the sheep!"

And he could be a working fool around the lambing shed when he saw Andy, and later David, approaching. This only alerted them that he had been up to something. David saw two dressed chickens hanging from a wire when he visited the ranch.

"What is this?" he asked.

"Dave," Tony answered, "my horse awful bad horse. He kick two chickens in the head and they die."

Sometimes he went too far. One old herder, who rode an old black horse when he came to camp, never caused anyone trouble, but Tony B.S. couldn't resist putting a cockleburr under the saddle blanket when the fellow was away from his horse. When he came back and mounted the horse, John said, "He was thrown forty feet into the air, and as soon as he lit, he quit his job."

Pablo Aramburu

Where Andy chuckled, his daughter, Jessie Naylor, laughed. And she laughed as she told the story of her father and Pablo Aramburu, herder in the hills twenty miles above Idaho City where the Naylor sheep headquarters was later located.

"Dad had bought Little Kempner Meadows, which were filled with ore diggings.

"Pablo saw some prospectors taking their picks and shovels to the Meadows, and he excitedly called Dad and said, 'These men are digging out in the meadows. Shall I kick them off?' Andy chuckled, and said, 'No. Wait until they strike gold. Then we'll kick them off.' "

Tony Plaza

Another Tony, this one Tony Plaza, could always make others laugh. Even Andy.

Tony was afraid of lightning. In the herding hills one night of exploding rain and wind, lightning hit a pine tree and splintered it. The echo was so loud it was frightening. Tony knew that the metal stove in the camp would attract lightning. He had a bedroll and he stuck his head into it.

Another herder came along, nudged his posterior with his foot, and asked, "What are you doing with your head in that bedroll?"

Tony pulled his head out, looked up and said, "Well, if lightning hit me in the butt it wouldn't hurt half as much as if it hit me in the head!"

On one occasion Tony led a packstring of mules into a camp and immediately unhooked the animals and turned them into the haystack. Andy came out of a tent and said, "Tony, you're fired!" Tony started running around the field slapping the ground with a shovel. Andy said, "What are you doing, Tony?"

"Hell, I'm killing those suckers jumping out of the creek. They're eating a lot more hay than those mules do."

Andy couldn't keep from chuckling and he said, "Get your gear and get back to work."

Sandy Dalsel

Basques weren't the only shepherds in Andy's operations, although they were some of the most colorful. Nevertheless, some of the Scots herders could be just as tough.

John told of an old Scots herder by the name of Sandy Dalsel who worked for Andy. He was not only tough but courageous. He was afraid of nothing, John said. One day as he was working at the camp near Banks on the Payette river, where there were a lot of rattlesnakes, for some reason he reached into the grass to retrieve an article and a rattlesnake bit him on the finger. Sandy took a quick look at the finger, walked straight to the chopping block and jerked the axe out of the stump, put his finger down on the block and chopped it off just below the second knuckle. That he was aware there were a number of rattlesnakes in the vicinity takes nothing away from the courage it took to chop off his finger.

John Basabe continued to work for the Littles as he pursued his schooling. War clouds were deepening throughout the world and on December 7, 1941, the Japanese bombed Pearl Harbor. The United States was in the midst of a world war which, until then, had been fought through being of help to England and other Allies fighting in Europe.

It was on January 1, 1943, that John Basabe joined the United States Navy. He served for three years in the South Pacific and is proud of the fact that his ship was the *USS Idaho*. After the peace agreement was signed in 1945, John was shipped for a stay of forty days in Norfolk, Virginia. He had kept in touch with Jessie during the war and when he telephoned the Emmett office, he said, "I'm not sure of what I'm going to do, Jessie."

"Do? I'll tell you what you are going to do. You are going to come back here and you are going to run my outfit, the Highland Livestock and Land Company," Jessie answered in her usual direct way. She had long before established a maternal interest in the young Basque and had much to do with his training. John recalls that she had so much pride in her father and his abilities, that many times she would send John along with Andy on various errands, so that he might learn from him. "Jessie not only loved her dad, but she loved those sheep," John grinned. He had worked for Jessie at the Highland from 1945 until 1955.

But he was not grinning when he told of J.R. Simplot phoning and sometime later asking him to come and see him about taking over his Bruneau Sheep company. "I hated to tell Jessie, but I felt it was just too good an opportunity to turn down. She offered me a good deal to stay, but I felt I had to take Jack's offer. And I know that much of what I learned working for the Littles helped me to get the presidency of the Simplot Land and Livestock Company.

"You know when you fight brush fires side-by-side, like Jessie and I did on the old home place, and you finally get the fire put out, you feel you have done quite a job together. That's the way I felt that day. And I remember even fighting brush fire with Andy and the others.

"There was a place near Sand Hollow where we had fires time after time. We had to fill barrels with water out of the canal. There were fifty gallon barrels and we all worked like demons to get those fires out."

When Jessie died, John was a pallbearer at her funeral.

"I have a favorite souvenir from Jessie," John said. "She gave me a small bear trap I liked and I have it hanging on my wall."

John Basabe talked of the organizing of the Western Range Association, for which he has served as president. It came about in 1947–48 when the sheep and wool people were desperate for herders. Under contract of job security, the association brought Basques from Spain. From California, Colorado, Arizona, Nevada, Utah, Idaho, Montana, Washington, Oregon, and Wyoming, members joined. When King Carlos and Queen Sofia visited in New York and dedicated the Spanish Institute, the Basabes, as representatives of the Western Range Association, were among the guests invited to the dedication and banquet. They also had a private audience with them at the Waldorf Astoria hotel. John said that when the Royal couple approached them, the King said, "Cashio," which is "Hello" in the Basque language, and then proceeded to count to five in Basque.

Ruby Ysursa Basabe

Boise's Modern Hotel was a Basque Boarding House located at 613 Idaho street and was operated by Eustaquio and Guillerma Ysursa Ormachea. In the early twenties, the building was owned by a Mrs. Bush. Mrs. Ormachea was a sister to Asuncion and An-

During his 1950 visit to Idaho, Jessie Naylor took her cousin, John Crawford of Edinburgh, to the Highland Sheep Camp on Beaver Creek north of Idaho City. The seated herder is unknown. Standing are Domingo, another unknown herder, Ignacio in dark glasses, Jessie, Ruby Basabe, John Crawford, and John Basabe. They are standing in front of the supplies building that Manager Basabe had built.

tonio, who had married Ysursa brothers: Asuncion to Benito and Antonio to Tomas. The two couples took over the boarding house from their sister and brother-in-law, who wanted to return to Spain to live. Benito and Asuncion became the parents of a son, Ramon, and a daughter, Ruby. Ramon and his wife are the parents of a son, Benito, who, as Ben Ysursa is a long-time chief clerk to Secretary of State Cenarrusa. Ruby, an attractive and dark-haired woman, married John Basabe and they are the parents of Tom, Raymond and Marie.

In the boarding house meals were served from long tables at noon and again at six o'clock in the evening. Ruby said that from forty to fifty herders stayed there when not out on the ranges and many kept their clothing there during the year. It was their home-away-from-home.

"When the herders came in from the hills," Ruby remembered, "usually from ten days to two weeks at a time, even though they rarely were ill while out in the hills and living in tents, they would become sick in town." Perhaps the shepherds had lost their immunity to contagious disease.

Building The Valencia

In 1940, Benito and Tomas Ysursa purchased the land across the street at 612 Idaho street from the Davidson family. There was a vacant building on the property which at one time had been the office of Dr. Goon-Hoy, who advertised "Chinese Remedies and Herbs."

It was on this property that the Ysursas built a Basque restaurant called The Valencia. It was opened to the public in January 1941 and continued in business until 1966. They sold the building ten years later.

The food was so satisfying and plentiful that the Valencia became known throughout Idaho and far beyond. Legislators filled it during the early months of the year when they were in session. Boise business people frequented it on a year-round basis.

Whenever the Valencia was mentioned, someone would invariably say, "That soup. Have you tasted that soup?" It was made from stock and kept in a big kettle on the stove. There was always soup and *cocido* (pronounced kooseedough) served family style. Other items on the menu included *paella* (rice), garbanzos (the chick peas soaked overnight before cooking), Basque bread, and all kinds of steak, which was the most ordered item. There were also *chorizos* (Basque hot sausage), and heaped-high platters of fried chicken. The Valencia had a walk-in cooler downstairs, which was used to age the beef.

Ruby remembers that Andy Little was a customer who always ordered the garbanzos. The families ran The Valencia until their retirement.

Famous Fries Dinners

The Valencia also became well-known for its lamb fry dinners and men who enjoyed them wanted to be sure they would be notified when fries were on the menu.

During lambing time, the herder castrates the male lambs by biting off the testicles with his teeth. The method grew out of the need to keep down infections that were frequent when castration was done by knives.

The testicles are then fried and have become a delicacy in many homes and restaurants throughout the sheep-growing world. The recipe is essentially the same wherever served. The Ysursas served over one pound for each person, and would prepare about twenty-five pounds whenever they were on the menu. They were breaded, fried in deep fat, then mixed with scrambled eggs and served with potatoes or rice. A spicy sauce accompanied them. Soup and other side dishes completed the meal.

For those who didn't care for the extreme richness of the fries, beef tongue and tripe were served. Ruby said that the custom could have started during tough times when herders threw nothing away, eating everything edible of an animal.

After one of the early-day lamb fries, Andy and Walter Little Sr. were returning to their homes at Emmett, with Walter driving. They drove straight through and missed a curve at Linder, between Boise and Eagle, and Walter's big Buick landed in the swamp. After making one short attempt to get out and wheels skidding, he calmly said, "Well Andy, I guess this is as far as we go tonight." "Looks like it," Andy said and they both went to sleep.

As time moved on and the Valencia closed, Bob Naylor and David each held a stag event organized around a lamb and/or calf fry party for their friends. David's guests have included: Jack Simplot, Warren McCain, Rich Hormachea, John Basabe, Agri Beek (who was a lamb buyer for Armour Corporation), Smokey McLeod and son, Sandy; Bart Brassey, Al Teske, Max Yost, Mike Roach, Bernie Rakozy, Bill Campbell, Bernie Grattan, of Boise; Tom Davis and Frank Callendar of Cascade; Roy Murray, George Yost and John Gamage of Emmett; Drew Little, Walt Little and son, Rob, of New Plymouth; his sons, Jim and Brad; son-in-law, Ron Woodie; and Phil Soulen of Weiser. The parties have been held at either the Arid Club or the Ranch Club in Boise.

Sheepherders Ball

No one can remember exactly when it started, but it is thought that well-known Boise sheepman John Archabal put together the first Basque Sheepherders' Ball sometime in the early 1930s. They have become such a whooping and howling success over the years that more than a thousand are now attending the annual affair.

It is always held during the Christmas season and the first ones were truly for the sheepherders. The only guests would be the Governor and First Lady of the state and perhaps a member of Congress or a United States senator if they happened to be in town. Invitations were coveted by many non-Basques. The Basques have melded so well into the American and Idaho culture, that this great entertainment displays to them just how much other nationalities want to be associated with them.

Early dances were held at the Riverside Dance Hall and the Basque Center, but the crowds became so large that they moved to the Fairgrounds pavilion. Now, many non-Basques and Basques-by-marriage attend. Some of the young Basques who have moved away from Idaho and Boise will drive hundreds of miles to take part in the festival, which has been a part of their lives since they were old enough to dance, to be with family members, visit old friends and generally whoop it up. The most popular band, organized in the mid-fifties by Jim Jausoro and Domingo Ansotegui at a boarding house in Nampa, was asked back year after year.

Courtesy Basque Museum

Hundreds of thousands of the highly-seasoned Basque sausages called chorizos have given off the aroma of garlic, pimiento, and cayenne pepper cooking with pork, from this old coal and wood-burning stove which is still in the kitchen at 607 Grove Street, Boise. Now the first Basque museum in the United States, the building was the original home of the Cyrus Jacobs family. In the parlor on April 21, 1895, Mary McConnell and William E. Borah were married. Her father and Jacobs were close friends. Joe Uberuaga started the Basque Boarding House there at the turn of the century.

Weight-lifting was a part of the entertainment. For many years, Bene Goitiandia held the title of champion weightlifter in the western states. To gain the title, Bene had lifted 304 pounds of steel to his shoulder nine times in ten minutes. At one contest, he lifted the same stone thirty-two times in ten minutes and 205 pounds fifty-seven times in ten minutes, one after the other.

Sheep auctions are held for the purpose of paying expenses and to help special cases. One year it was to aid a young man who had lost a leg in a farm accident. At another time, a thrift shop which had burned to the ground was given funds toward rebuilding.

The Basque Center

Adelia Garro Simplot (Mrs. Richard) is a Basque dedicated to preserving the history and culture of her race. She has gone so far as to purchase the old brick home at 607 Grove Street in Boise, a former Basque boarding house that was condemned in 1983, and to make it available as the first Basque Museum in the United States. Adelia is president of the Basque Museum and Cultural Center, which has as its purpose, "To enrich our melting-pot heritage and preserve the Basque culture in Idaho and other western states; and to educate about this unique group."

The house is the oldest surviving brick house in Boise and was built by teamster and businessman Cyrus Jacobs in 1864, one year after Idaho became a territory. Jacobs transported supplies to the gold miners in Idaho City and later was elected Boise mayor. In 1918 the Uberuaga family purchased the building after the death of Jacobs and it was the place where most Basque immigrants stayed between the time they arrived in Boise and secured work.

The sheepherders also came in the from the hills and ranges to spend Christmas and New Year holidays at the home. When the Center was dedicated, the Basque provinces minister of culture Josu Legarreta flew to Idaho to take part.

The Center is located at 611 Grove and an additional building at 605 Grove has just been purchased, to become a part of the museum. It will be needed as the Center is working with the University of Idaho on the transfer of thousands of books for a library. There will be extensive printed materials and a video library of Basque music and oral histories.

When Basque provinces President Jose Antonio Ardanza Garro, was in Boise in March of 1988, he planted a shoot from the sacred tree of Guernica in the yard at the Basque Center.

Adelia is a native Idahoan of Basque ancestry, reared in Boise and a graduate of Saint Theresa's Academy. She also attended Idaho State University and Boise State University. She and Dick have four children, Ted, Laurie, Will and Anne.

The Basques contributed to Idaho before Andy Little came, and kept on giving long after he died. They were as important to Andy as they continue to be to their Idaho homeland, the seventh province of the Basques.

CHAPTER TWELVE

SHEEP, SENATORS, AND MUTTON MOGULS

ANDY LITTLE BECAME AN IMPORTANT MAN BY RAISING SHEEP; INDEED, many of Idaho's leading citizens started out in the sheep industry. And many remained. Others returned to the ranch after careers in the halls of government and power. It is a good way of life any which way, to stay in, to be from or to go to.

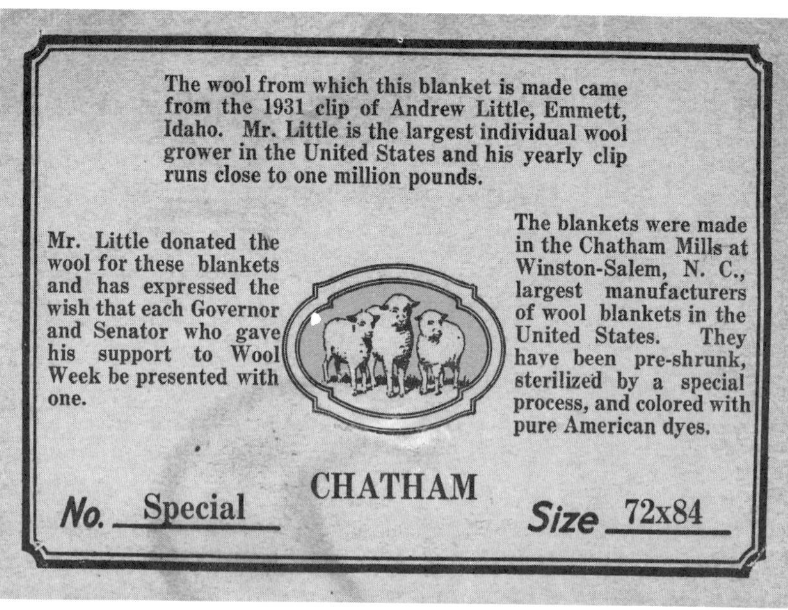

The wool from which this blanket is made came from the 1931 clip of Andrew Little, Emmett, Idaho. Mr. Little is the largest individual wool grower in the United States and his yearly clip runs close to one million pounds.

Mr. Little donated the wool for these blankets and has expressed the wish that each Governor and Senator who gave his support to Wool Week be presented with one.

The blankets were made in the Chatham Mills at Winston-Salem, N. C., largest manufacturers of wool blankets in the United States. They have been pre-shrunk, sterilized by a special process, and colored with pure American dyes.

CHATHAM

No. Special

Size 72x84

The card which accompanied an all-wool blanket woven from the 1931 clip from Andy's bands near Emmett went to the members of the U.S. Senate who supported the designation of Wool Week.

Andy does his homework, with his day's mail in coat pocket, enjoying a good cigar. Picture taken in early thirties.

James Laidlaw

James Laidlaw was often called Jamie or Jim. He was that kind of a man. People felt friendly toward him. Just as Andy Little, his friend and father of his son-in-law, David Little, Laidlaw landed in Idaho from Scotland with two sheep dogs and the clothing he could carry in a handmade trunk.

He was born in 1868 at Peebleshire, Scotland, not many miles from Moffat, but it is not likely that he and Andy knew one another until meeting in Idaho. A young man of twenty-three, he arrived in 1891 at Malta, Idaho, where he went to work as a herder on a sheep ranch. It took him but two years of saving his money and finding a partner, Bob Coates, for him to go into business. They started out breeding purebreds and ranging 2,000 leased sheep. Laidlaw continued in the business, steadily improving his bands and operations, until his death many years later.

Thousands upon thousands of range rams for use in flocks all the way from Texas to Canada and from California to Nebraska, were shipped by Laidlaw.

In its book *Sheep and Man, An American Saga*, the American Sheep Producers Council reported that "Laidlaw and Coates, vying with each other to see who could spend the least cash, winter-pastured their flock around the area of Malta, the present day town of American Falls, and Minidoka. During the summer, they would trail as far as Cape Horn, north of Stanley."

When the partnership broke up, Jim owned his own sheep and continued in the way in which he had started. He trailed his bands on horseback in all kinds of weather. He wouldn't have known how to shirk work even if he had wanted to. He built up the bands until he was one of Idaho's largest owners, with 20,000 head.

Like so many Scots, he soon brought family and encouraged friends to come to Idaho from the old country. His brothers, John and Will, and neighbors of the Laidlaw family arrived to be employed by him. He also sponsored herders from the Basque lands of Spain as early as 1904.

A year earlier, Jim Lindsey, one of the Scots to join his crew, formed a successful partnership with Laidlaw. Laidlaw had a large flock of Lincoln ewes, which he had purchased in a search for a

Courtesy Idaho Wool Growers

James Laidlaw of Muldoon and Boise, breeder of purebred sheep and "The Sheep Queen of Idaho" Emma Yearian of Lemhi enjoy recalling the early days in the wool industry at the 57th annual convention of Idaho Wool Growers in Boise on November 13–17, 1949.

larger-framed, meatier sheep. The partners started experimenting with cross-breeding. In 1912, to increase the fineness of the wool and secure a sheep better adapted to range conditions, they bred the Lincoln ewes to Rambouillet rams. Within three years, they were so pleased with the results that they took crossbred rams to show at the Panama-Pacific Exposition in San Francisco. By the time they returned, the crossbreds were called Panamas.

So popular did the breed become in the West, that many of them are stocked on ranches today. The Panama was noted for its ruggedness, and the ewes made an eighty-five mile trek every winter from the Muldoon ranch near Sun Valley to their lambing sheds northeast of Rupert. The Panama is one of only two recognized breeds to originate in the United States. Laidlaw continued to improve the strain during his lifetime.

Jim Laidlaw was also the first to run his sheep on the north side of the Snake River on the Minidoka desert. In addition, he built the first roads into that area and the Laidlaw Park and the Little Laidlaw Park grazing areas were named for him.

It was in 1907 that Jim Laidlaw and Genevieve Treadgold were married. She had been teaching school at Carey. The following year they bought the Braymer ranch at Muldoon, and added extensively to it over the years as it remained the headquarters for the sheep and livestock operations. It became one of largest ranches in the state, and it became the family homestead. A portion of the Little Wood River flowed alongside it. At its peak, the ranch covered 21,000 acres of deeded land with 20,000 sheep and 500 Angus cattle roaming its hills and valleys. Jim imported the Angus from Scotland. He was one of the first to believe that sheep and cattle could range together with benefit to both.

Jim Laidlaw and his Border Collie "Butch" arrive at the Muldoon headquarters ranch ready for a day's work.

Mutton moguls and partners, Scots both, Brockie and Laidlaw were interested in experimenting with different breeds to improve the stock. They were partners for twenty-seven years.

Lindsey sold his interest in the partnership in early 1920 to Robert Brockie, another Scot, and this joint effort was to last for twenty-seven years. Brockie was as interested as Laidlaw in experimenting with different breeds to improve the stock. It was the Suffolk upon which they eventually settled as the best for Idaho ranges.

Ben Darrah of Shoshone took Laidlaw up on his forecast that if the commercial range ewes were crossed with Suffolk-Hampshire rams, they would produce three pounds more per lamb at shipping time than any other cross. He did this by breeding 2,000 of his ewes to Hampshire rams and another 2,000 to the Suffolk-Hampshire cross rams developed by Laidlaw and Brockie. It turned out that Laidlaw was right. The lambs from the Laidlaw and Brockie cross outweighed the others by an average of nearly four and one-half pounds. Laidlaw, in addition to developing the Panama breed, bought the first Suffolk stud buck in the West.

Arthur H. Caine was chairman of the Idaho State Sheep Commission from 1937 to 1976, and the University of Idaho's Caine Veterinary Medical Center at Caldwell is named for him. Caine was high on Jim Laidlaw and his sons, with whom he worked. Art said, "Jim Laidlaw never borrowed money—he *loaned* money." Art recounted a conversation he had years ago with Jim who was telling him of loaning money to a mutual friend. Jim said, "I didn't even have a promissory note."

"Well, then," Art asked, "what kind of security do you have?"

"Security, hell. They *told* me they'd pay it," was the response.

John McMurray, banker turned wool buyer and then insurance dealer, described Laidlaw and Brockie as "movers and doers" in doing a lot for Idaho and the economy through the sheep industry. "I wrote the first insurance policy that Jamie Laidlaw ever put on his men and trucks, "John said. "I walked right out in the fields near his headquarters ranch at Muldoon, and found him in the center of the sheep and the men, and wrote up that policy right then and there. That was how he did things."

The Laidlaws became the parents of James Alexander "Sandy," Fred M., Annabel (Mrs. E.A. Roberts) and Gerry (Mrs. David Little). Small wonder that both the sons entered the sheep business and that one daughter married a livestock man.

It was not long before they owned their own sheep outfits and both sons were well-known for their business acumen. When Jamie died Sandy became the owner-operator of Muldoon. Fred had the adjoining ranch which was referred to as the old Post Office Ranch. The Muldoon post office had been located there.

At one time Fred shipped eighty-four purebred Panama lambs to Venezuela for establishment as a part of the Venezuelan agricultural development. They were a part of that flock developed by his father and purchased by the Venezuelan Ministry of Agriculture to further development of that country's sheep industry, already counted as a major part of the economy. Fred sent one of the rams as a gift to Marcos Perez Jiminez, then president of that country.

When the Fred Laidlaws sold their ranch including the home that they had built, their daughter Sally, now an attorney in Oakland, California, was saddened to see the home place go. Later, she bought back the land on which the house still stands. As has been said, "Once you've been in the livestock business, it never gets out of your blood."

The pioneer's death occurred on February 16, 1950, in Boise, where they had established another home many years previously. He had been in ill health for a year, but had attended the Idaho Wool Growers Convention, which he always enjoyed with the opportunity to visit lifetime friends. Because of his vision in seeing that sheep could be improved, and taking the lead in sponsoring an untried breed that in a few years proved him right, he was named the first president of the American Suffolk Sheep Society and still held that position at the time of his death.

Long before death, Jim Laidlaw let it be known that he was to be buried on "The Knoll" at the Muldoon ranch. Sandy said that if his dad had known how expensive and difficult a job it turned out to be, "he would have turned over in his grave."

A special road had to be built, a contractor hired to blast out a hole in the rock large enough for the coffin. The rock kept tumbling back in, and Sandy reported that when they had finished the project they could have buried a pickup truck.

A number of old Scots friends were in attendance at the burial. Before the coffin was covered they each took a drink from a bottle of Scotch and when it was finished, they tossed the bottle alongside the coffin. Sheepmen are a lively bunch.

When Mrs. Laidlaw died, the cremated remains were also placed in the unusual rock-enclosed grave and placed in a cement wall. There is a rock spire jutting up from the forward part of the wall and overlooks the ranch. Jim Laidlaw made and set the corner posts for the ranch's fence nearly seventy years ago.

In the fall of 1960, Sandy sold the huge ranch to Mary Thomas Peavey Brooks, then of Chicago and Muldoon. Her Flat Top Sheep company was put together primarily by her father, the late U.S. Senator John Thomas of Gooding. Mrs. Brooks had not only kept the ranch together, but added to it. With the purchase from Laidlaw, her holdings were nearly doubled and the combined ranch size is about 75,000 acres within some 115 square miles.

Thomas-Peavey-Brooks

The day that well-known, Idaho-born sheep rancher Mary Brooks was sworn in as Director of the United States Mint and raised her right hand to take the oath of office, she rested her left upon a Bible held by another, equally well-known Idahoan and sheepman, U.S. Senator Len Jordan. Administering the oath was Secretary of the U.S. Treasury David Kennedy.

Twenty years later, being interviewed in her home on Strawberry Lane in Boise she said, "Once you have been in the livestock business, it never gets out of your blood." The smiling, well-coiffed, white-haired woman has held many positions and offices in her life. Ranching and livestock have been only a part of an active life and a distinguished career, but the part to which she refers most often. Mary Thomas Peavey Brooks not only was born and reared in Idaho, she never got Idaho out of her blood, despite a number of years spent in Washington, D.C., and Illinois.

The varied roles she has played throughout her life have included those of student, wife and mother, farmer, banker, sheep- and cattle-operator, rancher, Idaho state senator, mother of a state senator, daughter of a United States senator, wife of a U.S. senator, and director of the United States Mint for Presidents Richard M. Nixon and Gerald R. Ford. Her activities and positions with the Idaho and National Republican party make a lengthy list.

Mary's Idaho sheep story actually begins in Kansas, through her father. Born in Phillips county, Kansas on January 1, 1874, John "Jack" Thomas was the firstborn son of Daniel and Mary Elizabeth Sparks Thomas. He was the first European-descended child born in an area that later became Prairie View. John graduated from the Phillipsburg, Kansas high school in 1891, and taught what was called "short school" for two years in order to earn enough money to attend Nickerson Normal School. He served as county superintendent of schools at Phillipsburg from 1898 until 1903.

So well-known had John Thomas become that in 1906, President Theodore Roosevelt appointed him registrar of the U.S. Land office in Colby, a position he held until 1909. In the same year, he and Florence Jessie Johnson of Scott City were married on October 25. They had met while working on their educations to become teachers. It was after they moved to Idaho that their only child, Mary Elizabeth, was born.

Answering the challenge to "Go West, young man," on New Year's day in 1909, Thomas arrived in Idaho carrying his savings, then a fortune of $2,500. He got off the Union Pacific train at the town of Glenns Ferry, took the ferry across the river to look over the land. He was not satisfied with what he had hoped to see.

He was thinking of returning to Kansas when told to take a look at Gooding. He boarded the train again and looked up Frank Robert Gooding, who was just completing his second term as Governor and for whom the town was named. Frank and his brother Fred W. were engaged in farming and livestock, which included extensive sheep holdings. The Goodings told Thomas that Gooding county had a great future with the main line of Union Pacific running through it, rich agricultural land, numerous springs and a colorful history. It was an area where the famous Ben Halladay stages had operated in the early 1860s.

Thomas was impressed. He put his life savings into the banking business, running the First National Bank, and owning the Shoshone, the Lincoln and the Jerome National Banks. His daughter, Mary, still has a $1500 bill of that day with his signature on it. During his banking days he was appointed to the Federal Reserve Board and as a director of the First Security Corporation in Ogden,

Utah. It was to First Security that he later sold all three of the banks.

He started the telephone company in Gooding as well as beginning a new career as a livestock man. Seven brothers and sisters all followed him to Idaho and Frank Thomas operated a sale yard in Jerome. A nephew, Earl Bolte, came from Kansas at the age of seventeen and went into banking for his uncle, becoming a well-known member of the community and state.

The Goodings and Thomas were lifetime friends and all three were active in Idaho's Republican party. The Goodings were born in England and emigrated with their parents to Michigan in 1867, moving on to California ten years later. The brothers came to Ketchum, Idaho in 1881, and seven years later they relocated to the area to be named Gooding. They went into the livestock business there and Frank became politically active. In 1888, he also began raising sheep and was elected the first president of Idaho Wool Growers in 1893. In 1911, he was named president of the National Association.

Frank served in the state senate, becoming Idaho state Republican chairman and governor. In 1920 he was elected to the U.S. Senate, but was appointed to an early session when Senator John F. Nugent resigned. He was re-elected in 1926, and served until his death June 24, 1928. John Thomas, mayor of Gooding, Republican state chairman and on the national committee, was appointed to fill Gooding's term.

Elbert Stellmon of Lewiston and Lapwai remembers a Republican convention being held in Kellogg in 1928 to name a successor to the late Senator Gooding. Elbert was then twenty-four years of age and here is how he tells it: "Guy Bissell, I think of Gooding, was wearing a great big red hand-tied bow tie that caught the attention of everyone. He had a loud, sonorous voice, and he walked to the podium and said, 'Ladies and Gentlemen, the man I am going to nominate for the office of United States Senator from Idaho was born in the state of Kansas, the year the grasshoppers ate the cowhide hinges off the cabin door!' " Stellmon says that after these sixty-two years he still thinks it was the most amusing introduction he has ever heard. And it had the desired effect.

Thomas ran again in 1932, and the internationally-famed Senator William E. Borah stumped the state for him. But Thomas was defeated, along with many other Republicans, in Franklin D. Roosevelt's Democratic sweep.

John Thomas went back to ranching.

When Borah died in office in 1940, Thomas was again called upon to return to Washington. His 1942 bid for re-election succeeded. He, too, died in office on November 10, 1945, and was followed by Congressman Henry C. Dworshak, Burley newspaper publisher, also a champion of agriculture and the sheep industry.

Mary laughs as she remembers how much her mother enjoyed rural life, always keeping a cow and growing a large garden. "During recesses of the Congress, Mother had Dad out weeding and working in the garden like a hired hand."

John Thomas started buying and selling yearling lambs in 1928. Both lamb and wool buyers purchased his stock and John McMurray, later to become a sheepman with his father, was among the buyers. As Thomas increased his flocks and began shipping ewes as well as lambs, he purchased forty acres east of Bellevue, near present day Sun Valley resort, just to rest the sheep after a twenty-three mile drive over the Muldoon Summit. They shipped out of Ketchum and took the bands to stockyards owned by Jack Lane and Bill Newman.

In 1929 First Security banker Lynn Driscoll of Boise told of a mortgage he had and which he felt Thomas could buy, on about 8,000 acres of land out of Bellevue and which was held by the Livestock Bank in Chicago. Thomas immediately boarded the Union Pacific and rode to Chicago and made the purchase. The acreage ranges from out of Bellevue, up Slaughter House Gulch to Muldoon and adjoined the other big ranch, Flat Top Sheep Company.

During these days, Thomas became acquainted with a number of other Idaho sheepmen. Mary remembered well Jack Lane in pre-Sun Valley days when he operated a large red store to serve livestock operators at a corner on Ketchum's main street. Groceries, sundries and any hardware items he felt sheepmen might need were stocked. Jack, also a former Kansan, "finally got so rich," Mary said, "that he'd sit in a corner of the store where the sunlight came in and read the *Sheep Market News*. Sheepmen would come in everyday to learn how rich or poor they were.

"When tourists came in, Jack would say, 'I'm sorry, but we don't sell to tourists. We deal only with sheepmen.' It was true. If you weren't in the sheep business, he wouldn't sell to you.

"In his early days in Ketchum, Jack knew all about how the sun shone down on that area, long before Union Pacific discovered it and built Sun Valley. He placed huge wood blocks facing south outside the store for his sheepmen friends to bask in the sun as they visited."

In the meantime, Mary was graduated from the University of Idaho. She and Art Peavey Jr., had met, dated and fallen in love. They were married and moved to Wallace for a short time and then to Twin Falls where they worked in an abstract and insurance business. They were working for the Hartford Insurance Company in Salt Lake City when the Great Depression hit and both lost their jobs in a staff reduction.

Returning to Gooding at the invitation of Mary's father, who bankrolled Art in a temporary business, the young couple began to work into the sheep business. At that stage of the Depression no one would cash checks for the school teachers. Art, with a loan from Thomas, founded a small business to do so.

"As we began to acquire some small funds," Mary recalled, "We would go out and buy little pieces of pasture. We made some money on them." The Peaveys and Thomas had lambing sheds at Rupert and were running about 20,000 head of sheep.

In 1933, John Thomas Peavey was born and life was looking up for the young trio. Baby John was a sturdy little boy and liked nothing better than travelling in a pickup with his Dad to look over the sheep and ranges. To complete the family happiness, a daughter, Betty, was born in 1936. She was five when tragedy struck.

While Art was duck hunting on the Snake River, during the fall of 1941, his boat overturned at Salmon Falls. Forgetting the weight of the shotgun shells in his hunting jacket and the heavy boots he was wearing, he jumped into the river in an attempt to swim to shore. He didn't make it.

After a time, John Thomas said, "You'd better get into the sheep business, Mary. You have the children and their future to consider. We've got all this investment that we need to hang onto. Young John may want to become a livestock man, too." As it turned out, he did.

"So," Mary said matter-of-factly, "I got into my saddle pants, put on my cowboy hat, and went to work."

Sam Burke took Mary under his wing. Burke was well-known to the family. John Thomas had loaned him money to buy yearling lambs. Burke promptly repaid Thomas, and Thomas soon hired him. He showed Mary the Thomas rangeland and holdings.

She was wondering what she would do to be of help while learning the business. She soon found out. As they drove into camp they visited with an old fellow who had been killing coyotes and saving their tails, for which the county agent was paying a bounty of five dollars each.

Mary tells the story: "Sam said, 'Now here, Mary, this is something you can do. Take these tails and mail them in to the county agent and collect the money.' I put the tails in a paper bag and dropped them into the trunk of my car and promptly forgot them. Several weeks later, when I opened the trunk lid, they were pretty ripe. Nevertheless, I mailed them into the county agent, explaining that I would be sending more in later.

"Within a few days I had a letter from the agent informing me that hereafter when I had coyote tails, 'DON'T MAIL THEM IN . . . just call and let us know how many and I'll take your word for it!' "

Mary was a "quick study." She absorbed much of sheep lore, mastered many of the intricacies of that life, and her children were also learning. Her children grew to adulthood and married.

Betty married Gordon Eccles, the son of Ruth Eccles Purdy and stepson of L.N. "Bud" Purdy of Picabo. Purdy was also engaged in the sheep business.

In 1941, Mary's mother, known as Jessie to friends, many of whom she had escorted throughout Washington when they visited, died of a cerebral hemorrhage. In Washington, she was intensely interested in the committee hearings on Capitol Hill and enjoyed the White House and diplomatic receptions and met with the group, simply called The Ladies of the Senate. She was buried in the family plot in Gooding.

In 1944, Senator Thomas suffered an ailment which affected his eyesight. Mary left the ranch and took the children to Washington to serve as her father's eyes and, often, his ears. When farmers and sheepmen visited the seat of government, Mary was more adept at talking with and helping them than many members of the Congress who had not experienced ranch and sheep life.

The Senator was a seatmate of Illinois Senator C. Wayland "Curly" Brooks. They often visited and Thomas had told Brooks of his daughter and the tragic loss of her husband. Brooks had lost his wife and also had children.

When Senator Thomas died his seatmate was one of the first to offer help and condolences. Later, he telephoned Mary and said, "Mrs. Peavey, everyone that I know in Washington has seen to it that I have met all the rich widows, all the fat widows, all the skinny widows and any other widows in town. I don't know you, but I knew your father and have heard all about you. Would you do me the honor of coming to dinner with Senator and Mrs. Gerald Nye and me?" The rest, as it is said, is history.

As Mrs. Brooks, Mary became directly involved in the Republican politics of Illinois and Senator Brooks had a new interest in Idaho. One of his sons, now living in Boise, became a doctor of veterinary science in Meridian, Idaho.

Upon the death of Senator Brooks, Mary returned to Idaho and the ranch. She also has a little house in Ketchum, which was headquarters when she ran for the Idaho State Senate in 1964. She describes herself as the original "walker," conducting a door-to-door campaign in Ketchum and Hailey. She also called at all the ranches in Blaine county, leaving a brochure and asking the residents of the county to vote for her. The local newspaper published a picture of her showing the holes in her shoes, which had been re-soled during the campaign.

On election night in November, returns from the East made it evident that Republican Barry Goldwater was being defeated in a landslide. Mary and some of her supporters were sad and worried about her own race. However, when the Idaho returns were in, she had handily defeated her opponent.

While serving in the Idaho Senate, Mary continued to visit the sheep ranch and keep track of what was going on. In 1960, she had purchased the old L.L. ranch at Muldoon, adjoining the Flat Top ranch owned by the James Laidlaws since 1907.

Her son, John Peavey, has been the sole owner for the last ten years. Dennis Burke, who had worked for the Flat Top as foreman, held that position for the Peavey-Brooks operation. They purchased the cattle Sandy Laidlaw had at the ranch. John handled the cattle and Burke the sheep. For several years Peavey and his mother were in the cattle business, and are now back into sheep to the extent of a band of about 3,500.

Now his sons, Art and John Thomas "Tommy" Peavey, who was graduated from the University of Idaho in 1989, with a degree of agriculture, are working on the ranch. They are the fourth generation of the Thomas family to be working in livestock. John Peavey was appointed to the Idaho Senate by Governor Don Samuelson. Defeated when he ran as a Republican, he switched to the Democratic party and has served in the state Senate for a number of years.

President Nixon named Mary as Director of the Mint in 1969 and she served in the same capacity for President Ford. She was the only woman mint director in the world and responsible for the manufacture of the country's coinage. She was also in charge of the manufacture of military and historic medals and coins for foreign nations and collectors. She was the only woman in the world with the keys to Fort Knox and laughed as she frequently told the story.

Mary also arranged for the transfer of the old government assay office in Boise to the ownership of the state of Idaho. Built during the gold and silver rush days, the assay office had belonged to the U.S. Mint.

A lot of talking and writing is being done today on the sheep industry as a "dying one." Mary Brooks takes a different stance. "There will always be a sheep industry. It is not dying, but it is changing. Despite all the synthetics in the world, we are always going to demand and need wool. We will always have big cities, along with the smaller ones, where the residents will demand roast leg of lamb, racks of lamb, and lamb chops.

State Senator John Peavey and his mother, Mary Thomas Peavey Brooks, inspect the feed and cattle situation at the Flat Top Ranch near Muldoon. On top of the knoll is the burial spot and monument to Mr. and Mrs. Laidlaw, from whose family the ranch was purchased.

"It remains an interesting business. It gets and stays in your blood.

"With sheep you have two crops—wool and lamb. Many of the ewes have twins and occasionally triplet lambs. When you are in cattle, you have a lot of money in one cow and if she loses the lone calf, she is of no monetary use, in fact, she costs money to have around for another year. The sheep industry is still a good one," the many-faceted Mary Brooks concluded.

Gooding-Smith Sheep Ranches

A jet-propelled thinker and doer, Jean Munro Smith, has inherited and runs a good-sized cattle operation on 20,000 acres at Little Camas in the foothills of Camas Prairie. Jean lives in Boise, seventy miles equidistant from the large ranch and to her 400 acres at Grandview. Along with managing these pieces of land she turns the cattle onto Bureau of Land Management desert in the spring.

She became the head of the operation in 1980 when her husband, Bill, died from a heart attack. He was loading cattle at Grandview, before putting them on the desert.

"I simply could not do without those wonderful Basques!" she exclaims. Basilio Susareta, foreman for the Smith operations for nearly forty years, is her mainstay. His wife, Eusebia, is the cook for the ranch. From Basilio, who is sixty-two, down to Pete Celya, thirty-nine, she has all Basque employees. "They loved Bill and had become used to seeing me with him in our trips to the ranches, and I knew I couldn't do the job without them. I just can't tell you how great those Basques are," she added. She says that several years previous to 1986 through 1987 were poor years for cattle, but that those years have been good.

As with Jessie Little Naylor and Mary Thomas Brooks, Jean Smith's livestock career actually had its beginning with earlier family members getting started. In Jean's case we go back to Fred Gooding, brother of Governor and Senator Frank Gooding, marrying Mary Griffin. Mary Griffin's father had come over the old Oregon Trail and spent a short time in Oregon. Then he returned to the Idaho area of Ketchum to make his home. Mary and Fred Gooding became the parents of two children, Edward and Alta Elizabeth, known as Betsy for most of her life.

Jean said that Mary enjoyed telling the story of meeting her future husband one day as she was driving a flock of geese to one of the ore mines near Ketchum, where she knew they would be eagerly bought by the miners. Fred Gooding was doing the same thing with a herd of cows. Somehow, Gooding's cows got into the midst of Mary's geese and scattered them to the four winds. By the time she got through telling him off, he thought he could fall in love with such a spitfire.

Betsy's future husband, D. Sidney Smith, known, as later was his son, as "Sheep" Smith, with so many other Smiths in the state, was born September 3, 1885, on a farm near Kirkville, Iowa. Upon graduation from Wesleyan University with an engineering degree, he came to Idaho in 1908, and worked as a surveyor on a number of irrigation projects. He became the manager of land sales for the North Side tract, which included the towns of Gooding, Jerome, Shoshone and Richfield. He became a member of the board of director of Shoshone's first bank, which was established and owned by sheepman John Thomas and they were lifetime friends. Smith also helped form the Sagebrush Hair Tonic Company, Ltd., of Shoshone.

Sid and his wife, Betsy, and her brother, Edward Gooding, inherited the huge sheep operation called Gooding and Son from Fred Gooding. It then became the Gooding-Smith sheep business and consisted of seven ranches holding about 30,000 acres. Ed decided to get out of the sheep business in the late 1920s, and sold out to the Smiths, who became sole owners. Sid established the Smith Land and Livestock Company.

The Fred Goodings had owned a big summer house in the middle of the town of Ketchum, where several generations of family members gathered in the summer. It was during those months that the sheep were driven on to the Bear Valley region for grazing. The property upon which the summer headquarters was located adjoined that land purchased by Union Pacific Railway for the establishment of Sun Valley lodge and recreation center.

Sid was always active in the sheep industry and was a director of the Idaho Wool Growers association, serving as vice president in 1928, and president from 1931 through 1934.. He was a member of the executive committee of the National Wool Growers Association. His fellow sheepmen named him to the Hickman Hall of Fame in 1956.

He helped establish and served as director of the Idaho Livestock Production Credit Association. He was also a member of the Idaho Cooperative Board of Forestry and the Sawtooth Grazing Association. It was while driving for his politically active father-in-law, Fred Gooding, that he became interested in politics. He was to remain active in the Idaho Republican Party for the rest of his life, serving as its treasurer for a quarter of a century.

When Sid Smith accepted a job or an office, he did it well and was willing to stick with it so long as he felt he was of assistance. For forty years he was chairman of the Lincoln County U.S. Bond sales drives. As a charter member of the Shoshone Rotary Club, he held a record of more than forty years of perfect attendance.

Gradually, Smith began selling off the sheep ranches. By the time his only son, Bill, was graduated with business degrees from both Stanford University and Harvard Business School, he came back to Idaho and started his own sheep business. It was at Stanford in 1938 that Bill met Jean Munro of Santa Ana, California. They were married in 1943 and lived in Shoshone and Ketchum. In autumn 1948, they moved to Boise, moving 14,000 sheep at the same time to a ranch which they had bought at Grandview. They purchased John Archabal's Wood Creek Sheep Company which adjoins the cattle ranch owned by industrialist and potato magnate Jack R. Simplot, who has also been in the sheep business. They began cutting down the sheep numbers and started into the cattle business.

Jean now has a 1400 cow-calf operation and raises purebred bulls. She and Bill had a son and daughter. Sidney Munro "Skip" Smith is married to a veterinarian and they are running cattle on a Washington ranch. They also have a son and a daughter. The daughter, Marcy married Bill Campton, who is a professor at Kearney, Nebraska. They have three daughters.

Len Jordan in Hell's Canyon

Len had herded sheep as a youngster. In the midst of the Depression in the spring of 1933, with his wife and three small children, one a baby, he went into Hells Canyon to Kirkwood Bar. Len told the story this way: "I was in Grangeville in 1932 and one day Wade Humphrey, the father of Fred, who was to become president of the Idaho First National Bank many years hence, told me that Mike Sloviaczek had just walked into town from his sheep ranch between the Salmon and the Snake Rivers. He said Mike was down at a local bar talking about selling out.

"Mike had married a widow with quite a few kids and just wasn't making it on the sheep ranch. Also, some of the kids needed to be in school. I went down the street on the double and found Mike in the bar drinking a beer. I said, 'Howdy, Mike. I heard you want to sell that band of sheep at Elk City. I might be interested if you'd be willing to waive your summer grazing allotment.' We talked for awhile and he was eager to get into town. He had 1800 sheep in his winter band. We made the deal right there, and I was in the sheep business."

Len and partner, Dick Maxwell, had bought the ranch at Kirkwood Bar. The Jordans later bought out Maxwell's interest in the Bar and the sheep. This unusual ranch was on the Idaho side of the Snake River Gorge, just below Hell's Canyon.

The USFS made it possible for the owner of a very few acres of hay land to run thousands of sheep or cattle. If the government range was used continuously and properly by the land owner it came to belong to the deeded land and could be transferred to a new owner when the land was sold.

The Jordans had title to less than a thousand acres, which ran along the river for ten miles and, in some places, reached to the divide between the Salmon and the Snake Rivers. It was an extremely steep range and the USFS had assigned it to sheep with a fee to be paid for each head grazed. On this land they had 3,000 ewes expected to lamb within a matter of six weeks.

Jordan and his herders took sheep to summer range in mountains to the east, which required three weeks of laborious travel, crossing rivers and prairies, deep timber and farm lands.

Ordinarily, Grace Jordan, their three children and a woman to help on occasion, and Len, when he could be home, made up the household. But during the lambing, the household rose to fifteen, and sometimes even higher. The lambing rush started at the lowest place on the range, because the earliest grass was there.

Their second year on the ranch the lamb drop was heavier because Len had the first year to learn the range; there were fewer dry ewes. Just as many lambs were born by night as by day, so Len put on a night man. Grace said she became a dietitian for lambs as every day a weak or orphaned lamb was brought to the door, sometimes it was a pair.

A lamb for whom no mother, natural or foster, can be found is a bummer. The bum lamb cries for a mother to feed him, yet he locks his jaws when offered a nippled bottle and it is necessary to force them open to feed him. Many of the bummers do not survive and those that do are alienated from the other sheep and if put with a band refuse to follow a leader.

Grace Jordan had never heard of a "graft" until Hells Canyon ranching and learned that it was an event of taking the skin of a dead lamb and slipping it onto a motherless one. It is then placed with the mother ewe of the dead one. She smells and nudges it, acting for all the world as though she knows it is not her lamb. As the lamb persists in nuzzling her udder and as it smells like her lamb, she permits it to feed. A day or two later, the pelt is slipped off and by that time it smells right to the ewe.

During the second year of lambing they were eager to see any improvement in their Rambouillet strain that might be attributed to the Hampshire bucks put with the ewes in November. The bucks had cost twenty dollars each, a small fortune in 1935.

The shearing was another interesting time to Grace and the children. Excitement built as additional cooks and helpers were hired and loads of food and supplies arrived by boat. The Jordans had the continual fear, during shearing, that the Snake River might suddenly drop and the resultant inability to ship the wool out by boat.

Shearers must always be treated with consideration for they are sorely needed. It takes a strong man to shear a strong sheep, and the best of shearers can find themselves in a wrestling match before the valuable fleece falls to the floor.

Unlike the early days of Andy Little, the Jordans had the benefit of engine-driven clippers, enabling them to finish clippings in one or two days. The wool-trompers, however, were as in the old days, and stood in the long hanging sacks stomping down the fleeces. Jordan used the horses to haul the huge and heavy bags of wool down to the river landings for shipment.

It was in 1938 that the government fixed prices, and the value of the wool made a sliding drop. One can understand why the Jordans might think too much government interferes with the lives of working Americans. Worse, that was also the year they were told that they might have trouble selling their wool, unless it could be certified sheared by union crews. The disgusted couple speculated where they might find the sheep-shearer's union hall in the brakes of the Snake River canyon. The Jordan's weren't the only sheep ranchers so beset, and all were learning to meet new government rules and regulations.

Not only did the government cause them trouble, but there were coyotes. The cougars were even more dangerous. Cougars would attack horses as well as sheep.

Then there were unusual hazards and costs of shipping wool from a Hell's Canyon ranch. Most other ranchers didn't have to shoot the rapids to market. Eventually, the Jordans were able to buy the Bar from Mrs. Reid.

The Jordans hung on. They did better than survive; they prospered.

It was in the canyon that Mrs. Jordan taught the three children through the Calvert School correspondence course. All three did well and went on to become university graduates. Joe graduated from West Point. Lessons arrived on the river boat and the children, with a mother who had already taught grade school, instructed them in spelling, geography, history, math, English, writing, art and even Greek mythology. All this was on a rigid schedule to which they daily applied themselves.

As World War II neared, prices for the sheep gained and the Jordans sold wethers for seven and a half cents and ewe lambs for nine and a quarter. Young men were enlisting and they feared that soon they would be herding their own sheep. Patsy, their daughter, was about to enter high school, and her parents had agreed that they would move out of the canyon at that time.

Grangeville was the selection of their future home. In 1943, they sold Kirkwood ranch, lock, stock and barrel and bought a twenty-five acre tract with views of the prairies and mountains from all sides. Len stocked it with beef cattle and began producing grass seed and peas. They built the home of which they had dreamed during the years of canyon living.

An interesting and exciting life lay before them. Their lives would not have not been so interesting, had not much of it been lived while ranching sheep in the deepest river gorge on the North American continent.

Back on the "outside" admirers and friends of sheepman Jordan encouraged him to run for the state legislature. He did so and was successful, even though he was a stalwart Republican in a heavily Democrat county. Nevertheless, residents of the county had come to know the qualities and character of the Jordan family during their days on the sheep ranch. Both the Depression and World War II were over and Idaho, as all America, was attempting to get back to normal life.

Governor C.A. Robins asked Jordan to chair a committee to study the state's outdated highway system and recommend a long-term program. That committee laid the foundation for Idaho's modern highways.

Although Jordan was defeated in the next campaign, many state senators and representatives who had observed his tough and honest stance on issues urged him to be a candidate for governor. During the campaign his seasoning as a sheepman in the canyon was always praised. Jordan was billed as "the only new face in the race." Young Bill Campbell was his campaign manager. Adopting the slogan, "Roll, Jordan, Roll," Jordan did just that, defeating five others in the primary election. Advertising man Eddie Casebeer highlighted Jordan's ranching background and in one picture, which clearly showed Len's bowlegs, the caption was "He didn't get those legs from riding a pork-barrel." In November, Jordan defeated another well-known and highly-respected Idahoan, Calvin Wright, then director of the Internal Revenue Service.

Things were happening on the Jordan homefront, as well. Son Joe, valedictorian of his senior class, was appointed to West Point by Congressman Abe Goff of Moscow. In his senior year at the Point, a group of young Idahoans working in the nation's capitol was teased about driving to Philadelphia for the Army-Navy game primarily to hear the announcer say, "In advance of the West Point band, Cadet Joe Jordan of Idaho carries our country's flag into the stadium."

Steve entered the College of Idaho, later to work for General Electric, and Patsy was married to Charles Story.

Under Idaho law, Jordan was unable to succeed himself as governor and was appointed by President Dwight Eisenhower as chairman of the International Joint Commission. The work of the commission is the cooperation and development necessary to make proper use of the waters that either cross or form the boundary between the United States and Canada. The great Columbia River, into which flows much of the water from Idaho's rivers and streams, is one of those. In 1957, Jordan resigned from the commission, moved back to Idaho and bought into the seventy-five-year-old Circle C ranch at New Meadows, owned by the Campbell family.

At home on the range, Jordan quickly got back into the saddle and worked much harder than he had planned. After two years he sold back his interest to the Campbells and bought 320 acres between Mountain Home and Boise for dryland crops. He also fed 500 head of cattle near the Snake River.

Henry C. Dworshak, Idaho's longtime Congressman and Senator, died of a sudden heart attack at his Washington, D.C. home in July, 1962. Always a champion of agriculture and the sheep and cattle industries, it was logical that his successor would be a man who thought much as he did. Len Jordan, the obvious choice at a Pocatello nominating convention, was appointed by Governor Robert E. Smylie to fill the vacancy.

Idaho's other senator was Frank Church, a Democrat who worked well with both Dworshak and Jordan. Idahoans are independent in political thinking and often match a Republican with a Democrat in electing candidates to office. While vocal and sometimes ferocious in promoting their chosen political party, all but those on the extreme right or left seem pleased when party lines can be crossed by good men and women for the benefit of Idaho.

Jordan was re-elected to his Senate seat, defeating Democrat Congressman Ralph Harding, and was sworn in by Vice President Hubert Humphrey on January 10, 1967. Among those on his staff was Carol McGregor, daughter of the Gordon McGregors of Boise, who later married Andy Little's grandson, Harry Bettis, and moved to the Willow Creek sheep ranch.

Declining to run for re-election in 1972, Jordan was the recipient of many tributes and other measures of gratitude for his service to Idaho and the United States. Len Jordan understood sheep and understood people. He did well with both.

In reminiscing about Andy, Jordan said, "No wonder that the Little sons and daughters and their children hold closely to the work ethic. Andy was a strong sire, and he was aggressive toward succeeding and worked hard. He had a fine, strong wife and they passed on to their children equally strong traits. And it wasn't just genetic. Their young people observed hard work with good rewards during their growing years. In turn, they passed this on to their children.

"I think a lot of it is that the Littles have never been ostentatious. Sure, they drive nice cars but they aren't above shoving a sick ewe or ram right into the back seat of one of those nice cars and taking it to a vet if there is no one on hand who can take care of its ills."

The A.G. Butterfields

In Fern Coble Trull's interesting monograph, "They Dared to Dream," she introduces the story of Aubrey G. Butterfield with the fact that the man who was to become his father-in-law, Thomas C. Galloway, brought the first sheep into Weiser Valley. He trailed them in during the 1860s, but lost the entire band during a hard winter. It was another twenty years before anyone had the courage to bring in the next band.

By September, 1890, there were heavy sheep shipments from Weiser and 60,000 were listed for the entire state. It was in 1892 that Butterfield purchased 4,400 sheep from Alex Watson. At that time ewes sold for $4.25 and lambs for $2.20. Hay was $4.50 a ton. Butterfield worked hard to cut expenses during his sheep-raising career. With this in mind, in 1893, he began the building of a water-storage reservoir on his home ranch on the Weiser flats, so he could raise his own hay for the livestock.

The following autumn, Butterfield sold and shipped a few of his French Merino rams. They were described as being "as large as mules." Editor Lockwood of the Weiser newspaper of that time wrote, "Time will come when he will be shipping out splendid bucks and ewes, instead of shipping them in." This came true many times over. Through his sale of registered sheep in many other countries, he and Washington County became known.

In 1902 the assessment rolls for the county showed 11,500 sheep were owned by Butterfield. That same year he sold 200,000 pounds of wool at twelve cents a pound. Jeremiah Williams of Boston was the buyer. Also in 1902, the business reached such proportions that the Butterfield Livestock Company was organized. A few of the owners were from Great Britain. He then had 15,000 sheep, with Rambouillets and Delano Merinos well represented. That year's wool crop was 230,000 pounds, selling at fourteen cents a pound. The company purchased high-grade Hampshires and Merinos the next year.

The first machines used for shearing, giving a cleaner wool, also appeared at the ranch in 1903. Butterfield said that "close attention and good management" accounted for his increasing success. In 1903, Idaho followed only Wyoming and Montana as America's largest sheep-producing state. There were 4,541,815 sheep registered, worth an average of $2.65.

Things were going great on the home ranch and in the grazing hills and valleys, but with the board of directors it was another story. Butterfield went to Boise to attend the 1922 board of directors meeting and found that some of the stockholders, including the Britishers, were not satisfied with the financial return they were receiving on their investment. Competition was coming from the importation of foreign sheep, paying little or no duty, and high railway shipping rates. Interest was shooting higher, and the stockholders refused to refinance the company's loan.

At previous meetings, Butterfield and his friends on the board had controlled the vote. What he did not realize was that a congenial individual had moved into the area and quietly bought up the stock that Butterfield had traded to others for feed. He sided with the English and Boise board members.

Butterfield later told his foreman, Ted Ballard, "They sold me out, Ted." The company was not in financial danger, but the group wanted someone they could call their own as chairman. According to old-timers, Butterfield was far from down and out and continued to operate on his own.

The Siddoways

No history on the Idaho sheep industry could be complete without mention of the four going-on-five-generation Siddoway sheep family. In early 1880s, the patriarch, James W., and his wife came from the Vernal, Utah area to Teton City, which he helped found. He got into the sheep business almost immediately after settling there. Their son, James Clarence, was born in 1889. He and Ruth Bean Siddoway were married in October, 1917. They lived many years at Teton City, named for the Teton peaks just across the border in Wyoming. They became the parents of six sons, three of whom moved to California to live; and one daughter, Diana Siddoway Richman, who makes her home at Teton.

Jim Siddoway had followed his father into sheep. His son best known through his activities in the sheep business is called Bill. Glen "Doc" Holm was teaching animal diseases in the College of Agriculture at the University of Idaho when young Bill registered there. Doc said that no student enjoyed campus atmosphere more than Bill. When asked what Bill was majoring in, the prof said, "I think it's fast horses and pretty women." He later commented that, "The Siddoways and Canadian thistle are taking over eastern Idaho."

Though named Raymond Kenneth, no one has ever called him anything but Bill. He grew up in the business and has handled every phase of a successful sheep business. He is now seventy-two years old and guides his son, Jeff, whenever needed. Jeff not only followed his father in sheep-raising, but is now president of the Idaho Wool Growers, a post held by Bill from 1965 through 1967. He had been vice-president for three years preceding. Bill went on to become president of the National Wool Growers, as well. Bill speaks out in behalf of sheep and sheep people whenever he feels it is needed. He does so with such wit and charm that he is called the "Will Rogers of the Sheep Industry." His fairness in doing so has also won him the Idaho Wildlife Federation's Sportsman of the Year Award and the Associated Sheep Producers' Silver Ram award.

Jeff served as vice-president from 1985 through 1987 and was followed in that position by Brad Little, Andy's youngest grandson. Brad will become president at the completion of Jeff's term at the end of 1990. The Siddoways currently have bands totalling 10,000 ewes. It is Jeff's eleven year old son, J.C., whom he expects will become the fifth generation Siddoway to become active in the family business. J.C. has already trailed sheep to camp and learned to herd. He is on his way.

The Soulens

During the autumn night there had been wind and rain, and there were misty spots to drive through along the highway from McCall to Phil Soulen's sheep-shipping point high in the mountains. As Mike Roach drove the fifty miles to Squaw Meadows on the Payette National Forest a glorious sun managed to squeak through, sending rays out from fleecy white clouds. The varied reds, oranges, yellows and greens glistened from the bushes and shrubs, making Phil Soulen's high mountain sheep loading camp a pleasant place to be.

Mike parked his wagon, joining other vehicles, across the road from three huge four-story vans, into which the sheep would be loaded in a few hours. Smoke was filtering its way straight up from the cook tent and a few feet away a group of herders were surrounding an outdoor warming fire. The baa-ing of lambs, still with the ewes in two large bands, could be heard.

Squaw Meadows is a typical Idaho sheep-shipping area with great fully-limbed conifers, fir, lodgepole and some spruce, surrounding a lush green meadow, now turning into the autumn earth colors. People were stooping their shoulders to step into the cook tent for a cup of the camp coffee brewing on the tin stove. It was duly noted that thick slabs of ham were frying and that the batter for sourdough hotcakes was ready to be poured when the ham was done. Dozens of eggs awaited their turn on the griddle.

In addition to the wooden box cupboard, the cook tent had on either side two cots for sleeping, and the tin stove with its thin black pipe angling up through the canvas top. Two large wooden grub boxes, the much-needed water bucket, tin forks, and a selection of cutting knives made up the cooking arsenal for the young Spaniard who was the cook.

As the crew began to line up for breakfast, two large slabs of ham, at least two eggs, sourdough hotcakes and camp-made bread, and a cup of good hot coffee were handed to each of them. A leg of ham was quickly disposed of as the hungry horde settled down to eating. The midday meal is even larger.

Tom Boyd, well-known buyer for Superior Packing Company, and father of Stan Boyd, Idaho Wool Growers Executive Director, was on hand to check and count as the sheep went into the truck. The sheep were pushed into the pen area in the meadow by the herders. It was a narrow slot through which they ambled, rambled or moved from a slow walk to a dash as they were prodded. Both Tom and Phil counted. The truck driver also does another count as they enter from the inclined ramp.

They are separated into two groups: the fats and the ewes with the feeder lambs. Those not fat enough for shipment will be sold as feeders. They usually run from 20 to 30 percent of the band.

It is noted that most of the lambs have cut ears as a notch is put in one ear during the springtime castration process. This is called "marking the lambs," Phil said. "We do the marking in the spring and chalking in the fall. I mark the ears according to age and have been selling off those that reach six years. That is why we use the swinging gates at the opening to the chutes, to catch the keeper-ewes and the ewe lambs which will replace the sixes.

"First, we run them as yearlings and then they go into the breeding process. We can also tell by the earmarks who owns each band. If you see a young one without an ear notch, you can be pretty darned sure he was born on the trail. All the wethers are cropped on the right ear. The ewes are notched in a different position, which also signifies their age as well as if they have an underbite or an overbite.

"The blackface ewe lambs are given a slit ear and they then go in with the wethers. In six years we have used up all of the various marks and notches, so we just start all over again. If they are not marked, Frank and I checks their mouths for age."

Boyd was having the fats shipped to Dixon, California, where Superior has a large operation from which many Californians are supplied with lamb, mutton and articles from wool.

Phil Soulen makes his home in Weiser and is owner and operator of the Soulen Sheep Company. He looks much younger than his about sixty years, despite the thousands of hours spent in the beating sun, the steady tattoo of rainstorms, and wading through feet of snow, all in the interest of caring for his sheep. A handsome man with a finely featured profile, he nevertheless has the rugged western look of a sheepman and his skin is the color of lightly tanned leather. His wide-brimmed hat provided protection from the elements.

This was Phil's ninth and final shipment of the May lambs. Along with his Basque foreman Frank Aguirre were: Phil's only son, Harry, named for his grandfather-founder of the sheep company; his second daughter Margaret Soulen; Brad Little, grandson of Andy and the husband of Phil's oldest daughter, Teresa; and Mike Roach. There were ten others, all busy herding, guiding, checking, counting, and loading the sheep.

Phil's wife, Erlene Clyde Soulen, was raised on a large farm near Moscow, and her parents, Lola and Earl Clyde, were among the best-known and liked people in the entire region. Margaret has worked for and with her father for several years, starting when she was two years out of the University of Idaho. He calls her his "Jill of all Trades," and indicates that it would not be possible to keep the operation going without her. Margaret still works as the bookkeeper for the company. It was obvious that she not only knew what she was doing in handling the sheep, but that she enjoyed her prowess, as who wouldn't . . . man or woman?

Sheep people are a sturdy lot. Harry Soulen and Brad Little had not yet been to bed when they arrived at the Meadow from Boise. They had attended a Boise fund-raiser for Public Television until late the previous night. They then decided that rather than try to sleep they would drive the 150 miles and help with the corralling and loading.

Rolled canvas with wooden staves were carried by several of the workers to make pen fence where some of the sheep were being kept. Round, loose chalk in red, blue and green was being used for marking different types. While running through the chute, a quick cross was marked on the back or the head to denote something amiss. Perhaps the sheep was lame or crippled. Those are chalked as well as the cull lambs. The latter are those with a spoiled udder or a bad bumble foot. Some of the aged ewes are also chalked.

"Don't chalk any wethers," Phil shouted as the herding began. He explained, "If a fat wether (a castrated male) should get to the shipping lot with a chalk mark, they might think something wrong with the animal, and reject it."

Not missing a movement in the loading, Phil went on to say that he had taken on an extra string of sheep this season, and had cured a hoof disease many of them contracted from long blades of grass caught in their hooves. They were run through a disinfectant of formaldehyde, and it did the job. Not one of them developed foot rot, which can be a troublesome and expensive disease within a band.

About seventy percent of the lambs were feeders, not fat enough to slaughter. They would be taken to winter feedlot quarters at Letha. Some of the lambs were ten to twelve pounds underweight. They will go on self-feeding at the feedlot where they can eat what and how much they want. First it will be alfalfa pellets and then grain rations. Within thirty to forty days they will be nice and fat. Each of the huge vans on hand hauled 500 sheep. This was on a Sunday, and the previous Tuesday 2,500 lambs had been shipped; another shipment was due the following Tuesday, and another on Thursday.

Frank Aguirre and Phil check the mouths of the ewes for age. They were cutting out the six and seven year olds to sell as running ewes: the ones considered old but still sound. "Lots of people buy the aged ewes to replenish their stock. When they get to be ten to twelve years old, they lose their teeth and it is difficult for them to eat enough to remain strong. Some do well on a family ranch where they are fed hay," Phil explained. The black and the bell sheep are used as markers in the band.

Many sheep outfits sell to the wool pools, where animals from many bands are put together to be sold. But Phil sells directly to the Pendleton mills. The Soulens and their crews grade the wool before breeding and then put the Suffolk with its coarse wool with the Rambouillet bucks with fine wool. Ewes with coarse wool are placed with Suffolk bucks. Then the fine wool ewes are placed with fine wool bucks to develop an even finer grade of wool. Phil says that if a wool grower does this type of mix four or five years and then goes back to breeding Panamas, the mix will last for a number of years.

Phil is talking about Idaho sheep herders: "Most of the good herders like Bill Rice and Allen Wilson came from Virginia and Tennessee. After the Southerners came the Basques, who made fine herders and equally fine citizens. They were intent upon giving their children as complete an education as possible. Hence, most of the younger Basques went into business, the professions, or into government work. Added to these factors, the Spanish government was no longer permitting Basques to leave their homeland as the Spanish economy improved to the point where many of them could find well-paying jobs there.

"Then came the Peruvians. The Western Range Association was now hiring Peruvians on a three-year contract. Most of the Soulen herders now are from Peru. The Basques had become such a large part of the southern Idaho culture, that many of the sheep people were hesitant to hire the herders from Peru. They found, to their pleasure, that the Peruvians adapted quickly to their new land and also seemed to be naturals with the sheep. For a long time they had to work with a green card. First, they worked on a contract after arriving from Peru, and finally got the green card which entitles them to work on any job, going back and forth between working places.

"The Immigration service didn't quit handing out those green cards until the boat people from Southeast Asia started arriving by the thousands. The Peruvians need to be taught how to do the job. My agreement with Western Range Association is to pay $600 a month, no matter what they know nor what, if any, experience they have. On a three-year contract it is possible for them to save $10,000 to $15,000."

Phil sheared 13,500 ewes and bucks one year. His Snake River ranch is wild country. It is located on Sturgill Creek and he tells of seeing thirteen elk going "almost straight up" the mountain that fall.

Occasionally during the day, the sun would disappear and a light rain would fall for a few minutes. The sheep did not care for that feel of wet wool in which they are encased.

The conversation is interrupted by hearing Brad pleading as he drove the ewes toward the loading shoot, "Go on girls, go onnnn." As everyone laughed, he explained, "It is just too wet and you would know they are ewes, as they are fastidious. They just don't want to touch their wet wool to another sheep's wet wool."

Each herder has his own yell, whistle or makes a trilling sound from deep in his throat to keep the sheep moving. When one large and beautiful ewe managed to get turned completely around in the chute and was heading back down, Phil picked her up by the neck and turned her in the right direction. When she was dropped into the proper spot on the chute, Phil gave out with his particular yell and she rushed on up the incline and into the van.

"If the whistle, yell or trill doesn't keep them moving, a quick prod with the shepherd's crook will get the job done," Brad said as he did just that. "Grandad Andy always carried a cane or a short crook so he could reach out and grab a sheep and turn it around. Dad says that Grandad never lost his interest in helping with the sheep as long as he was able."

The blackface ewe lambs were put in with the wethers because they are not considered good breeding stock. "Wool is too coarse," Phil explained. "The blackface is a Suffolk-cross and the wool is finer."

At that moment, Tom let out a yell as a few of the ewes he had been siphoning off were jumping over the chute and getting into the very group from which he wanted to keep them away. Whenever a ewe's sides touched both sides of the chute, out she would go. She was considered a "slaughter ewe." One frisky lamb leaped from the grassy spot where she had been put and landed back into the chute, scrambling up the incline. Tom said, "Likely her mother was cut out by me and went into the van."

One of the herders yelled a question.

"What did the lamb market do yesterday, Tom?"

"I don't know. The USDA offices were closed on Saturday."

"I just wondered if we are rich or poor."

The typical loading camp attire includes denims tucked into rubber boots just above the calf of the leg; a sheep-lined leather or denim jacket over the shirt and underwear; an old weathered Stetson or a hard-brimmed hat, except for the brightly colored stocking caps worn by the Peruvians, which is quite a contrast to the black berets worn by the early-day Basques.

While all the activity was going on, the Basque cook had made bread from a cup of water, a package of active dry yeast, a little salt and flour. He mixed it in the Dutch oven in which it would be baked. After allowing it to rise for nearly an hour, he popped the dough out, kneaded it down, and put back into the oven. As he placed on the lid he settled it into the earth where he had put coals left over from the morning fire. A covering of more coals and a layer of dirt on top of that and an hour and ten minutes later hot bread was ready for a hungry crew.

The cook said, "Don't use butter. Use *mantequilla*." It was tasty. A generous helping of lamb stew, cooked with potatoes, carrots, garlic, onions, rutabagas, tomatoes and a few beans, announced by its mouth-watering aroma, as it was also taken from the hot ground in a Dutch oven, that we were all in for a treat.

During the morning hours just inside the tent flaps, the cook sat on a low stool with a wooden cutting board on his lap, chopping up the onions and other vegetables which he dropped into just a smattering of vegetable oil before mixing together for the stew.

He said that usually the ovenful of bread would last about five days. But, with the size of the crew working that day, he would need to bake again the next day. The main fare in the sheep camp is varied and plentiful enough to keep the workers well fed. Potatoes, beans, beef, ham, and roast lamb, cakes and pies from today's popular mixes, and plenty of coffee make up the meals. The cook said, "Sometimes cook the fish. From French Creek. Lotsa fish. Sometimes too mucha fish, they say."

That day, Mary, the wife of Frank Jones, who was working as a herder for Phil, had sent a large chocolate sheet cake in by the truckers. The cook was thinking of going back to Spain for several months in December. "I will then come back for three years more," he said, "after visiting in Oviedo, a Basque state where is my home in the Pyrenees. Maybe about ten miles from the town of Oviedo."

All the water for drinking, cooking, and washing was packed in from the creek. The cook explained that the mountains in that area are just too steep for the wagons, so the packstring brings in everything. Wooden boxes used to hold the canned goods were packed in canvas covers with straps for handling when moving time came. The canvas covers for bedrolls, boxes, etc., are made to order by one of Idaho's most remarkable stores, John's Leather Goods in Weiser. Canvas stools were used as chairs and could be collapsed easily. Each herder has his own small tent for sleeping and these, too, are easily moved. Two horses and four mules hauled the camp gear. During December, January, and February, the wagon is used for preparing food on the desert; in March it's at shearing camp, and the rest of the time the cook lives in tents.

The cook and herders get to bed anywhere from nine until eleven o'clock at night and normally are up at six in the morning. During the shipping season, it is up at four.

An innovative lamp, made in the shape of a banjo and carved from a single piece of wood, was used to light the cook tent. A tin jar lid held in place by three long nails, driven one-fourth of the way down, held a white candle in place. The cook carved the lamp with his jack-knife, adding a cross-hatch design along the neck or handle.

Artwork seemed to be all over the tent, signifying that creativeness is in the sheep camps of the high-country as well as in the art colonies of the cities. The lid of an aluminum coffee kettle had etched cattle brands, with the date May 27, 1977. Names engraved include: Mary and Frank Jones, Phil Soulen and his Diamond brand, Bud Wilson, Bill Rice, who had been foreman for both Soulen and George Stolder; Lee Shephard, who runs Soulen's Sturgill Creek ranch and which he calls "cowboying"; "Cougar Bill" Rolland, a trapper who worked for Soulen as a herder; Jack Hanson, government trapper; the famous C.C. brand, signifying Crane Creek or "Coo Coo" (Scottish for cow-cow), the cattle brand of the late Harry Soulen.

A favorite memory picture of the day is of Harry Soulen II, a trim and handsome young man named for his sheepman Grandfather Harry Soulen, hoisting and carrying a huge and recalcitrant ewe, who simply would not move into the loading shoot as she should. The Soulens are well-known for not asking any task of their employees that they would not be willing to do.

Harry II is a graduate of the University of Idaho and was working with a mixed breed of Black Angus and Hereford cattle. He has imported Texas Longhorns for breeding purposes. He says that the calves are born easier. He works with 2,000 cattle and also has sheep. He is the only son of Phil and Erlene Clyde Soulen. Their daughters are Margaret, Helen, and Teresa. Margaret married Dorsey Campbell's son, Steve (who has a cattle trucking outfit at Caldwell); he and Margaret have a handsome and sturdy son, Sam, of about eight. Helen, a CPA, married another CPA, Ray Stevenson of Bainbridge Island, Washington. Teresa is Brad's wife and mother of Adam and David.

Phil said that each herder has a map of his grazing area and is to remain within that area; and that the U.S. Forest Service sends a field man out regularly to check the area where they camp to be sure it is not being overgrazed. Nor can they graze where young trees are growing. For each herder there is one camptender, who handles two camps, spending four or five days or up to fifteen, if grazing is good, before moving on. When he feels the grazing limit has been reached, he moves each camp for the herder.

When the tender is away from one camp, the herder does his own cooking. The tender does the cooking at whichever camp he happens to be. The camptender is exactly what the title signifies. He tends the camp, meets the foreman at a designated spot in the hills or on the plains to get the groceries he ordered ten days ago; puts in another order for provisions as the foreman returns to the home ranch. Estimating that three pounds of meat was required each day for each man, the tender has a good idea of what is required. One Basque herder was remembered for the fact that he ate a dozen eggs for breakfast each morning.

Shoes, boots, shirts and other needs arrive with the groceries. The foreman handles checks for them, depositing their money, bringing whatever personal things they might want. Herders and tenders work seven days a week all year long. They are given a two weeks vacation with pay. Many do not get away from the camp and sheep during that time, but they are paid anyway.

As other Idahoans who like sheep and want to see them around forever, Phil Soulen said, "The U.S. Forest Service has the wrong attitude in wanting to shift sheep out of the forests, and in thinking that people do not want to see sheep. Sheep are the heritage of Idaho. Those who do not understand that, cannot possibly know Idaho nor what it means."

Beulah Johnson Soulen

The second and third generations of Soulens (fourth, when Margaret's and Teresa's boys are along) come naturally by their enjoyment of the sheep life. Beulah Johnson Soulen, mother and grandmother of the clan, came from North Dakota to McCall, Idaho, with her parents when she was two years old. She grew to young womanhood and was married to Harry Soulen, a graduate of the University of Idaho's College of Agriculture, where his father was a professor and later principal of Moscow high school and yet later an inspector for Idaho's high schools. Harry returned to Idaho after teaching physical education in Dillon, Montana. After working as Washington County agent with headquarters in Weiser, he was offered a job with Swift and Company in Colorado.

Harry's sister, Beth, or "Pood," as she was nicknamed, married Enders VanHeusen, who had an interest in the gigantic Mesa Orchards.

Beulah was relaxing with Erlene at the Soulen home on Payette Lake, just watching her great-grandson, Sam, grow on the Sunday afternoon that the rest of the family and crew were loading sheep on the mountain. As she told the story, a good friend of Harry, a fellow by the name of Wise, had been foreman of a large sheep spread on Crane Creek for Swift and Company, and became ill with yellow jaundice. He offered to sell out to Enders and Harry just before he died. So, they carried on the transaction with Hardiman Duff, manager of all Swift's lands in Idaho.

"Enders and Pood took one-fourth and Harry and I took three-fourths. Fourteen thousand ewes and hundreds of acres in the Crane Creek territory was the spread. We were young and had nothing to lose but 2,000 old ewes, so we borrowed money from the Land Bank and made the purchase. But we had some tough times. In fact, two years after we bought, the government gave us a dollar for a pelt. We killed and skinned the old ewes for that amount. But, through the years we seemed to survive."

In fact, the Soulens survived very well. Even more, they survived, they overcame, and they prospered. When the depression hit and old timers wanted to quit the land, Harry was forward-looking enough to buy up a number of homesteads. Some of them were selling for ten cents on the dollar. And a number had cattle to go with the ranches. Beulah remembered that they had also bought the lambing camp at Letha from Swift in 1928.

"At different times, when needed, I cooked for the workers," Beulah said. "In the spring when they sheared in May and June, I would go out and cook. The operation is all changed now and we shear in March and April. We take the sheep to the desert to the lambing camp now and they shear before the lambing on Crane Creek."

When told that she must be proud of having helped build up such a business, Beulah said, "Well, Andy Little, who was a great guy, had hundreds of thousands. But we haven't expanded much as to sheep numbers. We always raised our own lambs for replacement. Years ago we used to go to the stockyards in McCall and ship by rail to Omaha and Denver. Now the McCall stockyards have all been torn down and everything is shipped by truck. The summer range runs from McCall all the way to Burgdorf on the west side of Payette lake.

"The reason we built our McCall home is that the phone service was so bad and when we had to ship our lambs back East, Harry and the other men would have to spend all night at the phone station just to handle the shipments from various points. The only way we could get a phone of our own was if we built where we did, on the south side of Payette lake near where the Shore Lodge is now located. Phil was only six years old then.We cut our own logs and had them planed."

Beulah told of a well-educated old Scotsman by the name of Jock Singleton who only worked during the time of herding. "In the fall he would come in, find a hotel and get drunk and never seemed to sober up until he went to herding again. My duty was to pick him up and take him back to the lambing camp when I moved there. We rented a house and lived in Emmett for two years when Phil wasn't in school. Jock was staying at the Carter Hotel and I told them I'd be there to pick him up at one o'clock. I got so busy readying the house, turning off the water and other chores, that I didn't get there until three o'clock.

"By that time poor old Jock was very drunk. As I drove along, I noticed he was gripping the dashboard of the car. I asked, 'Jock, are you scared of my driving?' He just clung on and said, 'Well, I don't know of anyone I'd rather die beside than you!' We'd get him sobered up and he would be fine until he had to come in the next fall. But, he died during one of those drinking spells . . . got pneumonia and died. He was a very well-read man. I think he must have been a professor at one time."

The Soulens lived in Mesa one winter when they lambed out the old ewes and then moved to Weiser where they bought a house on Liberty Avenue and lived there until building in McCall. Phil and Erlene were already married when they built the home, but their only daughter, Norma, was married there to Roscoe Rich Jr., another uniting of two well-known Idaho sheep families. They have a son, Tom, and a daughter, Diane, whose husband owns and operates a school for veterinarians in Denver.

When Phil took over the business, he added to the holdings and also went into the cattle business. Beulah said that Phil acquired about 700 cattle, "to eat up the brush," as he would say. "Harry used to say, 'The sheep made the money to support the cattle in the old days.' For a long time, the people went to beef and the sheep market declined markedly. Now, the people want gourmet leg of lamb and chops and the market has gone up."

Beulah remembered Harry going with one of the Faulkners and a Weeks to Australia and New Zealand to look over the sheep operations there. "Those countries eventually, with the help of subsidizing of the sheep industry by the United States government, put many sheep operators in our own country out of business. You couldn't get me to eat Australian or New Zealand lamb for anything!"

After Harry died, Beulah felt she couldn't afford a foreman and would oversee the ranches while Phil took over. Now she is content to enjoy her home on the lake. "It's a little too big for me now, but I'm going to stay right here. I feel comfortable."

Governor Steunenberg

George Crookham Jr. of Caldwell, internationally-known seed producer and distributor, remembers hearing that his uncle, Governor Frank Steunenberg, had sheep but has no recollection of the size of his flock or band. The Idaho Wool Growers was organized in 1894, but does not have on its records the sheep ownership of the Governor. Some connected with the industry say that they believe his sheep ownership "was quite large" or "considerable," but none can be exact.

Steunenberg was a thirty-six year old editor of the *Caldwell Record* when he became governor. He stood six feet tall, was a non-smoking teetotaler who weighed over 200 pounds. He served from 1897 until 1900.

Perhaps it is because all attention has been focused upon what happened after he was out of office that caused those who may have known of his sheep activities to forget. He was assassinated in

1906 when an attached bomb exploded as he opened his gate. In 1899 strikers for the International Workers of the World, often called the "Wobblies," then billed as the Western Federation of Miners, seized a mail train and dynamited and destroyed the Bunker Hill and Sullivan concentrator at Wardner. As the Idaho National Guard was fighting in the Philippines at the time, the only troops available to the governor to maintain law and order were federal. He called them in and it took three years before peace was restored.

The Miners Federation hired Harry Orchard to do away with the Governor. Ironically enough, Orchard passed himself off as a sheep broker, studied the governor's habits, placed the bomb and killed him. Orchard confessed and implicated the Mine Workers Association and Big Bill Haywood, organizer of the I.W.W. Clarence Darrow came from Chicago to help prepare for Haywood's trial. James Hawley was one of the leading lawyers for the state. He later became governor. William E. Borah, already establishing himself as a fine attorney, distinguished himself and later served Idaho in the United States Senate. Borah and Andy Little were destined to become good friends and the former was often a guest in the Little home.

The Sheep Queen

Emma Russell Yearian of Salmon, who had been given the title "Idaho Sheep Queen" by action of the Idaho Wool Growers Association, and Sheep King Andy Little did not meet until January of 1938. By that time, both of them had lived in Idaho for a number of years, but neither were great meeting-attenders, preferring to stay at home and look after their sheep.

In an Associated Press article from the Little home in Emmett by Walter R. Bottcher and published about six months previous to their meeting, Bottcher wrote: "How many sheep he owns, the extent of his farm holdings, his wealth, no one but Andy Little knows.

" 'I don't talk about those things,' he told Bottcher, as he leaned back in his chair, puffed away on his pipe and interpolated frequently his dislike for publicity."

On that January day in 1938, Andy and Emma were attending the annual Idaho Wool Growers meeting. The *Idaho Statesman* photographed the two of them visiting and appended a note that, "The picture of Andy Little is the first he permitted to be taken in many years." The picture was captioned: SHEEPDOM'S ROYALTY EXCHANGE SALUTES.

Andy was opining that, "Times are not as good as they once were," and he was correct. But, Mrs. Yearian said that the preceding year, 1937, had been the best sheep-season since the World War I. She agreed with Andy that the prospects for wool growing in 1938 was "dubious."

In an interview with the *Salt Lake Times*, while attending the convention, she went on to say, "But that's one of the reasons why the sheep business is attractive to me. It's always a gamble. We never know just what the next year will bring." The *Times* described her as "The kindly-faced, former State representative."

Mrs. Yearian, whose husband, Thomas, was a cattleman, began sheep raising in the early 1900s "because I needed the money." Emma was born in Kansas, February 21, 1866. She came to Idaho in 1887 from Illinois, where she had received a normal-school education to prepare her for teaching. She taught at Tendoy in 1888, then moved to Lemhi, where she married Thomas Yearian in 1889. Six children were the issue of their marriage, and when the youngest was three years old, the Yearians went into the sheep business. There wasn't enough money in cattle at the time.

A Dillon, Montana bank loaned her enough to buy 1200 ewes. Purchased in Montana, the sheep were driven across the divide into Idaho by Emma, her husband, and her son Russell. Back at the ranch, Thomas continued to run cattle. The sheep were Emma's. Her success and honesty encouraged the Dillon bank to continue to finance her sheep operation, because it was said that her word was as good as gold.

She continued running as many as 10,000 sheep, sprung from that original band of 1,200, because "I love the outdoors, love sheep, and love the land."

Despite protests that it would never work, Emma proved that sheep and cattle could graze in the same area. She had already proven that she, a Republican, and Tom, a Democrat, would exist amicably in the same household. Although he was a quiet and reserved individual, and Emma the go-getter type, she never did anything without his approval.

Art Caine of Boise served as chairman of the Idaho State Sheep Commission for nearly forty years and as secretary-manager of the Idaho Livestock Production Credit Association (PCA) for thirty years, beginning in 1934. He said, "The Yearians were about to go broke during the toughest times of the Depression and asked for some help. So, I drove up to Salmon and together we drove to the bank at Dillon, Montana, where they had done quite a bit of business. Mrs. Yearian had supplies and materials freighted in from Red Rock, Montana, to Salmon for many years.

"After a recitation by Emma of the financial reverses they had been suffering, the manager turned to me and asked, 'What percentage of this request do you think the PCA can take?' I said, 'About fifty percent.' He tried to get me to take more, but I just couldn't do it then. We were trying to save a lot of our good people. Finally they agreed to go along, and Emma Yearian continued to operate her sheep ranch."

L.N. "Bud" Purdy

"If you will go to the ranch and work there, *I'll* give you sixty dollars a month *plus* room and board." When William H. Kilpatrick Sr., the man who had built 5,000 miles of railway in the west, made this promise to his grandson, L.N. "Bud" Purdy, he had been anticipating the day for many years.

Bud was graduated in 1938 from Washington State College in Pullman, where he had taken a course in banking, and had just told his grandfather that the Old National Bank in Spokane offered him sixty dollars a month to go to work there. Bud was the son of the Kilpatricks' only daughter, Rachel, whose marriage to Leonard N. Purdy Sr., an engineer of Beatrice, Nebraska, where he had been captain of the 1913 University of Nebraska football team, lasted long enough to produce three children: Bud's brother, Bill, who now lives in Mombassa, Africa, and his sister, Christine (Mrs. Robert) Struthers of Twin Falls, Idaho.

Rachel and her children made their home with her parents in Redlands, California. From the time Bill and Bud were nine and ten years old, their grandfather sent them to the Picabo (pronounced Peek-a-boo) ranch in Idaho every summer. In 1927, the boys became derrick drivers during the haying season. Over the years they gained a general knowledge of all phases of work to be done.

Bud took to it readily and by the time he was offered board and room along with the sixty dollars a month, he accepted. In 1938, he started working with the 9,000 sheep on the Kilpatrick Brothers corporate ranch. He worked as a ranch hand for five years. In 1943, Leo Mercier, manager, quit his job and Bud was left in charge. The ranch had been formed by three of the four sons of the W.H. Kilpatricks Sr.: W.H. Jr., S.D. and R.J., the ones involved in railroad construction with their father. Only the youngest, J.M., who was a member of the company, did not join in the railway building and ranching.

The three brothers each secured 640 acres of desert entry land under the original Homestead Act of 1883. To secure title it was necessary to put water on the land, "putting it to higher use," according to the act. The brothers, who filed on a part of the land in 1883 and 1884 received title in 1887, by taking water from Silver Creek, which traverses much of the ranch, and using it to irrigate.

The father and brothers were also in railway construction and built lines for Union Pacific, Western Pacific and Great Northern railways. They built Sherman Hill tunnel between Laramie and Cheyenne, and the Aspen tunnel in Wyoming. "They also did all the major line changing between Salt Lake to Los Angeles for old E.H. Harriman," Bud said. It was in 1914 that the father started in the sheep business.

The business moved ahead and prospered under Bud's management. And the Kilpatrick family grew. By 1955 there were thirty-four heirs to the Kilpatrick brothers and sister. Most of the heirs wanted the company dissolved and the assets distributed. Within a year that had been done. Bud said that when the ranch started, a share could be bought for $100. When sold, the shares were worth $4,000 apiece.

Bud and his brother, Bill, purchased the original ranch at Picabo and the 4,000 acre Lava Lake ranch at Craters of the Moon. When Bill decided to remain in Africa (for a number of years he operated an advertising agency in Nairobi), Bud and Ruth purchased his interest. His sister Christine took the sheep then running on the Sawtooth National Forest and added them to the bands that she and her husband, Bob Struthers, have. The Purdys had grazed on the Sawtooth and Challis forests and the Shoshone Bureau of Land Management lands.

In 1901, Bud's uncle, W.H. Jr., started a commissary at the ranch. It eventually became the Picabo store, a modern and well-stocked business for area ranchers and tourists.

In addition to sheep, the Kilpatricks ran a shearing plant in the 1920s. They contracted with other sheepowners and at one time sheared 40,000 head at Picabo. The store is now run by Gordon Eccles, son of Ruth and stepson of Bud Purdy. His wife is the former Betty Peavey, daughter of Mary Peavey Brooks and granddaughter of sheepman and U.S. Senator John Thomas. They have two children.

When asked if any of the grandchildren are interested in the ranch, Bud said that Matt and Will Neal, sons of daughter Christine and Richard Neal, are now studying animal husbandry at the University of Idaho. Ruth and Bud have been endowing a scholarship in Forestry, Agriculture and Range Research at the University for a number of years. A son, Mark, and his wife live in Boise, where he teaches. They have two children.

Roscoe Rich and Sons

Soda Springs and north to the Blackfoot River and on to the Snake River in the southeastern part of Idaho covers the many miles where Roscoe Rich Sr. ran his thousands of sheep. Other sheepmen did the same thing. A.J. Knollin, a vice-president of Swift and Company, ran many bands for the meat company. From 1911 until the Depression in the early thirties more carloads of wool was shipped aboard Union Pacific from Soda Springs, Idaho, than anyplace west of the Mississippi.

It was, like the Emmett Valley, quite an area and its people were rugged, hard-working and willing to do what was necessary to acquire and develop their sheep bands and care for their families and employees. The Kackleys were among the area residents to become lifetime friends of Roscoe and his sons and their families.

"Young Doc" Evan Kackley tells of his father, "Old Doc" Ellis Kackley who handled a medical practice in the area for forty-five years, from 1898, when he arrived in Soda Springs until his death in 1943. One cold and snowy winter day, "Old Doc" was called to a sheep camp. He drove as far as he could, strapped on his snowshoes, grabbed his medical kit and stepped into a huge open field and walked several miles to the camp. There he had help in preparing the kitchen as an operating room, a herder was put onto the table, and Doc removed his kidney.

Old Doc was graduated from medical school in the East and wanted to go West. "He had no money whatsoever," his son said, "and he decided he wanted to locate someplace where a doctor was truly needed. So, he started writing postmasters in the West and asking about just such a place. He found it. The postmaster at Soda Springs wrote that his community was one hundred miles south of Idaho Falls, seventy-five miles east of Pocatello, thirty miles north of Montpelier and it was forty miles south to Preston. They needed a doctor."

Kackley left immediately and never regretted a minute of it. He liked people and wanted to help them. He never sent out a bill and they paid him when they could or wanted. His office was his hospital, and he would operate right there. When he died there were so many people at the funeral that there were more standing outside the church than were able to get inside.

Roscoe Rich was a member of a well-known Utah family. He and his wife, Helen, made a host of friends in the sheep and wool industry throughout Idaho and the country. He was an outstanding public servant and was appointed to a number of boards and commissions during his adult life. Among the most important volunteer jobs to which he was appointed was chairman of the State Highway Commission, the first professional operation of the placing and building of the thousands upon thousands of miles of highway across Idaho's deserts, through the valleys and hills and across and through the rugged granitic mountains that cover much of the state. At the same time, he defied the federal engineers who were going to build a super-highway in as straight a line as possible from the Atlantic to the Pacific, explaining that "Idaho isn't built on a straight line."

It was not an easy task and a man of Roscoe's strength and integrity was needed to withstand the clamor within the state for "political" or convenience roads to be built where many people wanted them, rather than where they would serve the greatest number of people and at a cost Idaho could afford.

Roscoe and Andy became good friends and when the Depression hit Andy's empire in the early thirties, Roscoe was one of the strongest of those wanting to help him stay afloat. Roscoe and Clyde Bacon of Twin Falls, another friend and sheepman, along with Art Caine, accompanied Andy to Spokane to see officers of the Federal Land Bank relative to Andy securing a loan to save his business. Henry Mathews, head of the bank, listened, discussed, argued and finally said, "Well, tentatively, . . . we can do this."

Roscoe exploded. "Tentative, hell! This man's house is on fire and he's about to lose the whole outfit. There is nothing tentative about this. This man has more acres of land and heads of sheep than the dollars he wants to borrow. He has to have help and have it now."

The loan was granted and the bank sent an employee from Spokane to inventory all of Andy's properties. Alex Campbell remembered that he, as an officer for the First National Bank, was asked to accompany those making the inventory. When it was only half done, the man hired to do the assessment work turned to Alex and said, "There is no way we are going to find anyone who could do a better job of running these ranches than Andy Little himself. It is certainly not a case of mismanagement in any way." And Andy was expected to continue his system.

Roscoe's son, Roscoe J., remembers hearing that Art Caine was worried that Clyde Bacon would become angry and speak rashly if the Land Bank dawdled over loaning Andy the necessary funds. After they had left the meeting, Art smiled at Roscoe and said, "I never dreamed that it would be *you*." That was Roscoe Rich. A friend was in trouble and he helped.

Roscoe came from sturdy stock. His grandfather, Charles C., had been sent by the Mormon church with a group of church members to colonize the Paris-Bear Lake area. He was later sent to California and paid for his Spanish Land grant to settle an area there.

In 1896, when Roscoe was about three, his father, Samuel, an attorney who wrote the principal reclamation laws in eastern Idaho, moved with his family to Blackfoot. Roscoe was yet in his teens in 1914 when he entered the sheep business. He had attended the University of Idaho, where he played football, for a year and one-half. He decided that wasn't the life for him and went home, rode his horse up on the flats, where he met a Basque herding sheep.

The Basque was a partner with two men in Ogden, Utah, but was willing to sell the 4,000 sheep to Roscoe, who wrote up a contract on the back of a blank check. He paid the Basque one hundred dollars in earnest money, and wrote a guarantee that "a reasonable down payment would be made in Ogden within two weeks." He told his father what he had done. Before the two weeks were up, the Ogden partners said that they would not go through with the sale. The Basque reneged and said he did not have the authority to sell the sheep. Roscoe's dad proved otherwise in court. The herder, as part owner, *did* have the authority. Roscoe was in the sheep business.

He was a good operator and at one time had 18,000 yearling, as well as breeding ewes, for a total of nearly 30,000 sheep. Learning that "you have to have enough range to take care of the poor forage years as well as the good," he dropped down to 8,500. He raised his own ewe lambs because he felt that he couldn't buy as good a ewe as he could raise.

Roscoe trailed his sheep to and from Burley, where he and Helen and their sons made their home. It was a trailing distance of 200 miles from the Caribou National Forest near the Wyoming line at Freedom, where Freedom Peak juts over 10,000 feet into the sky. Both sons, Roscoe J. and Elwood, learned so much about the sheep business working with their father, that in 1946 they bought an interest. In time they became equal partners and upon his death, they inherited the remaining third from Roscoe C.

Elwood and his wife, Helen, have three daughters and a son, none of whom seem interested in the sheep business. Roscoe Jr. married Norma Jean Soulen, daughter of Beulah and Harry, well-known sheep people. They have a daughter, Diane Rucker of Denver; and a son, Tom, who, according to his dad, "Is working at the sheep business hard. I hope he is able to stay with it, as he likes it and is good. It is hard to get competent help and difficult to generate the money necessary to keep going."

Speaking of competent help, Roscoe J. told of Felix Jorajuira, a Basque herder who had worked for his dad, and then for Elwood, for a period of forty-two years. "He worked until he was seventy-five years old, then quit and got married!"

They don't make 'em like that anymore.

Roscoe discussed the hardships and tragedies that accompany the sheep life. "In the hard winters we would lose some. Then a bear got into a bunch of our sheep and ran them over a cliff, where they died. Once, an entire band was stampeded over a cliff with a huge loss."

Both Norma and Roscoe J. are still feeling bereft of the 1,850 ewes and lambs burned to death in an explosive fire on the Caribou forest near the Wyoming border on August 25, 1988. The fire was a lightning strike that smoldered for two or three days. The forest ranger and Tom Rich had discussed that morning that a disaster could occur if the smoulder blew up into a towering blaze. They talked about the drought situation that had been building up for the past two or three years, and the fact that when the moisture goes below twelve percent it is time to watch out. The moisture was down to four-to-six percent that morning.

Tom was moving his sheep down when the fire exploded. He and two of the men helped one band to flee the fire but the second band and two herd dogs were cremated. They also got the packstrings out, and the herders barely made it to safety. It was such an inferno that within twenty minutes from the time it broke into blaze, the fire had reached the top of the mountain and had started down the other side. Remains of sheep were found draped over logs they were unable to jump.

Despite all the heart-and-head-aches that go with the business, it is not unlikely that fourth generation, T.C., Tom's seven year old son, who likes going with his dad to take care of the sheep, will one day join him.

John Faulkner

Residents of the historical and picturesque little town of Stanley, situated in the heart of the Sawtooth mountains, can tell the time of year by what John Faulkner is doing with his sheep . . . herding, pasturing, separating, breeding, loading for trucking to market, or trailing to the home ranch at Gooding.

Wives of wool growers serving in the Idaho Legislature in 1961 plan a roast and smoked lamb dinner for Legislators and their spouses. Speaker of the House Pete Cenarrusa and wife, Freda, wielding a serving fork, watch to be sure that Howard R. Andrus (sheepman near Idaho Falls), Roy Laird (Dubois), Harvey Schwendiman (St. Anthony), Dick Smith (Rexburg), and Governor and Mrs. Robert E. Smylie (leading the line) are well-fed.

With 13,000 ewes and lambs, Faulkner is among the top three Idahoans in the sheep business today. Faulkner is another of the generational families to own and work with sheep. His grandfather, G.W. Faulkner, moved from a Boise dairy farm to Fairfield in 1914. G.W.'s son, Ralph, moved from Fairfield when the bank there failed. He went to Gooding where he raised sheep.

John took to the sheep business and has been a large part of what has happened within the wool world for nearly forty years. "It's a great business," John says with enthusiasm. His feeling for the sheep is contagious and his advice is sought by many. The University of Idaho conferred upon him an honorary doctorate in range management. He has served as president of the Idaho Wool Growers association and chairman of the National Wool Growers committee on public lands.

John's son, Mike, works with his father. They are also involved in the cattle business, as are a number of Idaho sheep owners. The ones who have remained through the dark days of Depression, recession, predator problems, cheap imports of wool and lamb from New Zealand and Australia, are of that stalwart breed of giants that built America and Idaho from the beginning.

* * *

Idaho's sheepmen have made many contributions to our state. Among the heads of the Idaho sheep business are great men of American history, captains of industry and leaders of our nation.

CHAPTER THIRTEEN

ALLEN WILSON: FRIEND AND PARTNER

A SLOW-AND-SOFT SPOKEN MAN WHOSE RUGGED BRONZED FACE WAS framed with sun and smile wrinkles, Allen Wilson was considered by all who knew him to be one of the top sheep and ranching men anyplace in the West. Drew Little's widow, Myrn, drove us out to the field in her jeep and found Allen working on a new fence post. It was a sunny day and he shoved his battered Stetson back on his head, wiped his brow, and gave us a big grin. "Now, what are you two up to?" he asked.

Allen reluctantly started talking about his life in the sheep business and 'lowed as how he knew a heap of amusing stories about Andy, and then quickly added, "But I ain't gonna tell 'em to you." He not only felt a deep loyalty to the entire Little family but particularly to his old friend and boss. But once he had started talking, he relaxed, laughed and reminisced without reluctance.

He told of his boyhood in Tennessee and how a heifer gone loco helped with his decision to come west. His father had started with just one heifer and a calf and was able from that small beginning to build a herd of twenty-five Black Angus.

"One day a heifer got into a tobacco field and ate the leaves like she was starved. She just went plumb loco. That isn't all that sent me west, but it sure helped. And I came to Idaho and started to work for George Miller on a ranch over at Parma. He paid me a dollar a day. For that dollar, I milked cows, harnessed six horses, irrigated during the day and did the very same thing in reverse every night. It was a daylight to dark job. Every day. Sundays, holidays and all. For that one dollar.

Allen Wilson's friendliness was a hallmark of the man. He came to Idaho from Tennessee as a young man and built a reputation for being the best in the industry when it came to training and handling workers. Photo was taken in 1943.

"Later, I was working for another big rancher out of Parma by the name of Levi Stevens. He had 640 irrigated acres. I was irrigating about one hundred inches of water and keeping plenty busy. Then one day, when I was working at McCann Bar, along came Andy Little on his big horse. I knew who he was. I don't know if he knew who I was. But, without saying a word, he pulled his horse to a stop and just sat there and watched me handle that water and that irrigating. Finally, he asked, 'What are you making a day, son?' and I said, 'A dollar.' 'I'll give you two,' he said. I said, 'It's a deal.' And right then I started to work for Andy Little." And it was a good deal for both Andy and Allen and both prospered as a result. Andy bought hay, corn and pasture from Stevens.

"Yup, I made thirty dollars a month in Parma, no matter where or how hard I worked, and I just doubled my salary by going to work for Andy." Allen was twenty-two when he went to work for Andy, having moved to Idaho in 1920.

Andy's fine reputation for recognizing and hiring the best men is certainly borne out by the years which Allen Wilson spent with him, and later with his son, David, and finally with his daughter-in-law, Myrn.

Years later, David Little, who went into partnership with Allen a few years after the death of Andy, said, "Allen was probably the best hand ever. If Dad was extraordinary in handling men, so was Allen. He could take men others wouldn't hire or thought were absolute derelicts or halfwits and turn them into good workers. He did that by treating them like the kind of workers he wanted them to become. He kept at it and worked right with them until they knew the way he wanted something done. Even when he was in the camps, he would continue to work with them.

"When we formed our partnership, Allen had 2,000 sheep and I put in 4,000 and it was a good deal for both of us. Once I laid off a guy who had bad eyes and could hardly see. Allen turned right around and hired him back. I had so much respect for Allen that I only asked him, 'Do you think he can handle the job?' Allen only said, 'Yup', and that guy brought in one of the best lamb crops we ever had."

Allen continued his word picture of working for and with

Andy: "When I worked for Andy, we took care of at least 500 horses. He was building a huge horse barn on the Lower Bench ranch and I helped build that barn. During that time, I started to work at 4:30 in the morning and, sometimes, worked until 10:00 at night. I'd catch teams, put them in the barns, feed them and rub them down. At night we washed all the horse collars off, so the sweat wouldn't make their shoulders sore. We had 'em all fixed up for the next day.

"Actually, we had about 700 horses, as there were 500 pack horses and 200 work horses. I think he always had about five horses to every 1,000 sheep. The herders would go afoot, but the groceries and supplies were taken in on the pack horses. The camp-tender had a saddle horse and a bell mare and four mules. So, you can see, it took a lot of horses just to take care of the sheep. Andy had about fifty string of those camp horses. He had a big band of brood mares. Then he had a lot of extras in those big Belgians and Clydesdales that he used for the ranch work: the plowing and cultivating, and putting up hay and just everything horses could do. Andy was sure proud of those big Belgians. But he just plain liked animals. He liked sheep and he liked dogs. He always had a good dog riding with him in the pickup or car.

"Well, next, I went with a Basco out to feed sheep at the Butte ranch. We were lambing about 6,000 head on the lower ranch at Big Willow. And then that spring I took a band out and herded them back around Clipper Flats on the Lower Bench and then back over to the Butte Ranch, then 'way up to Elkhorn and the Salmon River."

Allen was asked how often he saw Andy out in the sheep camps. "Very seldom. I worked out for two years and the only time I ever did see him was when he would drive by in that Buick or his big old Stanley Steamer.

"But that didn't mean he wasn't keep track of things. If you did your work he would never say a word. But, boy, if you didn't do it right, he'd let you know pretty quick. I remember one time when I rode a little old mare from the McCann ranch on the Big Willow to settle up on my pay. It was getting along toward evening and I went into his office and said that I'd like to settle up. He said, 'Who the hell are you?' I told him my name and he got the book out and looked at it. Then he looked up at me and said, 'I sure should know you from the looks of these books.'

"Y'see, I'd worked there for over two years without drawing a penny and hadn't settled up for supplies and stuff yet. He was accustomed to most of the herders, young guys, spending their money when they got it. I guess he thought I had spent mine. I wasn't married yet, so I sent my money back to Tennessee and had my dad put it in the bank. And that bank went broke."

Allen switched back to settling up with Andy, and said, "Then he asked me, 'When are you going back?' and I said, 'Tonight. Right now.' and I got on my little mare and rode back to the McCann. Well, the next morning, here he was about nine o'clock. I think he figured I wouldn't go back at night. But once he figured out you were telling the truth, that satisfied him. He liked you to say exactly what you meant, too.

"Once when I was tending cattle over on the desert, I came in to the home ranch to get groceries. I wanted to get me a few more oats, as I didn't want to get in very often. I'd told Andy the night before that I would like to get a couple of sacks of oats. 'Alright, boy,' he said. So, I went out the next morning and got me four sacks, and I see him coming, swinging that cane of his. I had the mules headed out when he come up, looking in the wagon and said, 'I thought you wanted two sacks of oats, boy,' and I said, 'Well, I got two more.' 'Well, just turn around and unload two,' he said. So, I did, but I just had to come in again a little quicker, so it didn't make much difference. But if I'd said I was going to take four, he'd probably have said, 'Alright, boy.' "

"I herded sheep for two years and I saved some money. There was no reason for all the herders not to make good money. I guess they made it, alright, but they spent it pretty fast. They lived in camp all the time, but most of them spent their money the minute they hit town. Darned few kept any. John McNish ran a commissary where the herders could charge their necessaries to Andy. Stuff like blankets and their clothing. Not many people knew it, but Andy paid for all that stuff."

Allen went on to tell of his herding days with the Little

ranches, recalling that many herders came from the states of Tennessee and Virginia, "Right after the depression that followed World War I in about 1920. The southerners started coming in '25 and '26. We had quite a few sheep in Tennessee and Virginia in those days and most of the men had learned a little about herding.

"It seems like the Basques started coming in from Spain in the twenties, too. There were quite a few when I got here. In fact, I think when I started I was the only American here. But before long there were about half Basque who could understand one another in one outfit and maybe Tennesseans in the other outfit. Most of the Basques were sponsored by Scots sheepmen when they first came. By that, I mean that the Scots had paid the way of the Basques to come. Before long, the biggest part of the herders were Basque. They were good at it. Seems like they could talk to the sheep. Course, Andy could too."

Allen recalled that Andy was adamantly opposed to any kind of gambling or liquor of any kind in the camps. "But, when he wasn't aware of it, there were some big games and gamblers at the Butte ranch. I've seen some of them play all night long. And they played for big stakes. Both Ontario and Weiser were wide-open sheepherders' towns then. These herders came into Emmett, got their money and hit out for Ontario and Weiser for the cards games and gambling."

Allen said that he had hired and fired herders. "Not so many fired, but if they got to drinking too much, raised hell, or wouldn't do their work, I didn't want 'em around. One time, David and I bought a whole trainload of sheep up on top of that bench near The Dalles, Oregon, and he said, 'Where are we going to get herders?' and I said, 'I'll get 'em.' So, I went down to Ontario the next morning and I come back with all the herders we needed. There were about 6,000 sheep in that trainload. This wasn't the way we usually bought sheep and we went up there just to buy one band. But they looked good and were pretty cheap, so we just bought three bands. Union Pacific hauled them back for us."

It was downright enjoyable relaxing and listening to Allen on that sunny day. He told of herding with David and taking the sheep from the Emmett valley north to a spot near Yellow Pine. "It took us ten or twelve days to get there. We didn't stay in one place very long. You didn't want them to stay because you needed to get them to fresh feed all the time. We didn't rush them, but we moved them along. Sheep don't like changes and they don't like to be hurried. They need to be well fed or they won't bed down at night. They have to be taken care of like a family. That's why the Little family understood that a sheep could be cared for that way and that's just what they did. One howl from a coyote can cause a stampede by the whole flock as one takes off in fear and is followed by the whole bunch. They don't always know what they are running from, but they know they are helpless against coyotes, bear, cougars and mad dogs. So, they run. When a ewe about to give birth to a lamb is frightened into running, most of the time she loses the lamb.

"So the sheep just feel good to see the herder and his trained sheepdogs and the camptender or cook standing by. All of the Littles took good care of their sheep. So did the people who worked for them. That, or they didn't work for them," Allen finished with a grin.

"Another reason we needed to nudge the sheep along is that they get into a habit and would stay in the same area until there was no graze left. We just kinda headed them into fresh feed and kept them moving. When they wanted to go back where they had just been, we headed them the other way. One thing we knew that we didn't want was to over-graze. We knew we'd be back that way about the first of October, on our way back to the home ranch, and by then we wanted good feed to have grown up again. If we let the sheep go where they wanted, it wouldn't be long until there just wouldn't be good graze. Besides there'd be ticks and bugs and pretty soon the whole band would be pestered with vermin. We just have to keep moving them along. And that's just what we did."

Andy Little had set a program for moving the sheep. He had learned as a lad in Scotland that it was the single most important part of sheep ranching to keep them on the move. Every one of his sheepherders and all of his children knew that this was the only way to keep the grass growing and the bands in good condition. When the flocks were being taken to the high country in the summer, the campsite was set in the center of the grazing area.

The Little plan was to take the sheep to the faraway hills and mountain ranges during the summer months. Often the sheep grazed in meadows above timberline. It is not until the feel of snow is in the high mountain air that the sheepherders start moving the flocks down the hills and toward the home ranch.

Allen continued with his story on working for Andy. "I herded for Andy for two years then I tended camp for him for more than three. The sixth year I was with him, I became the riding boss and looked for the lost sheep and strays. In 1934, he named me foreman of the Van Deusen ranch, where we kept 35,000 head of sheep. Then, I took on his Little Willow sheep, too. We kept 6,000 head there and I ran both of 'em. At the peak, we took care of well over 100,000 head. With the lambs and bucks we must've had nearly 200,000 at times. We split 'em up between the Van Deusen and Andy's original place in the Highlands back of Boise."

Everyone who worked with Allen Wilson said that he had inborn sense of livestock and was a livestock genius. "Few people have the gift for dealing with sheep and cattle that Allen had," according to Dave. "One day Allen and I went out where the herders were cutting out the ewe lambs. Allen took a look and said, 'There's a wether . . . what's that wether lamb doing in there with the ewe lambs?' The herder said, 'There isn't a wether in there.' Allen replied, 'Yes, there is,' and he was right. The ultimate gift in the livestock business is the 'eye of the master,' and Allen had that."

Allen relived a day in the life of sheepherding when he would get up at 3:00 a.m., go out to the sheep first thing, get them settled out on the grass where he wanted them to eat and get headed in the right direction for moving along, and then come back to the tent and fix his breakfast. He always looked to the sheep first. Allen said, "It's not hard to turn the sheep in the right direction. You kinda walk around, don't use the dogs much, whistle at 'em a little bit and wave your arm a little bit, and they'll turn." For Allen they did.

In the early days, Allen prepared his breakfast on a Dutch oven, as the herders didn't receive the galvanized tin stoves until later. "I'd dig a hole and build a fire and let the coals form. I'd put the Dutch oven on top of that. Depending on what I cooked, I'd sometimes heap more coals on the top, before covering it with dirt.

I made a lot of bread. Most of the time, I'd fill the whole oven with bread." He admitted that he "used to be a pretty good cook and fixed sourdough biscuits, bacon and eggs for breakfast. I had my sourdough, usually, in a kettle, but when I could I liked to have it in an earthen crock. It works better in a crock. He said that he and other herders were supplied with dried apples, beans, flour, coffee beans and a little grinder to prepare them, and sometimes mutton. They didn't have butter in the early days, so used bacon grease until getting margarine in later years.

"When I first started herding, I had only an A-tent, sheet metal or tin, with a couple of pieces of bent metal to put it on for a stove, Dutch oven, and the coffee pot. Now, the herder has an eight by ten tent, stovepipe, the cooking utensils he needs, at least two, and usually four, kitchen boxes. He gets dried apples, apricots, prunes, raisins, biscuit mix, flour, baking powder, soda and sugar and bacon and ham in boxes."

Allen had two or three dogs, black and tan shepherds and blue Australian shepherds, raised from pups, to help with the sheep. By the time the sheep have been directed to the graze, breakfast prepared, eaten and utensils cleaned and put away it was late morning. When asked if he then moved the sheep, Allen said, "No, they'd be getting hot about then and they'd buck up [go to sleep] in the shade and stay there until about four o'clock in the afternoon. The sheepherder then gets more sleep than he did at night, when he kept checking on the sheep.

"Those sheep would clip about ten pounds of wool apiece and Andy was shipping a million pounds a year. That's a lot of wool. In the late twenties, he was the biggest single operator in the whole United States, and mebbe even in the world. I don't really know about that last statement, but I *do* know he was sure a big man in the sheep business.

"But in late 1929 or early in the thirties, the bottom dropped right out of the market. It really got tough on Andy. He had a hard time, but he kept going. You ask, 'Why?', well, he really liked sheep. Besides, he *wanted* to keep things going. He had a lot of people depending on him. His family. Those hundreds of people working for him. He wasn't a quitter. He just wouldn't give up."

Allen Wilson and a group of herders who worked for him on the Little ranches pause for a moment in the midst of sorting lambs on the Upper Bench Ranch. Photo was taken mid-40s.

It was in September of 1926, Allen said, that Andy bought the Van Deusen ranch from two brothers, Dudley and John Van Deusen, and it was one of the biggest sales ever made in the valley. The newspapers reported that all of the Van Deusen brothers' holdings in Gem, Payette, Washington, and Valley Counties were sold to Andy at a total of nearly $1,000,000. It involved about 40,000 sheep and 21,000 acres of land. The Van Deusens had been in the sheep business for a quarter of a century.

It was in 1934 that Andy put Allen in charge of handling the Van Deusen. "We took on the Little Willow Creek sheep, too, and we kept 6,000 head of sheep there. I ran both of 'em. We took care of more than 100,000 at the peak. We split 'em up between the Van Deusen and Andy's place up in the Highlands in back of Boise. I know he shipped a million pounds of wool each year for awhile. That had to be a hefty ten pounds per sheep."

Allen then lapsed back into talk of the Depression days.

"You know," he said, "it's funny and sad at the same time, but now that wool is back up and people want to eat lamb and mutton again, the ranges just ain't there. Even the cattle have dwindled. Now they run in lots of about fifty to a herd. Everything just kept dwindling away. The last dwindle was those danged synthetics.

"Competition from Australia got as rough as the prices and the coyotes at home. There was competition from everywhere. Immigration policies got tougher and tighter and it was harder to get herders from the Basque country. It seemed like the government wanted to put us out of business. They done a pretty danged good job of it, too. There was just no more labor to be had. Sure, they said people were looking for work, but we couldn't find the kind of workers we needed.

"One great thing about Andy, though. Even when things were toughest for him, he would laugh and jolly other people up. He had an even better sense of humor when he'd had a drink or two. When he went on a business trip, he had a habit of taking a bottle of Scotch, and a cigar for himself and one for the guy he was going to see. He would leave his pipe at home and take good cigars. That was Andy 'talking business.' But, boy, he got a lot of it done that way."

If Allen credits Andy with laughter and ability to jolly people up when times were tough, others say that Allen had just as fine a sense of humor and liked joking with people. David remembers Orrie Limbaugh going out to herd with Allen at a time when a tough foreman by the name of Tom Crosswhite was in charge. Orrie, unaware of Allen's whimsical humor, started early in the day to complain about Tom. Allen let him continue for most of the day and just before quitting time answered another derogatory comment with, "Orrie, you oughtn't to talk about Tom that way. He's my uncle."

For the rest of the day, Orrie shot quizzical looks toward Allen when he felt that he wouldn't be looking at him. Noting this out of the corner of his eye, Allen remained silent and unsmiling. For several following days, Orrie steered clear of Allen until he felt that the comments about Tom had been forgotten.

Allen continued as the Van Deusen foreman for Andy until about 1939, whe he went to work for John Stringer in Ontario. He had both sheep and cattle. "Then," Allen said, "I was asked to be the sheep inspector for the State of Idaho. I was asked to be the range checker for the Production Credit Associaton. After that I bought half interest in the Connally outfit.

"I came up to Andy's funeral in February of 1941, and got to visiting with Dave and we talked some of getting together. We were good friends. When Dave was just a kid and I was riding boss for his Dad, he rode with me a lot. In 1944, I went partners with Dave. I brought my 2,000 sheep up here and we formed the Little and Wilson Sheep company. We hung together for nearly twenty years. Myrn needed somebody to help her after Drew was gone, so I went to work for her in 1965."

Myrn said that Allen was a good foreman and "he managed to hold that outfit together for me. Allen was a good man.

"The day Allen died," Myrn said, "he took that old jeep of his and drove over that very morning to check the bulls on the Canyon ranch, a little pocket of land near the Bettis ranch. He then went home for lunch, sat down in his favorite chair and just died. A nice way for such a good man to die."

Allen died on January 2, 1979, at age seventy-seven. Allen's widow, Helen Rose, died on January 25, 1990, after a long illness. She was buried beside the body of her husband in the Emmett Cemetery. She had lived the previous three years with her daughter and son-in-law, Kay and Jim Phelps, in Lewiston. Three other daughters and two sons and their families also survived.

C H A P T E R   F O U R T E E N

TOGETHER THEY STAND

NEARLY 100 YEARS AGO, A GROUP OF IDAHO SHEEPMEN GATHERED IN Mountain Home to discuss problems that could only be solved through group endeavor. It was a cold January day in 1894, but they knew it would be worth the effort to gather together the two organizations that had until then been meeting separately in southeastern and southwestern Idaho. Frank R. Gooding, later to become both a governor and United States senator, was named the first president.

From that time on, the Idaho Wool Growers Association (IWGA) has never ceased to function. There were times, particularly between 1918–1922, that it waned in activity. In 1923, a reactivation movement took place and the first full-time secretary was hired. Until then a paid part-time staffer handled the office affairs.

T.C. Clyde Bacon of Twin Falls was named president and he gained support to rebuild and strengthen the Wool Growers Association. Among those helping him were Nathan and Ephraim Ricks of Sugar City. A new constitution and by-laws were drafted and did not need revising again until 1956. As later-Secretary Mel Claar said, "The men behind the organization made it strong, not some fancy document. Sound judgment and guidance built a sturdy organization."

Much of the strength came from the stalwart characters involved. Men of the outdoors have become powerful individuals in attempting to control elements of environment, the hazards of drastic market breaks, and the managing of a business that extends over a wide area. Either that or they went into another line of business.

Wool growers were the big spenders in their areas. Of necessity, they spent hundreds of thousands in purchasing trucks, cars, trailer camps, sheepherder wagons, horses, dogs, all kinds of tools, groceries and other supplies. They must all be farmers to produce the greater part of their feed. And, as in the case of Andy Little, they were orchardists and vegetable-growers. They employed laborers as herders, camptenders, shearing crews and extra help at times of winter feeding and lambing time.

In latter years, the changing land pattern called for the shipping of about eighty percent of all range lambs from feeding grounds to market by truck. The wool must be hauled by truck to railheads in the spring and fall. These big spenders must also be big savers to prepare for any drop in the market or disaster in the hills or on the ranges.

In early days of Idaho and the West, sheep and wool were leaders in the basic industries which developed resources. Still important, these industries do not wield the power they once held. Farm sheep flocks are increasing while range sheep numbers have declined.

Exactly fifty years from the day Idaho Wool Growers was organized and Frank Gooding became president, his nephew T.H. Gooding took over that office. Vice presidents are elected with the thought that they will become president at the end of the term.

Other presidents were: John McMillan, Boise; Fred W. Gooding, Gooding; C.O. Stockslager, Shoshone; Tom Stanford, Carey; E.A. Van Sicklin, Weiser; Worth Lee, Mountain Home; Hugh Sproat, Melba; T.C. Bacon, Twin Falls; Roscoe C. Rich, Burley; D. Sidney Smith, Shoshone; Merle Drake, Challis; Harry Soulen, Weiser; J.H. Breckenridge, Twin Falls; David Little, Emmett; John W. Noh, Kimberly; Andrew Little (son of Jim), Howe; Wilbur Wilson, Hammett; Ray W. Lincoln, Twin Falls; R.K. Siddoway, St. Anthony; Walter Little, New Plymouth; Roscoe J. Rich (son of R.C.), Burley; Phil Soulen, Weiser; John Faulkner, Gooding; Stewart Cruickshank, Parma; Maurice Guerry Jr., Castleford; Marvin Cox; Jeff Siddoway, St. Anthony, who is slated to be followed by Brad Little, Emmett.

Maurice Guerry Jr. is a member of an old-time, classic Basque family whose father came to Idaho in the early twenties. He took a number of sheep in lieu of salary and secured between 4,000 and 5,000 acres of deeded land. Guerry speaks Basque fluently and his American name is a shortened version of Mauricio Garro Guerricaechevarria, a thirty-one letter spelling of the Basque family name.

Volunteer secretaries served until 1914, when John Rhidenbaugh became a part-time paid employee and worked until 1924. Donald McLean served until 1928, when M.C. Claar became a full-time paid secretary. Lew Williams followed him. Then Stan Boyd, son of buyer Tom Boyd, joined IWGA.

Throughout its history the IWGA has been affiliated with the National Wool Growers Association, the oldest livestock organization in the country. Roscoe J. Rich is proud of the fact that he and

Photo by Georgia Layton, Burley

Courtesy Idaho Wool Growers Association

Working together for the good of Idaho Wool Growers for nearly 100 years, officers of the association in the years 1971–73 were left to right (seated): L.M. Williams, secretary; Roscoe J. Rich, Burley, president; Phil Soulen, Weiser, vice-president; (standing) Kenneth Westfall, John Faulkner, and Laird Noh, directors.

Three bonnie Scots, John MacQueen, operator of Kirkland Stockyards near Chicago, Andrew Little of Emmett, and James Laidlaw of Muldoon met at an Idaho Wool Growers convention and enjoyed reminiscing.

his father, R.C., are the only father-son team to have served as president of the national organization.

In Territorial days, sheep was an important part of Idaho agriculture, flourishing on the semi-arid land. In 1890, when Idaho became a state, there were more than 600,000 sheep and the numbers were rapidly rising. By 1895, there were more than one million. Within another five years that number doubled. The high point was reached in 1918 with 2.6 million head.

By 1950, the number had dropped back to one million and remained fairly stable at that number until the early sixties, when many ranchers found it more profitable to raise cattle. Synthetic fibers arrived on the scene and wool prices plummeted. Recruiting herders became more difficult as economic conditions improved for the Basques in Spain, and both America and Spain made migration difficult.

Of recent years, public interest in sheep and wool has increased. The shift to natural fibers in clothing, a desire for lamb on

Bob Naylor hoists an unshorn sheep toward the clipping shed at the Highland in April, 1949. This was Bob's twenty-eighth shearing.

the dinner table, and an uncertain supply of energy has brought this about. Idaho sheep ranchers continue to outstrip other wool states in high weight per fleece, with an average of 10.4 pounds of wool per head, compared with the U.S. average of eight pounds, as we entered the eighties. Idaho ranked first in average fleece weight and seventh in total wool production.

While the Taylor Grazing Act was a big factor in the sheep and wool decline, Stan Boyd says that there were other responsible factors, including the dearth of labor as the standard of living rose in Spain; the continuing loss to predators; and a change in the eating habits of the American public after World War II, when lamb was dropped as a staple from the American diet.

"Idaho still has all the potential in the world to grow if federal policies will accommodate the sheep industry. When we consider that sixty-five percent of Idaho land is owned by the government, it is obvious that there must be fair policies for the industry to thrive," Boyd said. "This source of food and fiber now provides

Andy Little and Emma Yearian, Idaho Sheep King and Queen, always attended the annual meetings of the Idaho Wool Growers Association.

cash receipts of $28 million a year in Idaho. With the multiplier effect of buying equipment, hiring help, etc., it becomes a $120 million industry."

Taylor Grazing Act

That change is inevitable is a recognized truth. And when that change threatens an entire industry, the battle to prevent it can be long and hard. Such was the fight joined by the cattlemen and sheepmen leading up to, during and following the passage of the Taylor Grazing Act. It was on June 28, 1934, little more than a year after taking office, that President Franklin Delano Roosevelt signed into law the act which had been passed by the Congress a couple of weeks earlier. Its passage was to have a significant, persistent and—some believe—injurious effect upon the sheep and wool industry of Idaho.

The bill's author Colorado Congressman Edward T. Taylor called it "the Magna Carta of American Conservation." Sheepmen all over the West called it "the beginning of the end of the American sheep industry." If neither characterization was entirely accurate, Taylor's bill was, at the least, a bit of both descriptions.

The Act proposed to "stop injury to public grazing lands by preventing overgrazing and soil deterioration, to provide for their orderly use, improvement, and development, to stabilize the livestock industry dependent on the public range and for other purposes."

Many factors contributed to the legislation, likely beginning with the increase in population. When the Homestead Act was passed by the Congress in 1862, giving 160 acres of public land to settlers who would live on it and bring it under cultivation, there were less than one million sheep in the seventeen grazing states. By 1880 there were 19 million sheep in those same states. From 1860 to 1930 Americans had nearly quadrupled in growth. So the very land which had seemed unlimited during the years of the great move westward was beginning to be in short supply.

But during those years of seemingly unlimited land the belief in and political commitment to open range with available grass had become ingrained in both the cattle and sheep people. As realization set in that homesteaders were taking the most productive land and leaving the more arid to them, rivalry between the cattle and sheep grew to such a point that often open war broke out between them. Not only were cattle and sheep killed, but human lives were lost on both sides.

In fact, Congressman Taylor, in pleading for his Grazing Act before the Congress, said that as a District Attorney in Colorado before being elected to the Congress, he had prosecuted eight murder cases which were the outcome of battles over the use of the range, primarily between cattle and sheepmen.

Although the charge certainly could not be made against Andrew Little, cattlemen complained that absentee sheep owners bought their bands, hired herders who lived in wagons and followed the herds to grass and water. It was left only for the absentee owners to rake in the high profits while they (cattlemen) owned, built up and improved operations at great cost to themselves.

The Idaho Woolgrowers were more than unhappy with the contents of the Act as it passed the lower House in the Congress and put on a determined drive to, at the least, make changes before it was heard in the Senate. In the bulletin issued for members, the Woolgrowers reported, "It was a much different piece of legislation than originally introduced, but there are still several needed changes. The bill offered better protection to our industry than the first bill, but many changes should still be made."

The growers' organization worked unceasingly to block passage of this bill until it contained, "provisions to protect and help the industry and not leave it at the mercy of unfamiliar eastern bureaucratics (sic). Most western representatives opposed passage of the bill until more protection was offered, but with no avail."

One of the complaints from the woolgrowers was that Congressman Thomas C. Coffin of Idaho's Second Congressional District failed to vote against the bill. Elected as a Democrat and serving during the first term of President Franklin D. Roosevelt, Coffin chose to oppose the measure.

The *Woolgrower* magazine article exclaimed, "It seems the Easterners just want to put some more control on us, and besides it was the President's command that the bill be passed."

Many of the woolgrowers had been able to come to an agreement with the officials of the U.S. Forest Service for sharing lands they administered. The next sentence expressed a hopeful note: "There is still hope some changes can be put in the bill to insure western ranch and range interests they will not be put out of business. Consolidation of all grazing regulation in the Forest Service was also desired but the bill authorized the regulation of the public domain by the Department of Interior." Andy Little supported the final bill.

Congressman Taylor realized early on that his bill had small chance of becoming law if he could not show the support of reliable ranchers from the West. Lady Luck was riding on Taylor's shoulder the day that the Gary Cooper-type tall, lean and slow-spoken Farrington Carpenter strolled into his Capitol Hill office. A Colorado attorney with degrees from both Harvard and Princeton, Carpenter nevertheless had a western drawl and "he looked like a cowboy."

Taylor told Carpenter how his attention had been drawn to what he described as "proper use of the land and better care of the remaining public land" as a result of the Midwest dust storms and drought during the Depression of the 1930s. He went on to discuss with Carpenter how the majority of the public land was in the West and that the public eye had definitely moved westward. During the House floor debate, Taylor had said, "We are rapidly permitting the creation of small Sahara Deserts in every one of these [midwest and western] states today," and added that there were places in southern Colorado where nothing was left but sand drifting back and forth "with every breeze."

Carpenter acquiesced to the Congressman's appeal for help and testified in favor of the bill. He was appointed the first administrator of the new grazing service soon after the passage of the bill.

After Senate passage, the sheepmen requested a meeting with officials of the Interior Department. Several sessions were held with both sheep and cattlemen expressing their opinions. Little wonder that Carpenter was met with a generally favorable opinion as he quickly demonstrated his understanding of the western way of thinking. He called for public meetings in the small towns of the

West and set up grazing advisory boards composed up of an equal number of local sheep and cattlemen. He explained that neither was to have an advantage over the other. Carpenter also said he wanted the first level of appeal to be locally.

On December 17, 1934, more than 700 Idaho sheep and cattlemen met in Boise with Administrator Carpenter in a seven-hour session. Carpenter showed that he had made diligent study of the law to add to the knowledge he already possessed as a rancher and the problems that confronted all of them. When many of the stockmen urged a slow and cautious procedure, Carpenter agreed. "It is far better," he said, "to hammer the range for a few more months or even a year, than to do an injustice to the industry and you individuals who make up the industry."

Sheepmen elected to the statewide advisory committee to work with the Interior Department in classifying lands included two of Andy's brothers, James D. Little of Arco and Walter C. Little of Emmett, and Henry B. Soulen of Weiser, whose granddaughter, Teresa Soulen, was to marry Andy's grandson, Brad Little, many years later. Others were Leon Contor, Idaho Falls; J.C. Siddoway, Teton; H.L. Finch, Soda Springs; B. Thomas Morris, Pocatello; Roscoe C. Rich, Burley; T. Clyde Bacon, Twin Falls; Merle Drake, Challis; S.W. McClure, Bliss; Angus McRae, Paul; Worth S. Lee, Mountain Home; and Asa Williams, Boise.

All of these men were considered to be among the "big" sheep owners. In a later session a proposal was accepted to add medium-sized operators to the committee. With the approval of Carpenter, those added were Tom Bicandi, Boise; J.B. Gray, Nampa; Don Frederickson, Gooding; and the Twin Falls County Agent Harvey S. Hale. Among the members of the cattle committee was L.M. "Docky" Bettis of Gannett, Andy's son-in-law.

Board members advised on policies and practices that would affect their operations. Through this, the district rangers were able to allot specific areas of the federal range for use by the local livestock operators. The itinerant herdsman, who had proven such an aggravation to the sheepmen by only making use of the land in following the grass growth, lost his privileges to use the range. It was in this way that Ferry Carpenter let the cattle and sheepmen organize the West into grazing districts. The boundaries were established to run primarily along natural barriers and boundaries. History was made by them. Until then no one, even those in the government, seemed to know just how much land the United States owned, nor where it was located.

A few of the remaining oldtimers remember that when Carpenter praised someone it was with the words, "He knows which end of the cow gets up first." If he spoke in disdain, he'd say, "He doesn't even know which end of the cow got up first." He struck a responsive note with the sheepmen when he used that statement to describe his superiors in the Department of Interior.

Every woolgrower in Idaho was continually urged to keep in close touch with what was transpiring with the new legislation and of the grazing regulations and control that was to come with the rules adopted. Regardless of effort, the sheep industry did decline.

Many, if not most, of the sheepmen to this day feel that the government did not live up to its side of the bargain struck for their support of the act. There are, as has been cited, other reasons. Still the Taylor Grazing Act is blamed by many as "the beginning of the end."

C H A P T E R   F I F T E E N

THE MEMORIES ENDURE

REMEMBERING ANDY LITTLE, HIS SHEEP OPERATIONS, HIS FAMILY AND his colorful quips, is something many Idahoans like to do. Some knew him well, others only as an acquaintance, and yet others felt they knew him through what they heard from those who did know him and his family.

Joe Albertson

Joe Albertson knew Andy Little well. Every American within earshot of an Albertson's store can hum, if he can't sing, the musical jingle, "It's Joe Albertson's supermarket . . . ," which has become a slogan for the grocery king.

Andy Little bought his foodstuff for the ranches and herders in amounts to last for one year. He bought a year's supply of ham and bacon at one time. On one occasion only, he bought a year's supply of dried codfish. He even ran an advertisement in the newspapers asking for a regular supplier of cured ham and pork. To supply the Notus, Emmett and Cascade ranches, he did business with George King from 1915 until 1934, without one face-to-face meeting. All their business was done by telephone.

Joe Albertson's father lived in Emmett for awhile. Joe worked the Caldwell-Boise area and on as far as Liberal, Kansas, for the Safeway grocery chain before being made a supervisor at Emmett. Knowing of the large amounts of food that Andy Little needed for his giant sheep domain, Joe sold in a single transaction 6,000 pounds, or a carload, of Safeway's private brand coffee to the Littles. It is not surprising that Joe became known as the greatest coffee salesman in the Safeway chain. He won a national award for the most coffee sold that year.

Hard-working and ambitious, Joe moved on from the programs and philosophies of Safeway to those he had been building as he worked in the grocery business. He resigned from the chain, a huge one for the early thirties, took the $9,000 he had been able to save, borrowed $5,000 from his aunt, and started his own store. Located at 16th and State streets in Boise, it remains the flagship for all the Albertson stores throughout the nation.

Continuing to build upon his progressive plans, and taking a large crew of hard-working people with him as he climbed the success ladder, the Albertson Corporation has been on the Fortune 500 list of leading businesses for many years and is now the sixth largest food and drug chain in the United States, doing billions of dollars in business in its more than 500 stores.

As big in his philanthropies as he was in coffee sales, Joe and his wife, Kathryn, "literally saved the College of Idaho from closing in 1976," when it "was down on its knees," according to Robert E. Smylie, former Idaho governor and acting president of the College of Idaho in 1973–74. Joe and Kathryn each gave a $500,000 check to keep the college in operation. Smylie said, "They have given millions more to the college."

Smylie went on to say that Joe also worked as a hod-carrier to help build Strahorn, the first library at the college. Both the Albertsons attended the College of Idaho and have continued to contribute so that other young people could receive such an education.

The Albertsons' latest gift is a magnificent forty acre walking park (no cars permitted) along the Boise River, across the boulevard from Ann Morrison park in Boise. Two wildlife islands, surrounded by water, permit the viewing of birds of all kinds.

Warren McCain

Warren McCain, who has been the Chief Executive Officer for Albertson's for nearly fifteen years, got his start in driving a horse-powered derrick to stack hay for Andy Little's ranches near Emmett when he was just ten years old. Warren is proud of what he was able to do as a boy and says, "That was quite a feat for a young fellow of ten. I drove the horses that pulled hay up on that old wooden derrick, a boom with a forklift on the end, and stacked the hay.

"I stacked lots of hay during a summer and that was my first paying job. We worked from sunrise to sunset and I was proud of that one dollar a day I earned. There was a forklift and derrick on every farm Andy operated. Bernie Gratton had the same job on another farm."

In discussing Andy Little, Warren said, "As a young boy, I thought Andy Little was the most awesome fellow I would ever meet. He was a legend even then. He was a hard-nosed and tough manager and just had to be one of the best. All of the Littles knew how to work. Drew and Dave worked hard and Jessie was the ramrod that kept things going."

It is heart-touching to hear the pride in his voice, when Warren speaks of what it means to him to have the middle school at Payette, which he once attended, named the Warren E. McCain School. It is a measure of the man that he feels the same pride in the officers and employees of the Albertson chain.

While he doesn't call it that, the secret of his success is summed up in a statement he made about builders. "As I grew older I realized that Andy Little was a strong link in the chain of Idaho's successful builders. Other links include Joe Albertson, Harry Morrison of Morrison-Knudsen, Jack Simplot, the Skaggs family, the Davis brothers of Winn-Dixie chain stores, Duane Hagadone of newspaper and hotel fame, and others like them. And each one seems to encourage and inspire others coming along the chain. Andy Little was good to Joe Albertson, and Joe was good to me, and I hope I have been able to help others following after me."

He has.

Joe I. and Bill Guthrie

One of the first friends Joe I. Guthrie made after arriving in Idaho in 1909 from Marshalltown, Kansas, was Andy Little. Joe's son, Bill, said that his father had a keen mechanical mind and had built a Fairbanks Morse engine while in the hardware and implement business in Kansas.

"Dad and Andy hit it off right away and became good friends," Bill said, "and both were interested in the Black Canyon gravity-flow dam that was built the year before Dad arrived, which brought irrigation water to the Bench. Andy had tens of thousands of sheep on the Bench, and plans were being made for development in that area. The water came in one ditch, siphoned down the hill of the canyon and the upper part of the valley, then across the Payette River, where the old siphon bridge is still located just below the powerhouse at the park."

Bill tells an interesting story of happenings that led to the family moving to Idaho: Joe's mother, Ada Hayman Guthrie, was one of the "early liberated women" and, with her cousin, W.M. Hayman, was working for the land promotion division of the Great Northern Railway. The two were handling Great Northern property sales on that wide stretch of land from New Plymouth through the Emmett Valley and on to Boise. At the same time, community leaders were laying out a townsite of 640 acres at Hanna, eight and one-half miles northwest of Emmett.

"They had a high-powered promoter as their leader and made great plans for putting the land buyer in the townsite and planting a huge fruit-orchard as a community project for all. A year later, when about ten families were living there," Bill said with a wry smile, "the promoter became even more high-powered and flew the coop with the funds. That was truly the end of the road for those involved."

Joe Guthrie had bought 100 acres seven miles northwest of Emmett from his mother's cousin. The following year, he was hired to manage the 640 acres and he planted hay and grain. The dreams of abundant ripe fruit falling from the trees died a-borning. No orchard was ever planted. They lived at the "company ranch" in the center of Hanna for a few years, until it was sold to Jim Clinton, who also had a home in Boise. During that time, in 1911, a daughter, Harriet, was born on the ranch to the Guthries (years later to become Mrs. Jim Patrick). On September 23, 1919, William, was born at the home place, a distance of one mile from the ranch.

Bill worked with his father until Joe died of a cerebral hemorrhage in 1941 at the age of sixty-seven. Mrs. Guthrie died at age eighty-nine in 1968.

Bill's first memories of working with the sheep are those of trailing lambs up and down the three-mile road to Letha in the fall and spring of each year. "The road to Letha was knee deep in dust in the summer and the same depth of mud in the spring. We brought the lambs back in September and fed them until spring. We marketed a few carloads at a time from mid-December until the middle of March. Then we went to farming the hay, grain, silage and from forty to fifty acres of apples.

"As a young boy, I managed to get into lots of mischief with the sheep. Andy never permitted his children to make pets of the animals, but Dad didn't mind that my sister and I taught our sheep to pull us on a sled in the winter. You know, sheep *can* be trained; they aren't dumb. A little bullheaded maybe, but so are a lot of people, and both can be trained. I also broke sheep to work and to follow me around."

Bill recalled winning first place in the pet lamb show at the Gem County fair when he was only a four year old. "I had a letter of congratulations signed by the first Gem County extension agent, A.L. Berry, and Dudley Van Deusen as fair treasurer. I also had a check for $2 and the fact that I remember it still is an indication of its importance in my life. In Berry's letter, he wrote, "We hope in the future to make the Gem County Fair the best fruit and livestock show and sale in southern Idaho." For many years, they did just that.

Joe Guthrie bought feeder lambs in the Steens Mountain country of Oregon, where there is little forage. His desert type lambs were lighter than those raised by Andy, which fed on lush grass and all went to slaughter right off the range. The grass-fat lambs are choice meat and shipped in June or July. Guthrie shipped his lambs from Oregon to Emmett on Jack Whalen's little "Punkin Vine" railway. According to Bill, Whalen later sold that little set of tracks to the Oregon Short Line, which later became the Union Pacific. Whalen had written into the sales contract that he would have a lifetime job as conductor.

Bill continued with the sheep story: "The lambs would go out in mid-August or early September. We would go to Steens Mountain and contract for them to be received in mid-September. We kept a minimum of two extra men, and often three, year-round.

When the lambs got to the Emmett area on the little train, they were fattened and trailed back to Letha for shipment east. They went to Mississippi River points for slaughter and then on to St. Joseph, Mo., Omaha and Chicago for sale. A shipment of 3,000 went in the spring of 1914. It took about ninety days to fatten, feeding off and on all winter long, until-mid March. Our dogs were always offsprings of the Littles' fine border collies.

"Dad sold Andy some hay, while he was wintering ewes on the Payette. It was a wet and muddy winter. George Smith was feeding the ewes for Andy when the mud got so deep and squishy that the team could not pull the wagonloads. They needed two big loads every day to feed those ewes, as it took four pounds of hay for each ewe. George was feeding 3,000 then, so we needed to haul six ton a day. That is a heavy job for a wagon and a team. So, Dad loaned George our team and then the four horses hitched together had plenty of power to pull the hay-filled wagon through that mud," Bill said.

"One day while the four-horse team was hard at work, Andy came along on his saddle horse," Bill said, in recalling the celebrated memory which Andy had. "Andy knew every horse he ever owned and I mean KNEW with capital letters. What an amazing memory he had. Some said he knew every sheep, but that would have been impossible. I think it was said only to point out what a memory he did have. But he did know that two of those horses were not his.

"So, he reined in his riding horse, put his crossed wrists on the horn of the saddle, looked over the two teams carefully and said, 'Morning, George. Where did you get the extra horses?'

'Joe loaned them to me.'

'What is he charging you?'

'Nothing. He just loaned them to me.'

'That's nice. We'll bring him a fat lamb.' "

Within a few days, Bill reported, a dressed lamb was brought to the Guthrie kitchen and his mother pronounced it beautiful. Furthermore: "When it was roasted and while being eaten it was pronounced delicious." Bill went on to tell how Andy had learned butchering as a boy at the Little family sheep ranch in Scotland.

His brother, Jim, had worked as a butcher in Moffat before the brothers moved to Idaho.

Bill Guthrie and Bobby Little became fast friends in their boyhood and remained so until Bobby's death in a truck accident.

Paul Peery

Paul Peery tells of the people and places contained in the memory-provoking collection of pictures lining the walls of his Gamage Barber Shop, which was originally owned by the Gamage family and is the oldest continuing business in Emmett. It opened in 1902. Paul explained that Dave Vahlberg started the collection in the basement of the Jackson Studio, where he had hopes of opening a museum for the town. When that didn't work out, he finally placed the photos on the barbershop wall.

Paul is the son of farmer Harry E. Peery and the family lived at the lower end of the Bench, above Andy's No. 2 ranch. "I was just a kid going three miles to the Cooper school and I can still see that road during the spring lambing on the Little ranch. Thousands of sheep were moving to the No. 1 pasture from another on the Lower bench and they passed No. 2. There were old silos, lambing sheds between the two ranches, now owned by Clayne Cooper, a son of Emmett, who donated an acre of ground to put the school on, hence the name. Our ranch bordered just a part of the Little's.

"My brother, Marvin, and I rode the same horse to school each day. When our brother, Norman, started school, Dad had to get another horse. Marvin became an artist for the Boeing Corporation in Seattle. We virtually waded through sheep and every few yards there was another band. We could always count on there being sheep right next to the Falk's Store bridge, which was used as a trail to the hills from Parma, where Andy wintered his bands. Pablo Arambaru told me once that they moved as many as 200,000 sheep a year from several different outfits along this trail. It was from the lambing to pasture and back to the lambing sheds."

Paul remembered his wool-tromping days. "Even after graduating from barber school, I still tromped wool for Andy. The burlap bags were huge, measuring three feet in diameter and eight feet in length. The sacks were placed upright on a rack. The fellows who did the shearing also tied the fleeces and the first of them were just thrown into the bottom of the sack. Meantime, I would be tying the bottoms of my trouser legs to keep the wool from getting into them, and then would jump into the bag and start tromping. I had to make those bags 'tighter than a drum.' Other fleeces were tied, tossed in and tromped until the bag was full. It took four husky men to roll one of those full and huge wool bags up the planks from the shearing shed and load it onto the freight wagon. I worked as a tromper at the Aikman, the Butte and the Van Deusen ranches."

The photos Paul has on his barbershop wall include Andy Little's sheep crew at the Lower Bench sheds about two miles west of Falk's Store, with the cook and bunkhouses in the background. Among those in the picture are Ed Larsen and Walt Steivers of New Plymouth; the cook, Jack Brady; "Pinochle Joe" Anacabe; Jack Bell, "Big Joe" and Antonio Murelaga, brothers (Tony later owned the Merino Bar in Boise for a quarter of a century); Felix Gabiola and Santiago Achurra.

Another photo shows the intersection of Main and Commercial Avenue on April 22, 1908, as Governor Frank Gooding makes a visit after giving the dedicatory address at the opening of the gates of the old Canyon canal near Horseshoe Bend.

As a young man, Paul Peery was working for Charlie Daugherty, who had between 500 and 600 sheep on a place between the Little's No. 1 and No. 2 Bench ranches. Peery remembers: "One day we were shocking hay when I looked up to see Andy Little going by in his brown four-door Buick sedan, driven by George Smith. As he was Emmett's most famous citizen, I said, 'Hey, there goes Andy Little.'

"Charlie, who had worked for Andy when he first came from Ireland and decided it would be smart for him to get into the sheep business for himself, didn't even raise his head. 'Never you mind about Andy Little, Paul, you go right on shocking hay,' he said." It was obvious that Andy wasn't the only hard-working sheepman in the area.

Eddie Cruzen

"Bigawd, that Andy always knew what he was doing and what was going on, whether he was looking or not." Eddie Cruzen, a friendly and breezy conversationalist, enjoyed Andy and was also a friend of the other family members. A fine livestock man in his own right, he talked of the virtues that made Andy Little a success.

"When Andy showed up at one of his ranches and a fella was breaking his neck to show what a good worker he was, Andy knew that he didn't do a damned thing when he wasn't there to watch. He was a tough manager. That is why he was a success. But he was also a generous man and an appreciative man. If anyone ever helped him in any way, even a little favor, he never forgot it."

There was a sale of state land in Boise on the very afternoon that Andy's funeral was being held in Emmett. Eddie said, "The Littles and I had previously agreed that if I couldn't be at the sale they would represent me and vice versa. So, I bought the land in Long Valley that both of us had been leasing from the state. Later when Jessie and Drew and I got together in Boise, I gave them the news that they had ten acres and that I had bought thirty.

"Better than anyone I ever knew, or ever would know, Andy knew the value of land and what it would be worth in the future. His favorite phrase, when we talked about land, was, 'The only land I want is that bordering mine!' I think there were about 760 acres at his ranch at Norwood and he kept his bucks there. Young John Basabe came to the Norwood when he was only fifteen year old and herded the bucks for Andy. A lot of those young fellows got their start with Andy."

Ike Westcott

Most of Andy's close friends were sheepmen or cattlemen, but one whom he enjoyed a great deal was Ike Westcott, who started the first gas and oil service station in Idaho. Ike was a colorful character who had played big league professional baseball. At one time Ty Cobb was his manager. An over-sized, and sometimes outrageous, sense of humor made Ike one of the most talked-about Idahoans throughout the state. His jokes and pranks spread like wildfire, but on a few rare occasions a friend gave as good as he got from Ike.

Dr. Ellis Kackley said that Ike told the story of Andy becoming very ill at one time during Prohibition days, and the doctor feared he might not make it. Andy, canny as he was, asked someone to have Ike come to the hospital and visit him. When Ike arrived, he said that he was startled by Andy's appearance as he acted as though he couldn't raise his head and feebly beckoned for Ike to come near.

In a muted voice, Andy said, "Now, Ike, when I'm gone there will be six pallbearers at my funeral, and I have buried six bottles of good old Scotch. After you fellas have put me away, I want you to go down and dig up those bottles and have a joyful celebration as we have had so many times together."

Ike nodded his head and they began to visit concerning other things. Being a practical man, particularly regarding pre-Prohibition Scotch, Ike finally said, "You know, Andy, that I will do what you ask, but you won't be here when the fellows and I go to dig up that Scotch. You'd better tell me now where you buried it so that when the time comes I will be able to locate it."

Andy hesitated for a moment, and Ike said his bright blue eyes began to twinkle and his voice was firm and clear as he said, "But I *may* make it. In fact, I'm feeling better already." And, as Ike told the story, "That oat-eating Scot never did tell me where he cached his supply of Scotch!"

George Smith

Both Andy and Adis liked sports and sporting events and admired athletes who participated. George Smith had been quite a runner as a young man in Scotland. He and Andy had known each other there and they became great friends in addition to being employee and employer. Allen Wilson delighted in memories of incidents with George acting as driver for Andy.

"Andy really liked George and he had him as his driver for years and years. After listening to Andy on some of their longer trips, George would come back and say, 'Me and Andy think this, or me and Andy think that.' "

There were four Smith brothers to emigrate from Scotland: Bill, Charlie, George, and Tom. They were born in Hoick (Hawk) and George was nineteen when he arrived in Idaho. Tom's wife remained in Scotland with their baby, Agnes, until she was two years old. Then they came and lived with Tom's widowed mother, Margaret Smith. George was the first of the brothers to arrive. All of them found jobs with the Little ranches. Bill worked at the Aikman on Willow Creek. The Smiths lived in a two-story home on Fourth street, not far from Andy and Adis.

George had learned something of the mechanics of an automobile in addition to herding sheep. He kept Andy's cars and trucks in running condition. He also kept the ranch machinery in good repair, and especially at shearing time.

Because of his interest in mechanics, George called often at the Murray garage, where Grace Tappan was the bookkeeper. George was a jovial sort and became acquainted easily. It was not long before the acquaintance of Grace and George ripened into something deeper and they were married. Dave Murray had taught Grace his system of bookkeeping and she worked at the garage from 1919 until 1927.

Grace described George's work with Andy as busy with long hours. "George would drive one of Andy's cars home to Emmett after dropping Andy in McCall or any of his ranches along the way. He was hardly ever home for the evening meal. It seemed like George and Andy were forever getting stuck in those early-day muddy roads. But they always laughed about it."

Andy was happy to have automobiles in which to travel. A 1909 photograph published in Boise's *Idaho Statesman* newspaper showed Andy leaning into a horse-drawn wagon to brace it against a hillside and prevent its falling off a primitive rocky road. He had been driving at an angle along the hill to prevent high-centering along a muddy roadbed.

Often the roads would become impassable within an hour or less, if the rain or snow began to fall heavily, or if a blinding dust storm arose. If the snow was heavy, wagon wheels were often replaced with snow runners. But this, too, could be tedious when the route ran through spots of bare ground. Travel wasn't easy.

The *Statesman* had also reported that the driver of an eastern stage lost the track about twelve miles from Boise and wandered around all night in search of the road. The track had been blown full of snow, the storm and darkness blinded both driver and horses so that it was impossible to proceed. About five o'clock in the morning they did reach the Twelve Mile Station, from where they had started the night before. They took a fresh start from there and came on through by daylight.

When the car became his general mode of travel, Andy bought gas from his friend, Dave Murray, at the Emmett Garage. All of those connected with the garage, including Dave's sons, Roy and Jim, and their families have fond memories of the Little family.

Every car that Andy purchased from them was a two-seater and included an old Hupmobile. Later, various makes were tried and included the Stanley Steamer, Studebakers, Cadillacs and Packards. These were used for family cars, but often carried cargo such as a sheep. Andy usually had one or two of the dogs riding with him.

Pickup trucks were purchased to take food and supplies from the grocery store and the commissary to the sheep camps. Eventually, flatbed trucks were bought for use at the various ranches.

High marks were given by friends and acquaintances to both Andy and Adis for many remarkable qualities. But, friends and relatives alike agree that both were "atrocious drivers." Andy once drove from Emmett to Boise without shifting into second gear.

George continued to work for Andy until the day Andy died. It had been a period of forty-five years of work, friendship and enjoyment of life. As the Little children grew to young man and womanhood they also drove for their father. There were other things for George to do. If he had done nothing at that stage of their lives, it would never have entered Andy's head to let him go.

Allen said that George had the reputation of being the best driver to come out of Scotland. "At least he could get out of close scrapes in a hurry. Once he hit one of those little bridges that are over all the creeks around here. But he jerked the wheel, swerved that car and gave 'er the gas. As he rounded the corner, he said, 'Oops! We made 'er, boy!' "

David Little remembers George as being about five feet and six inches tall, with a clean-cut appearance. His hair was light brown and his eyes blue. He was adept at water-witching, or water-fishing, as he called it. George successfully witched a well on Willow Creek for David.

Engineer Carl Tappan, who shared a home with his sister, Grace Tappan Smith, after both their mates had died, told of how George came into possession of the old Stanley Steamer car that he cherished for years.

George accompanied the sheep train back east one year and Andy met him in Chicago. Together they took the train to Indianapolis, where Andy bought the Steamer. "That was a pretty great car in those days," Carl said. "Once, coming down Freezeout Hill, he got to going so fast in that thing that he had to drive 'er into that sandy bank to stop."

Roy Murray, well-known Emmett car dealer, was enthusiastic about the old Steamer. "It operated with a steam engine and had a big boiler up front where the engine usually is. The motor was set right on the rear axle. Same principle as the pistons that drive the old steam locomotives. All you had to do was get up a head of steam and turn it back in there and it activated a crankshaft to turn it. It was a two-seater and I rode in it. But I always took a car from our garage when Andy wanted me to drive him to the Twin Falls area. But that Stanley Steamer was surely the car of its day. Like owning a Rolls Royce now."

George and Andy drove the Steamer back to Emmett from Indiana and there were many tales of their trip. A year later, Andy made a gift of the car to George, who kept it for a number of years. After it had served its purpose, George kept it in a pasture on Locust street. It became a real novelty and many people from as far away as Payette, McCall, and Boise came to look at it. After a few years, George traded the car for a Ford pickup which he used on the sheep ranch west of Emmett.

David Murray

Despite divergent political beliefs, Dave Murray and Andy were friends all of their adult lives. Dave was a Democrat and

Andy a Republican, a staunch supporter of the free enterprise system, and their debates were friendly ones. The Murray and the Little children became lifetime friends as well.

Gem County, for which Emmett is the county seat, was established in 1915, more than twenty years after Andy's arrival in the area. Murray served as Gem's state senator in the Idaho legislature during the 1931–32 session. He succeeded Finley Monroe, a Republican. In turn, he was succeeded by Democrat Sam Riggs, also of Emmett. Murray went into office with the state landslide for C. Ben Ross as governor. Ross served three terms of two years each and served longer than any other Idaho governor until the extensive terms of Robert E. Smylie, Republican, 1955–1967.

Murray was among the many friends invited to Andy's study for a "wee toddy" each Christmas Eve. His son, Roy, often drove him and on occasion would act as a driver for Andy.

Roy's son, David, when just a tot, was unimpressed with Andy's favorite trick for small children. Andy would hold his big pocket watch up to a child's ear and the ticking would amuse the small one. David just sat there, showing no expression. Florence said, "Roy and I were beginning to worry that David might not be too bright when Andy finally put his watch to his own ear, shook it, listened again, and said with a grin and a growl, 'Aye, and it's not working. Run down.' "

John McMurray

When John McMurray, whose father was in the sheep business, graduated from the University of Idaho in 1927, in the same class with Jessie Little and Herman Welker, he went to work for the Idaho First National Bank in Boise. He recalled that he was paid ninety dollars a month, and felt that he "was doing a pile of work for that amount." John, Jessie and Herman were all to become leaders among their generation of Idahoans. Jessie went to work in the family sheep business. Welker, who was later to be elected to the United States Senate, was an attorney and often represented Andy Little.

"There were a lot of young kids working at the bank and posting the accounts as a part of their duties," as John tells the story:

"After posting the financial record of Andy Little those kids would come and tell me how crazy I was to stay in banking when I could go into the sheep business with my Dad and get rich." John ruefully added, "My dad, John Sr., was not only in the sheep business but also in the Idaho legislature. So, it looked to those kids that I was some kind of a sap to be drawing down a mere ninety bucks a month and not building up any kind of recognition.

"I managed to stay with the bank for nine months and what those kids didn't know, and what I didn't know until later, was that most of Andy's money was borrowed! I found that out after joining my Dad in the sheep business in 1928. In fact, I got into the business just in time for the big stock market crash. When the bank in Oakley where Dad did business went broke, I took the caboose of a freight train to Boston. For awhile I attended the Harvard Graduate School of Business.

"Later, I went to our country's headquarters for shipping wool, Boston, and got a job at twenty-two dollars a week working in a wool warehouse. I could punch a typewriter, so I wrote letters to growers asking to buy their wool. It seemed that typing was the only thing I got out of college. Somehow, as life went on I began to feel that the ninety dollars the bank paid me wasn't so damned 'mere' as I had thought."

John came back to Idaho on a wool buying trip in 1933 and at that time, he recalls, the Littles were shearing 87,000 sheep. Another large operator of the day, John Archabal, was running 45,000 sheep. When he returned again in 1936, he said that the Little lambing camp was below Boise on the Snake River, as was the winter range. In the summer they would trail the sheep into the high country north of Boise. During the 1936 trip, John recalled that he bought a half-million pounds of wool in Idaho.

John McMurray who, many years later, was described by Idaho reporter and lawmaker Perry Swisher of Pocatello, as "having one of the most blessed personalities I have ever known," depicted Andy as having, "one of the most brilliant minds I have ever known." John credited Andy's great success to the manner in which he used that mind to organize and put into effect the efforts of hundreds of men of diverse nationalities and backgrounds, along with hundreds of machines and thousands of head of livestock.

The McMurrays and the Littles held in common the same political beliefs and he told an election-day story of Andy. The sheep king and one of his herders saddled their horses early at Squaw Creek and rode all morning the first Tuesday in November to cast their votes in Emmett. On the way back to camp Andy said, "I voted straight Republican." The herder concurred, adding, "except for that sonovabitch running for county commissioner. I wouldn't vote for him under any circumstance!" They cancelled each other's vote.

Colin and Smokey McLeod

Colin McLeod, whose son was Smokey, was among the many Scots who entered the Idaho sheep business. He operates along the Snake River at Marsing and makes his home in Caldwell. He has about 6,000 ewes and a greater number of lambs, due to the large number of twins born to the ewes.

Smokey is a good friend of the Little family and succeeded his father in the sheep business. He, too, worries that the increasing costs of machinery and equipment, the difficulty in hiring herders and other help, and the continuing restriction on many of the practices used on the ranches, may force him into closing down.

"Most of our buildings and lambing methods were established long before the Environmental Protection Agency or OSHA were even thought of. Dead sheep have always been a part of lambing, but because of all the new rules, I'm having difficulty finding a place to take the carcasses."

In addition, he wonders who would run the business after he can no longer do so. His son, Colin III, is more interested in cattle than in sheep.

Ivan and Elma Stover

After a few years in business with his brother, Ivan and Elma Stover of Washington County decided to branch out on their own and build a sheep and cattle outfit on Jenkins Creek. It was Elma who told Joy Beckman of Mann's Creek of the grisly spectacle that coyotes and bear leave in their wake among the flocks. "In those earlier days, we were permitted to protect the animals from the predators. A government trapper worked with us by placing bait laced with '1080,' a potent poison, in strategic places on the range. Today we don't have that protection and so they take a heavy toll on both lambs and calves.

"It sounds gruesome, and it was, but we lost many a calf because a coyote ate its tongue while it was being born. Once Jim Waldrop heard a calf bawling and rode over the rise to see two coyotes holding a calf down while two others feasted on it. A true message on a car sticker is, 'Eat lamb: 10,000 coyotes can't be wrong.' One time in camp I counted eight prime lambs which had been killed by one swat of a bear's paw. Many hunters wonder why the chukkar and pheasant populations have dropped so much. Coyotes love fresh eggs and baby chicks, whether they are chickens or birds."

Elma Stover is an Idaho native, born near the turn of the century at Van Wyck, now under the deepest part of Lake Cascade. Her father was James Wesley Auxier of Iowa and her mother Mary Elizabeth Piercy. They arrived in Idaho at Caldwell and went by the little train to Emmett. After a year there they went by freight wagon to Van Wyck, where her father built the Baptist church, the first in Long Valley.

"We had 1800 ewes, a Merino-Columbia cross to produce heavier fine grade fleece, and these were bred to Suffolk bucks for a heavier, meatier lamb. We April-lambed on the lower range and one year had a record-breaking 146 percent lambing. The weather cooperated and the ewes were the right age to twin. But sheep people just never know. A few years later, a false, early spring was followed by windy weather in April: We had our worst lambing.

"We went back to February and March shed lambing on the ranch to get an earlier shipping. In early June we started trailing to the Seven Devils reserve from our upper range on Monroe Creek. We trailed to Mann Creek Crossing to Sage and Keithley Creek out of Midvale, then came the hard part of the journey, climbing and crossing Cuddy mountain out of Cambridge. One year the second band was pushed by another on the trail until there was no chance to feed before starting the climb. They were hungry enough to eat the very poisonous new skunk cabbage, and several hundred ewes and their lambs were lost. The rest of the bands reached the head of Deep Creek on July 4.

"We had our own shearing plant on Sheep Creek, just beyond the Carter Hilliard ranch. Shearing began in early May and we contracted every year with George Garner and his crew. A cook shack was nearby."

Elma told of a distressing evening in the shipping process. The lambs were separated from their mothers at New Meadows about the middle of September and loaded onto double deck freight cars for shipment to Omaha, Nebraska. One shipping time, Ivan had left a worker to come down from the high country with the lambs while he drove his truck loaded with camp gear and the dogs to the ranch. He planned to meet the lambs when they arrived in Weiser that evening.

As Elma tells the story, the lambs didn't arrive. The train master at the Weiser depot told Ivan that the cars had likely been switched to through transit and would be at the Caldwell stockyards. He telephoned Caldwell. No lambs. So, he left instructions that when the lambs arrived to unload, water and feed them and Ivan would meet them by shipping time the next morning.

About one o'clock the following morning the phone rang, and Ivan answered to listen to a weary and irritable voice, questioning why he wasn't at the Weiser depot to meet the lambs. It turned out that the cars had been side tracked while the train returned to pick up a car of the cattle they had forgotten to hitch to the rest of the cars.

Ivan grabbed his suitcase and shipping papers, and headed for the train. He accompanied the sheep to Caldwell, Ogden, Denver and on to Omaha, where he met another mishap. Most of the lambs were sold to Jewish buyers and no one had realized that the coming Jewish holiday, Yom Kippur, does not fall on the same day each year.

"Ivan left the lambs on consignment and came back home," Elma said, "and that was one big reason why we switched to earlier lambing. We then hit an earlier market."

In telling of camp living, Elma said, that on the lower range the camp was moved by truck or pack string before the heat dried the range enough to use the roads. Pack horses were used in the Seven Devils, rugged and steep mountains. The herders and packer lived in tents with a hole cut in the ceiling, then reinforced with wire, through which the stovepipe extended. Ivan had tinsmiths make up his special campstoves so that they could be fired up inside the tents in cold or stormy weather. In addition to the fire box there was a stove large enough to bake those famous sourdough hotcakes and biscuits. The sourdough crocks with a fitted wooden lid and all the food and other necessities were furnished by the Stovers. The men furnished their own personal items.

Elma reminisced that the men lived on sourdough and beans in the very early days of herding. "However, our men lived very well," she said, "and could order whatever staples and food as they wished." This was much as the operation of Andy Little and other ranch owners. "A side of bacon was always on hand, and often they butchered lambs for fresh meat. And they knew how to care for the meat, always hanging it high in a tree where it would keep until they needed it."

The Stovers believed as Andy did that not everyone can herd sheep. It takes a highly skilled man who knows how to use the range to the best advantage and keep the sheep spread out to feed, but brought back together so that small bunches do not become lost.

Sheep must be salted regularly at specially designated areas. They are called to the salt by a special trilling sound. As they lick the salt, the bell sheep and black lambs are counted. There is ordinarily one bell sheep for every hundred ewes. If either bell sheep or black lambs are short in count it means some have strayed and it is up to the herder to find them.

He also needs to know how to train and use his dog, an important part of the outfit. A special bond takes place between them as the training takes place. The Stover sheep dogs were collies: Border, Shetland, or Australian, or a mixture.

At the time they started, the Stovers had less than a thousand acres of deeded land. They were able to buy the private land they leased, so that they had a home base of 6,927 deeded acres. This reached north from the first foothills for ten miles. As it increased in elevation they could move the bands as the range forage became available. Bureau of Land Management and Idaho state lands joined their acres so that they were able to operate on 15,000 acres in one large tract.

Their allotment in the picturesque Seven Devils included the area from Smith Mountain to Black Lake, the head of Deep Creek, some land on Rock and Granite Creeks, Six Lake Basin, Twin Lakes, Emmett Mountain, Witte Mountain, Echo Butte, and at the head of Lake Fork. The home range, called the "Thousand Acre Field," had a low grade of thermal heat underneath it which caused an early spring green-up. It could also be used later in the fall and sometimes all winter. It was found that both cattle and sheep could be run on the same range.

The Stovers sold their ewes to Vaughn Stringer in September of 1961. The Seven Devils reserve was also turned over to him. They ran cattle until 1976, when Ivan's health failed and they sold 5,607 acres of upper range to David Brooke. The two lower fields they gifted to their daughter Carol Lea Loveland, and two longtime sheep people retired to the home place on West Weiser Flats.

Grace and Ralph Jones

Grace Jones, ninety-one in 1988, and a widow of Ralph, with whom she worked in the sheep business in Cuddy Mountain/Weiser area for many years, is still full of enthusiasm for the rugged life. In talking of selling out as they grew older, she said, "I hope they [the people who now own their former ranch] enjoy it as much as I did, because it was a special life. I've had a chance to enjoy something the average woman does not have, the outdoor life, the livestock, the beautiful saddle horses, lovely country with lakes and trees. And I remember the trout the herders used to catch in those streams."

Grace told of their entry into the sheep life as a result of "losing their shirts" in a farming attempt on eighty acres at Meridian. As she tells it, "When we went out on the ranch hay was twenty-one dollars a ton and that fall it dropped to six dollars. When a farmer loses that much he has to be dedicated to farming, and we weren't. And I wasn't really a farm wife. But we'd had a couple of pet lambs we'd raised and they went for a very good price, more than for a calf. So, Ralph had the idea that there was money in sheep. We were just twenty-one years old, that was back in 1919.

"Some fellow who was fattening 25,000 lambs over at Wendell let Ralph come over and learn all he could. The first thing we did after he thought he knew the sheep business, was to buy 500 old ewes. We couldn't afford the young ones. We paid three dollars a head and now, I think, they're over sixty dollars. We rented a fair-sized prune orchard and we took those wooden prune boxes and stacked them one on top of the other, making divisions and protection from the weather, with feed sacks for a cover, and that's where we lambed out those sheep. Despite their age, we had pretty good luck with those ewes and the lambing.

"In those days you could run sheep on any of this sagebrush land. Any place you wanted. That was before that Taylor Grazing Act, the government deal, came into the scene. Ralph started herding at Melba and went clear across to this side of Mountain Home, and then turned back up into the hills. In those days if you had a ranch you could lease a forest right and we got it cheap. Nowadays there's nothing like that, so I'd say there's not much chance for young people getting into the sheep business today.

"That summer they took that little band of sheep over the mountains to the forest land above Lowman, a long stretch of country, and they stayed until fall. We had a tarpaper shack down below the rim on the flat, along the Snake River, and that was our first headquarters. I cooked for the men and by that time we had our little girl and boy.

"Ralph fixed me a deal so it was easier to get water for the house and I wouldn't have to carry it. Getting that water was something. One of the men would take the old stone-boat, made of big squared logs, put together, with planks on top, and put a fifty gallon wooden barrel on that. They took that down to the river and filled it and put tubs on top of the barrel to keep it from splashing, because it was steep back up. They'd pull that right up to the back door, and I had water.

"There was getting hay, which was a big job. The men would take four horses and go up on top of the bluff where the farmers had stacks of hay and haul it back down the incline. It was steep. They had to take what we called an iron shoe. Some of the old timers know what that was: a big flat, not exactly square, piece of iron they chained onto the wagon wheels to keep them from turning and sending the load down on top of the horses. It was that steep.

"We were lucky and didn't have any big accidents. It was a good place to live: sun shining on that sand and sagebrush and the lambs just thrived during the winter. In the summer we went back to the range, near Lowman. One time Ralph was looking at some ewes to buy over near Cambridge and when he came home he said, 'I found the most beautiful country in the world today. It was like paradise. And sometime, if humanly possible, we're going to buy that place.' Ralph had bought 4,000 head, including a lot of fine well-bred yearling ewes. He asked about the place that he thought was paradise and found it was owned by Sheriff Pfost of Boise, who had it leased. But the leasor said that Pfost wanted to sell.

"Ralph couldn't wait to get over to see Pfost and, sure enough, he made a deal." Grace went on to say that at that stage of their lives they needed another place, "like we needed two heads." But, because it was paradise, they bought half of it on contract. A year or so later, Pfost lost in a re-election campaign and wanted to sell out. "And that is how we came to buy the 12,000 acres under fence, and a thousand outside, on Cuddy Mountain. We had to scrape together enough money to buy his equity and that left us with a big mortgage. In those days things were a lot cheaper than now, and we got by."

Grace said that there was a house on the ranch and that it was a beautiful place, especially in the summer time. But, she said they had been just "patching and scratching and getting along" until then. The purchase moved them into the bigger realm of sheep and wool. "We got ourselves organized and got started on a bigger scale, and it was on Cuddy Mountain that we made our money."

They were still young, about thirty-five, and the boy and girl, Grace and Joe, were in school. Later they had two more children, Gordon and Ruth.

Aubrey Butterfield, who was well known in sheep circles, had brought in a lot of sheep from England and was doing experimental sheep development, had a lot of hay on his ranch. Ralph Jones made arrangements to winter his sheep on the Butterfield ranch near Weiser. Butterfield provided sheds in return for the purchase of hay. "We found it was a bad deal for us," Grace remembered, "because it is just too cold for lambing, and we took a big loss in lambs. We decided then we were going to spend the next winter close to the Snake River. We finally landed at Nyssa, which is all sagebrush.

"We trailed the sheep down from Cambridge, across the flats, across the river bridge, clear across to where the Speropolous ranch was. The Shirts brothers run their sheep there now. We rented a rolling piece of land that we couldn't irrigate, but it was ideal for sheep and we put our sheds there. That was before Taylor Grazing and we could go anyplace with the sheep. All we had to do was open the back gate, and away they went.

"Today, you can't do that. There is an upper ditch that takes in all the country down there, and it's all farms and homes. Every square is taken up by someone . . . row crops. The government came in and took all that land, put the ditches through and that was the end of grazing all across the country."

The Joneses used shipping corrals at McCall and divided the ewes and the lambs there. "McCall used to be one of the biggest sheep-shipping centers in the entire country. Incidentally, the shipping center was built by Andy Little, who shipped hundreds of thousands of sheep out of there. At one time he was considered the biggest sheepman of the world."

Looking back fifty to sixty years, Grace remembered hiring kitchen help when she cooked for seventeen men during lambing and shearing. One young couple enamored with the sheep came to work and remained on the Jones ranch for six years. "Just imagine making bread for seventeen men. We had no electricity, but one big, long table, with coal-oil lamps at each end. Those lamps had to be filled, wicks trimmed and glass chimneys cleaned every day. Seven men on each side, two at one end and one at the other. And, did those men ever eat! You can imagine. Fried beans are a specialty in sheep camp, with ham and hot bread.

"One of the things that fascinated me was those 'blue sheep dogs' Andy Little had imported from Scotland. I always said they had glass eyes, because their eyes shone, and that bluish tinge to their fur, made them just beautiful. I think we had fifteen of them at one time. They were wonderfully smart animals, and pretty soon the whole country seemed to have those blue sheep dogs. Andy and the other Scots people have a way with training their sheep dogs: They train them to jump through hoops, count sheep, and put them in the corrals. Ours were descendants of those the Littles had, so they were good dogs. Each herder had two of them.

Grace grew thoughtful and nostalgic for the days and sheep operators now gone. "There are very few sheep outfits left in the country," she sighed, "too many regulations, too much government, too much Taylor Grazing, too much . . . oh, just too much management by other people of our affairs, without knowing much about it. The sheep people were as interested as anyone else in taking good care of the range. We never got credit for it, but, of course, we were interested. It was our livelihood.

"My husband's father told him when we went into the business, 'you took the hardest way there is to live . . . you're subject to everything . . . the markets . . . the weather,' and he was right, but I'll never forget those days. It was just a real pleasant way to live. It was our life and we loved it, and we did it for sixty years. That is a long time, and I still think we were better off for it than if we had lived in town. I wouldn't want to be anyplace but my home. Maybe you could say I'm now reaping some of the benefits of the years gone by."

Some of the other operators in the Weiser area were Tom Carr, the Shirts Brothers, George Speropolous, his son-in-law, Ted Bokidas; Bill Rice, August Broaderson (whose daughter wed Bill Rice), Barney Lincus (who married a Broaderson), John Stringer (who died in 1984, after a full life in the industry and who ran sheep in both the Idaho and Oregon sides of the Snake River near Weiser and Ontario). His nephews, Bill and Vaughn Stringer, run sheep in the Nyssa area; Pat Conley, an Irishman, married the widowed mother of Orrin McMullen, who inherited the sheep outfit when Pat died; and a McMullen daughter married Delbert Koontz and they established a ranch on Weiser Flats; Endicott Dahlquist operates out of Grangeville.

Arthur H. Caine

The man for whom the University of Idaho named its Caine Veterinary Medical Center had an amazing memory. Art Caine was born August 11, 1893, about thirty years after the first permanent settlement of sheep in Idaho took place. He received a Bachelor of Science degree in animal husbandry from Utah State in 1916, and went on to earn a master of science degree in dairying from Iowa State.

It was after his service in World War I, that he worked in Joplin, Missouri for W.H. Eardley of the American Metals Company. His brother, George, heard of a livestock outfit for sale in Soda Springs and said to Art, "You go out there and take a look at it. If it looks good, I want half interest." Art was so impressed that he spent the rest of his life in and with the Idaho livestock industry. The operation was larger than the brothers had anticipated, so they formed the Eardley-Caine Livestock Company, in which the two Caine brothers, Eardley, and three Eccles brothers, Spencer S., George and Marriner of the First Security Bank, in Utah became partners.

Art ran the livestock company from 1919 until the depression year of 1934, when he was hired as secretary-manager of the Idaho Production Credit Association, designed to help finance the financially-suffering livestock owners. Clyde Bacon (president), Roscoe Rich (vice-president), Andy Little, and Harry Soulen were board members.

Art and Andy became fast friends. "We took many trips together and he loved people and had lots of friends. He always wanted to stop along the way, in the different towns and drive into ranches just to visit his friends. He used to call and say 'I'm going to visit the ranches to see how the crops are, do you want to come along?' I liked being with him and enjoyed seeing those eleven ranches on the Emmett bench, where each one was an entity in itself. The family houses, outbuildings and barns were all independent of other ranches. Each had a garden spot, fruit trees, and an irrigated pasture for milk cows, and sheep and cattle for lamb and beef to eat.

"Andy had one ranch where they raised some lovely peaches and he gave me a box of peaches for Mrs. Caine. When we got back to the home ranch, Mrs. Little looked at the box and smiled. She said, 'Now, Art, I'll give you some peaches that *are* peaches.' She picked two bushel baskets, one from her and one from Andy, she said. When I got home, I told Mrs. Caine I had a gift for her from the Littles and she said, 'I hope it isn't peaches.' She had been canning peaches all day. But when she saw those peaches she couldn't believe the size of them. Three of them weighed five pounds!"

David added to the story. "Dad was a great fruit lover. He planted 50,000 trees up and down the creeks and around the ranches. I remember the Damson plum jam Mother used to make. And we had peach, cherry and grape arbors. There were only about eight or ten peach trees at the Canyon ranch on Big Willow. We also had a small apple orchard at the home place."

Art marvelled at the self-sufficiency of each ranch. "They also had pigs and raised hay and grain to feed the sheep during the winter. The Littles held 'hog-killing' days in the winter when they butchered. Andy gave all the spareribs to his friends as the sheepherders wouldn't cook them. He cured the rest of the pork.

"When Andy had over 100,000 ewes, the most of anyone in North America, he never bragged nor boasted at all. I always thought that if he had been in the steel business, he could have been the Andrew Carnegie of our nation. He was, in the very best sense, a big man, farsighted, with vision.

"But during the depression, he was in differences with the bank. I remember that Crawford Moore was insisting that he pay up a huge loan and Andy said he didn't have the money, but had the sheep. Moore said, 'Being the biggest-sheepman in the country has gone to your head.' Andy replied, 'If I bring those sheep right down Main street into this bank, then *you'll* be the biggest sheepman in the country.'

"Later, Roscoe Rich, Clyde Bacon and I went with him to the bank in Spokane and Andy was completely honest and matter-of-fact about his resources. Those were very hard times and everyone had a limited amount of money. I think it was on this trip to Spokane that I ran over three birds, a pheasant and three quail. The next time I stopped by his ranch to pick him up for a trip, Andy walked out to the granary and got a gunnysack. When I asked him why, he said, 'Well, if you're going to be doing the driving, I'm going to have something to put the wild game in after you bag it.' No matter how tough the times, he never lost his sense of humor."

While working with the sheep people, Art became concerned with the economic loss to sheepmen because of vibriosis, which causes ewes to abort their lambs. His concern led to the development of a regional research project which brought together researchers from the western states in a coordinated effort. He became chairman of the National Wool Growers association committee on vibriosis and continued support from that association developed management procedures for prevention, treatment for controlling outbreaks and an effective vaccine.

He spent much of his career strengthening Idaho's livestock industry through betterment of education. Art became chairman of the Idaho Sheep Commission in 1937 and served until his retirement in 1976.

Alexander Campbell

Alex Campbell went to work for the Idaho First National Bank in 1909 and served as assistant cashier for a number of years. He also served as the bank's representative in dealing with the Regional Agricultural Credit Corporation, an agency of the RFC set up to loan money. After a year, he resigned from the bank to work for the Western Loan Company and continued to represent the bank on the RACC. Eventually RACC was absorbed into the PCA, and Campbell became assistant manager and secretary-treasurer of theBoise office.

Andy had financed at the First National and when it closed, he went to the RACC, which wanted to close out the entire Little operation. Had that materialized, the story of Andy Little and his children and grandchildren would have been much different. Friends such as Roscoe Rich, Clyde Bacon and Art Caine all wanted to help and made appeals in Andy's behalf. John Schoonover, bank president, only said that "big loans are a detriment to the bank," when Andy asked for a loan to save the work of a lifetime. It is fascinating to note the manner in which the Little operations dealt without money while staying afloat.

Andy's good friend, Luke Moore of the Golden Rule store, predecessor to J.C. Penney stores, took checks Andy had written to his employees when they purchased goods, and simply returned the checks to Andy to be repaid if and when he could do so. Bob Naylor, married to Jessie, who had left the bank during the reorganization days, had $3500 in cash, on which checks were written for the bare essentials.

"No one but Andy and Andy-trained Jessie could have run that operation of 120,000 sheep and thirty-two irrigated farms on Bob's $3,500. They truly ran that gigantic operation without money," Alex said.

"We made a lot of loans and burned a lot of midnight oil trying to help Idaho farmers and ranchers suffering from the upheavals of the Depression," Alex reminisced many years later. Because Andy was unable to receive the loan he needed in 1937, he sold 6,000 sheep and range to Donald McPherson for $100,000, taking $20,000 as a down payment. It was the only land Andy ever sold in his life. Later the RACC bought Andy some replacement sheep, but they "were certainly not the type he had been accustomed to," Alex said. "He and his brother, Walter, were well and widely known for the fine sheep which they raised."

Alex was a friend of Bob Naylor and worked with him at the bank. He also became a close friend of the Little family over the years. He had seen them through good times and bad. David recalls finally going to Alex for help when, early in his ranching career, he simply could not balance his books. He looked for errors for several night before taking his books and visiting Alex. Quickly looking down the lines of figures, Alex noted a transposition and corrected the mistake. His comment was, "Dave, when working under pressure, as you are doing, it is easy to make a transposition. Relax. Things are going to work out."

David said, "When Dad died, we were still financing with the RACC, because the PCA limit was $50,000. My first loan was for $52,000; Jessie's for $42,000, and later another $10,000; Drew's for $52,000." The land which Agnes and Docky had received as a part of the estate included irrigated farms on the Emmett bench (Walter Little had done well with irrigated lands) and the ranch at Norwood below McCall, which their son, Harry, still operates. Jessie also took a great deal of land, which she soon sold to Harry Soulen, while Drew and David liquidated much land they had inherited or later bought from their Mother.

"I considered Andy Little one of my very best friends," Alex said, "and his children became close friends. No one could go through the Depression experiences with a family like the Littles and see how strong they were and how they kept going in spite of everything, without coming to like and admire them a great deal."

Clyde Keithly

Clyde Keithly told of the time that Andy and his herders were trailing 2,000 sheep through Midvale. There were roads and ranches to cross, and there was lots of trouble opening and closing the gates. Clyde and two of his school friends, Boyd Newman and Bob Clare, rode their horses up to where the sheep were crossing, hoping to sign on for some work. Andy spied them on the horses and said, "Boys, we need some help in getting these sheep across the valley."

"We put in a full day's work," Clyde reminisced, "and Andy said, 'Thanks, boys,' and rode off. We hesitated for a bit, surprised that he didn't give each of us a dollar, the going rate for a day's work at that time. Then we rode up to him and said, 'We think you owe each of us a dollar.'

"Well now, boys, we didn't have any agreement on that," Andy said, and wheeled his horse and rode off.

The three boys decided to play a little game of tit-for-tat and, "That night the three of us rode up to where they were bedded down for the night. And we scattered those sheep from hell to breakfast. The next day, Andy was back in Midvale and looking for help rounding up the sheep. Boyd, Bob and I signed on, but our price had doubled overnight and we agreed that two dollars for a day's work was fair. We did pretty well. As I remember, it took us three days to gather in the bands!"

Clyde said, "It was not until a year later that my dad, Sam, found out about that whole incident. And I still got a good licking for it."

The Lakes

Going to the high country was not simply a sheep drive, with the Little bands it was a migration. It was also a slow process and took from a month to six weeks to get to the high area where the sheep grazed for several months. The sheep fed lazily as they traveled along each day.

John and Hazel Lake lived on a farm on the bench above Emmett and they cooked in the sheep camps for Andy. A favorite menu in camp was venison stew, when someone was lucky enough to bag a deer, along with sourdough biscuits. Andy relished the sourdough biscuits and was happy when they were on the menu when he stopped by camp.

Vera and Betty Lake liked to ride out from camp on picnics during the summer. They would take a couple of watermelons, tying each into a gunnysack, then tying both sacks together at the neck, toss it over the horse's neck at the saddlehorn and ride into the hills.

Even when they were down from the hills, John Lake often stopped by the Little home to visit. On one visit, after just a few minutes, John said he must be getting home. Andy and Adis urged him to stay for supper. His answer was, "When I left home, my kids were crying."

Andy chuckled and said, "John, I think they were crying for sourdough biscuits."

These and so many other memories that cannot be included, are an enduring part of the lives of those who knew the Little family.

C H A P T E R S I X T E E N

HEIRS OF THE TRADITION

DUSK FELL EARLY DURING THE WINTER MONTHS. ABOUT FOUR O'CLOCK each afternoon Adis would light the kerosene lamps. It was a daily ritual for one of the hired women to fill the lamps, trim the wicks and see that the glass chimneys were clean. The soft glow of the lamps warmed the house. Soon Andy would be coming in the door and he liked to wash up before the evening meal. If there was time he would go through any mail that had arrived, setting aside those matters he would peruse later in the evening.

His daughter Jessie said that he would riffle through the pages of the *Congressional Record* which was sent to him by his friend, Senator Borah, dubbed "The Lion of Idaho" by the reporters in Washington. Sometimes Andy would say, "Listen to this." Then he would read to those around him some section which was of particular amusement or interest to him. Everyone liked to hear him chuckle. He could become intense about items that did not amuse him.

Andy soon learned that conscientious reading of the *Congressional Record* was no guarantee of good humor. But it was an excellent way to keep current on what was going on with the taxpayers' money in the nation's capitol.

The *Congressional Record* was first published in 1873, three years before Andy was born. Averaging more than two hundred pages a day in 1989, during the years which he read the *Record* it was about fifty pages in length. It is a fairly accurate account of the proceedings of the Congress and is published on a daily basis when either or both Houses of the Congress are in session. Along with everything that is said and done on the floors of the House and the Senate, there is voluminous additional reprinting of editorials and articles from hometown newspapers, commencement addresses, mayoral proclamations, debate and oratorical winning speeches and any other items which members of the Congress want to insert into the *Record*. These items are usually red-lined by a member of the Congressional staff and mailed home to those constituents involved in the articles. The lengthy Supreme Court decisions take up many pages.

The late Washington columnist Raymond Moley once referred to the *Record* as "that fearsome receptacle of trivia." To many it is only that. But to Andy it was a fount of information and learning. Surely he was one of the most avid readers the *Congressional Record* has ever had. He took the necessary time to keep up with what was going on in the Congress and, through the *Record* and its reprints of editorials and articles, much of the rest of the United States.

Through his readings in the *Record*, local Idaho papers, and what he heard or had repeated to him of radio news by Adis, Andy formed his opinion that the Negroes of the nation were not being given their rights nor justice. David said that it was not just the Negroes, but that his father had such a belief in the freedoms and rights in America that he wanted to be sure they were not denied any individual or group.

It is a surety that Andy's diligent reading of the *Record* and his quotations from it had an influence on the children and their interest in government on the local, state and national levels.

Andy and Adis were determined that their children should have the best educations possible. Andy had attended grade school in a small red brick building within walking distance from his childhood home along the Selkirk, a part of the Annan River out of the small sheep and woolen mill town of Moffat. Among the easier of his lessons was a poetic way to learn the rivers of the Annandale district in which Moffat was located.

> The Annan, the Tweed and the Clyde
> All rise from the one hillside.
> The Tweed flows east
> And the Clyde flows west.
> And the Annan goes to the southwest.

The Annan River flows from the Tweedsmuir; muir is the Scots pronunciation for "moor" or "the highland."

Adis attended the school near Plunton Farm and the advanced cooking school in Edinburgh. Both had a natural curiosity of such strength that neither ever stopped adding to their educations through reading and learning from others.

Agnes Little Bettis

All their children attended grade and high schools in Emmett. The oldest daughter, Agnes McMillan Little, attended Emmett High, and then the University of Washington for two years and two years at the outstanding college for women, Wellesley College in Massachusetts. Boston wool buyers had talked of Wellesley to Andy and Agnes when they visited the Little home on buying trips. They were hospitable to Agnes and showed her about the area.

One Boston couple found their roads too slick to drive and the driver said, "I don't know what to do. I have chains but no jack to lift the car." Agnes replied, "In Idaho we just drape a chain over the tire and drive slowly until we can hook it together." They wrote Andy and Adis that their daughter was a genius.

Agnes, the firstborn, was named for her mother and the family name of her maternal grandparents. She was always known as Agnes and her mother as Adis. She and her siblings were taught to work through chores assigned by their mother and responsibility for completing them as well as toward her sister and younger brothers. Anything but outspoken, Agnes was affable and well liked by many. While living on the Bettis ranch at Gannett, she was described by one friend as, "the nicest woman who ever lived along the Wood River." Her youngest brother, David, said she got along with everyone regardless of occupation or wealth. People responded to her in kind and she was a popular woman.

One of her closest friends, Katherine Hunt of Emmett, told Teresa Little that Agnes felt close to Drew, but felt at times he was a "bit too rambunctious and exuberant." Agnes and Katherine learned to play golf on the first Emmett course, located by the dam. One hot day, one of Andy's drivers took them to the course. While they were golfing, he killed a rattlesnake with eight rattles.

Agnes may have been quiet and reticent, but she laughed when she told Katherine of her wedding trip. She and Docky drove to Baker, Oregon, and took a room on the second floor of a hotel. They had barely entered the room when the bellhop appeared and said Mr. Bettis was wanted on the phone. Docky went downstairs to take the call, since there were no room phones then. It was one of the Davidson brothers in Boise. The brothers took turns calling at half-hour intervals through the night. Docky was always heavy and would puff as he climbed the two flights of stairs. After one call he puffed back exhausted and dropped on the bed, which broke under his weight. An embarrassed young couple explained it all to an only slightly amused desk clerk, who had been doing as much running upstairs to deliver the messages. They changed rooms and quit answering the phone.

Agnes, as her mother, became an excellent cook and a gracious hostess. Katherine felt that she was so kind that people took advantage of her generosity. But no one ever heard Agnes complain. Docky suffered the loss of one eye when he picked up a dynamite cap that exploded. From then on, Agnes did some driving on their extended trips to California and Florida. She also drove their long sedan, loaded with supplies, out to the various ranches.

The story of how Agnes received an elegant piece of jewelry tells a bit of the romance her father carried in his heart. Andy would often stop and pick wildflowers to bring to Adis when he was on his way home from the range and ranches. He liked giving her gifts and always brought her something from his various trips. Once, from a trip to Chicago, he brought her a dazzling star-shaped diamond brooch that was later given to Agnes. In turn, it went to another Agnes. When his wife died, Docky gave the brooch to her niece, Agnes Brailsford, the daughter of Myrn and Drew.

Upon graduation from Wellesley, Agnes worked in her father's office on Main Street in Emmett. In back of the office was the commissary in which she also helped. It was kept stocked with groceries and supplies for the ranches and workers. Andy bought smoked codfish by the truckload for three or four years.

David remembers that when Agnes worked in the office he was in the third or fourth grade, and she drove him to school each

Andy Little and ever-present cigar, woolen suit, woolen overcoat, and a new snapbrim hat, is photographed with his oldest daughter, Agnes, at the family home in 1928.

morning in the family's Packard. On one trip he gave her a terrible fright. They had picked up Walt Little Jr. on the way to school and when Agnes stopped the car, David jumped out and ran in front of a car coming from the opposite direction. He was hit and knocked unconscious and everyone nearby was horrified. But he regained consciousness and quickly recovered.

Agnes and her brothers and sisters became proficient at riding horseback. She, Jessie and Drew rode the 72 miles from Emmett to Cascade one summer day, a feat few riders would undertake today.

A number of people have described Agnes as a gentle and peaceful person who did not like controversy. When Laurence Moore Bettis, an outgoing young man who was to become a banker and livestock owner, came into her life he more than made up for any reticence Agnes displayed. "Docky," as he became known early in life as the son of Dr. Harry Bettis (Boise's first dentist), stood firm in his beliefs and did not hesitate to speak up for and about them. His father was called "Doc" and for a long time, Laurence was called "Little Doc." Still later, it became and remained "Docky." He was the grandson of Christopher Wilkerson Moore and Catharine Minear Moore and the son of their first child, Alice, who was the first white child born in the small mining town of Ruby City in 1866. Alice's brother, Crawford, was an uncle-by-marriage of Robert Naylor, who married Jessie Little.

It was the grandfather who founded the Idaho First National Bank in Boise. He also built the palatial home on the corners of Warm Springs Avenue and Walnut Street in Boise in 1891–92. All this happened as a progression of his working life. He prospected in Florence and Elk City in 1862; moved on to Ruby City and Boise in 1863; and in 1864 the National Banking Act, which was to have a dramatic effect on his life, was passed by the Congress. The act made it possible for Moore and B.M. DuRell to set up a business in Idaho City to exchange gold dust and give credit to miners. The next year, they were granted a charter for the First National Bank of Idaho.

The young men moved rapidly and in June of 1867, they opened banking outlets in Silver City and Idaho City, both mining towns. In 1872, DuRell sold out his interest to Moore, who, as cashier, ran the bank. In January of 1889, he was elected bank president and within a couple of years built the Boise home. It was the first house in Boise to be heated with natural hot water. The Moore's second daughter, Laura, married J.W. Cunningham who, years later, joined the bank as vice-president. It was Cunningham who started the Idaho Power company, through establishing a little plant between Horseshoe Bend and Emmett, and which he sold in 1906 to Electric Bond and Share.

The Cunninghams moved into the Warms Springs Avenue home to live with her father after Mrs. Moore died in 1911. Since that time, the home has been called the Cunningham House. It is now owned by the only son of Docky and Agnes, Harry Little Bettis. Upon the death of C.W. Moore in 1916, his son, Crawford, became the president.

Laurence "Docky" was in the U.S. Army during World War I. He had attended the University of Virginia for one year but did not want to return. His parents protested, so he went into the bank to talk to Grandfather Moore. C.W. saw his grandson coming and walked out of his office to meet him. Before Docky could say anything, his Grandfather firmly said, "You are going back to school." At about the time the University opened in that fall of 1916, Moore died, Docky quit before the year had scarcely begun, and started home. He notified his parents that he was enroute. At the Chicago railway station, when he was making the transfer to an Idaho-bound Union Pacific train, he met his father at a turnstile. Headed home together, father and son spent much time talking of Docky's future.

By the time they reached Boise, Docky was prepared to get some cattle and operate on Three Creek south of Twin Falls and also into Owyhee County. His mother died in 1918 and Docky and his father spent a great deal of time together. "Mainly, it was talking a lot about sheep and a little about cows," he said. In 1921, Docky sold the cattle to go into the sheep business with his father. It was in 1923 that Docky got into a fierce argument with his uncle, Crawford Moore, and the bank foreclosed on the ranch which Docky had been running for three years. His father said it would be a good time for the two of them to take an around-the-world trip. Dr. Bettis' former partner, a man by the name of Valentine, ran the sheep for them while they were gone. Docky would laugh and say, "That sheep outfit made more money while I was gone than when I am here." That same year, he moved to Hailey and located on a ranch on Little Wood River. He sold it in 1940, and sold another sheep outfit in the Hailey area in 1946. Three Creek sold in 1947.

It was while under the supervision of his uncle, Crawford, that Docky had been urged to learn the livestock business by working in it. Moore had in mind his own learning experience during a decade spent in Colorado and that Docky would someday be a bank officer. So he was sent to Bruneau, Idaho and Nevada ranches, where he enjoyed ranching and livestock. He remained briefly at the bank upon his return and went into the livestock business, both on his own and with his father.

He and Agnes were married at the Little family home in Emmett. Their only child, Harry Little Bettis, was born in Boise on October 10, 1934. The lad had a rich heritage of livestock ranching and as soon as he was old enough began to learn all his father and grandfather could teach him.

A heart-breaking tragedy in the life of Docky and Agnes was that their second son died at birth: The umbilical cord wrapped around his head.

It was natural that Agnes worried that Harry, as an only child, would be lonely on the ranch at Gannett. She knew that he wished for playmates and he thought his cousins far away. One day she sent him to the home of a neighbor for a cup of cream. As she watched out the window for his return, she saw him pour the cream in the creek. As he came in the door he said that one of his cousins had appeared and taken the cream away from him.

While attending Stanford, Harry received a visit from his parents. They couldn't locate him anyplace. Finally they found him in the horse barn where he was cleaning the stalls to pay for his board! Harry has always been ambitious and a hard worker, dedicated to paying his own way.

His great-aunt Laura Cunningham doted on Harry. When he was small and visited her in Boise, she stayed in the room with him as he napped to be sure that he was breathing. Small wonder that she left the big family home on Warm Springs to him when she died and also put him in charge of her foundation.

When he left the bank, Docky held on to his 100 shares of stock, which continued to grow. At that time the Moore family ties held 2,059 shares out of a total of 3,000 in the bank. Docky was a director of the Western Loan and Investment Company and was elected to the bank board of directors in 1950.

Docky and I.E. Rockwell of Bellevue, also on the Wood River, enjoyed talking and arguing politics, economics and any other subject that came up. They looked quite a bit alike and were often asked if they were related.

Eloise Anderson, in a well-written history of the bank, "Frontier Bankers," told of Docky's continuing and hands-on interest in the bank. "Bettis, as the grandson of the founder, became a very vocal spokesman for the still considerable Moore family stock interests. At the time he became a director he was operating a cattle ranch at Gannett, but moved to Boise in 1958 and became an active director."

When Harry returned from Stanford University in 1956, after studying business and accounting, his father essentially retired and Harry began operating the family businesses. Like a sheep to lush green grass, he took to it. He said, "Both of my Grandads, Little and Bettis, loved sheep. So, I guess it got into my blood when I was born. There has to be a reason for all this misery," and he smiles as he continues, "There just has to be a better way to make a living." And Harry Bettis, sheep and cattle man both by birth and by choice, grins and chuckles in a manner reminiscent of Andy.

Even when he talks of his Grandad Little, he gets a twinkle in his eyes and a grin comes to his face. "Grandad Little raised dozens of real good work horses and he was very proud of his matched team of Belgians. His workers knew those horses had to be kept clean and shining. Yep, Grandad was quite a livestock man. No one like him."

But there *is* someone like him: Harry Bettis.

Harry said that when Grandad Little was going out to measure hay, he would take a long tape measure and by throwing it over the

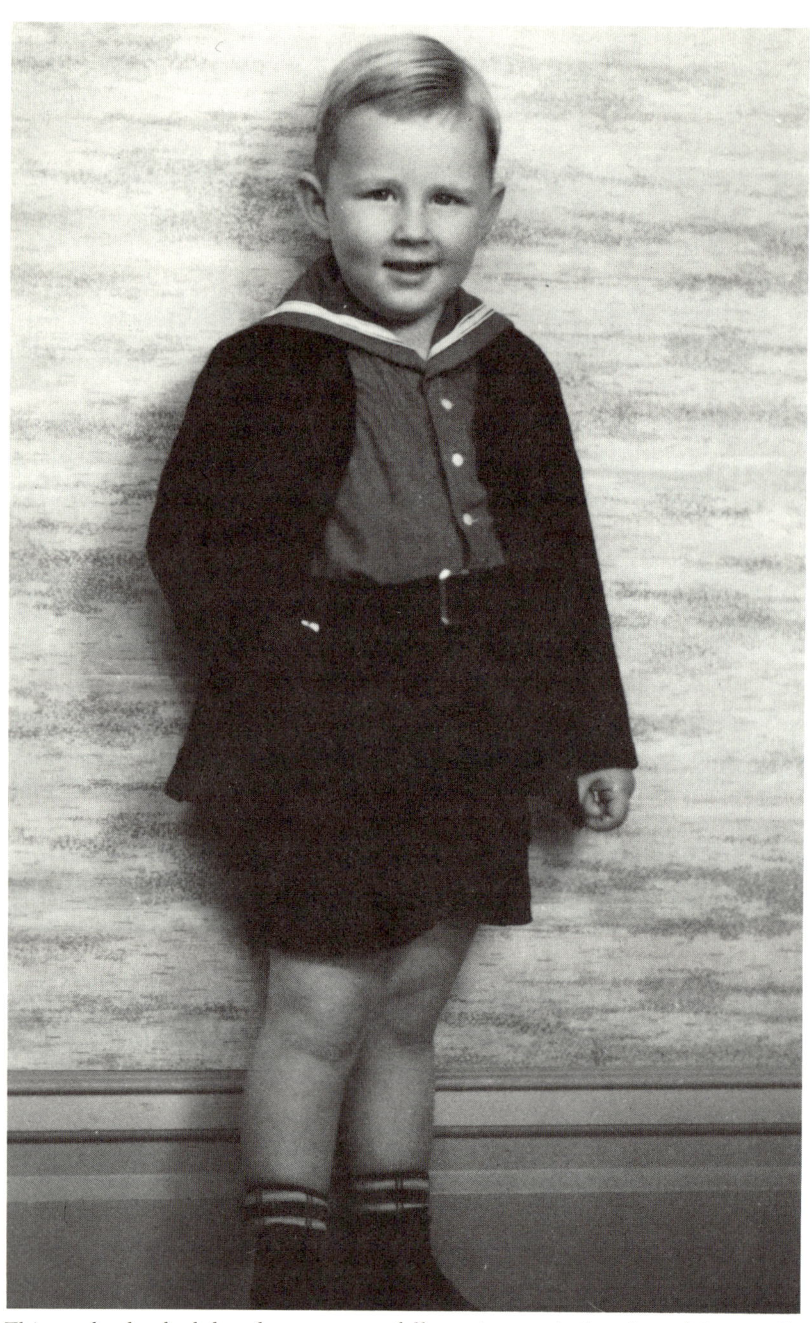

This apple-cheeked, handsome young fellow gives an intimation of the sturdiness of body and character that Harry Little Bettis was to display all of his life. Taken in 1940 when Harry was about six.

Courtesy Jack Rottier Photos

Jessie Naylor ran Andy Little's office as well as the Highland Livestock and Land Company which she and her husband, Bob, owned for a number of years.

known on campus. Jessie became president of the Delta Gamma sorority and as one of her former classmates said, "There was never any doubt of just who the president was nor what the sorority stood for and where it was going so long as Jessie was in charge." It was these same attributes that made her such a success later as her father's strong right arm and with her own operations.

A June 9, 1930, report of her grades in Philosophy at the University of Idaho, from which she graduated that summer with a Bachelor of Science degree in education displays a final average of 4.892 on the old five-point scale. That she was unusually bright there can be no doubt. She immediately went to work in Andy's office and became invaluable to the entire Little sheep empire. The first job to which Andy assigned her was buying supplies. Later he had her handle the payroll. She sold the wool, took the contracts and did the book work at an old rolltop desk in the office. When asked who did all this work before Jessie went into the office, Roy Murray said, "Andy, and he kept all those records in his head."

Through her kindness in helping the herders, Jessie was soon handling their finances. As a result, many of them accumulated a small fortune. Jessie paid their taxes, insurance and made any special purchases they wanted and turned over a nice nest egg at the end of the year.

Jessie could be very firm. One day she had a set-to with Ellis Harris, the bookkeeper, who became so angry with another employee that he threatened to kill him. When Jessie reprimanded him, he became furious with her. He was replaced by John Fry, who remained for a number of years. Elmer Astin was another office employee.

A clipping from the *Denver Post* of April 20, 1958, reported that she was "A woman trusted by hundreds of workers in the greatest sheep kingdom of the Northwest, built by her famous father . . . ." The 1970–71 winter issue of *Idaho Yesterdays* featured a story on the First Security Bank of Idaho and The Great Depression. In it was printed: "When Jessie, Andrew Little's daughter, received word that Moore had not opened his bank on that fateful Wednesday morning she immediately sent this message to all foremen: "Hire no men, fire no men, write no checks, the bank is busted."

Drew was handling the sheep of the Andrew Little outfit and assisting his dad with the range problems. This kept him on the move since there were twenty-seven irrigated, very productive ranches. A well-planned crop rotation, plus fertilizer from the sheep fed on them, was responsible for the fertility. Under single ownership, but divided into four units, the three others were A.L. Sheep and Land Company, the Highland Livestock and Land Company, and the Lake Sheep Company. There was a foreman for each of the divisions and each of the ranches had its own foreman. Jessie's husband, Bob Naylor, was assisting Andy in several areas, with most of his time spent on development of better land and crops.

The four sheep outfits were handled as individual units, each herd using the same lambing shed, equipment, feed yard and ranges. Every employee who had gone through the seasons with any of Andy's outfits was familiar with all phases of the cycle.

It is interesting to note that Andy had taken out a total of $5,108,676.84 in RACC loans from 1932 to 1937, and that all loans were repaid. Land holdings in those same five years included irrigated farm land: 5,646 acres; irrigated pasture: 4,654 acres; deeded grazing land: 49,964 acres; for a total of 60,264 acres of deeded land. Leased grazing land included 292,546 acres, for a total land use of 352,810 acres in addition to lands of the U.S. Forest service and the Public Domain. In 1932, the operations had a total of 84,691 grown sheep, and the number was not exceeded in the following four years. All of this was fascinating business to Andrew Little Jr.

Myrn Henley of Pomeroy, Washington, was teaching school in Emmett when she and Drew were married on November 27, 1936. She laughed as she told of spending her honeymoon driving a team of horses with a single wedge behind to break a trail to the sheep so they could get through a foot of snow.

Mrs. Little also laughed when she told Drew and Myrn that when the *Idaho Statesman's* society editor telephoned to learn where the bridal couple were honeymooning, she answered, "In the South. I didn't tell her it was south Idaho."

They lived at the family home, as did Jessie and Bob Naylor at that time, for a year. Myrn said that Mrs. Little and Jessie were both excellent cooks and that she learned much about cooking while living there. All three of them worked together in preparing meals. Drew could also cook and when his mother refused to cook the lamb fries, he took over. He procured the fries in the spring when the lambs were castrated. He washed them, dredged them in flour and bread crumbs with salt and pepper, browned them in butter, and then baked or steamed a bit and served them. He prepared a twelve quart galvanized bucket full of them at a time.

Myrn felt close to her father-in-law and Roy and Florence Murray said that Andy treated her as his own daughter. "He liked the way I liked the outdoors," Myrn said. "With his Scottish brogue he could never pronounce the name Myrn, so he always called me 'Mrs. Drew' or 'Little Miss,' when someone else was around.

"When Drew and I were living in the little house that used to be Grandma Little's summer place at Cascade, I had a little pet badger. At first, Grandad said, 'It will dig holes in everything, do away with it.' I said that I was going to keep it, and Grandad got so that every night he would come down from his camp and wear his oldest shoes. He would stick a foot out to the badger and the pet waddled over and untied his shoes. Grandad got a big kick out of that. He got so he would ask for 'Ole Cousin Badger,' as he called him. Drew and I felt that the badger was the nearest thing to a pet he ever had."

When his father died, Drew, along with other family members, inherited debt as well as much land and sheep. In 1938 he sold the Lake Sheep Company to Don McPherson, along with 20,000 acres of grazing land, to pay off the debt he had taken on.

After his parents died, Drew wanted more than anything to buy the family home where he had spent so many happy times. The home had been up for a sale for about a year and no one felt they could afford it. Drew kept saying he wanted it and Myrn kept saying it was too far out, too big, and "I hate housekeeping." Myrn resisted as long as she could, saying it was much too large for their needs and that they simply couldn't afford it.

She said that one day in 1950, she could tell he "had something up his sleeve," as Drew came in with a beaming face and said, "I got a $1.10 a pound for the wool. It's the highest market I can remember." Usually, they got about thirty cents a pound. That year they received about $60,000. She agreed that it was a fine price. "Now," he exclaimed, "if the rest of the family say we can buy the place will you move?" Myrn said her heart sunk but that she didn't want to dampen his high spirits, and she was sure they couldn't buy it from the estate for that amount, so said, "Okay, but only if you will let me remodel." He agreed and they bought the home for $70,000.

Drew and Myrn became the parents of two daughters and a son: Myrn Jean Gosse of New Plymouth, Agnes L. Brailsford of Hagerman, and Andrew Henley Little of Emmett. The Brailsford family was also in the sheep business near Jerome. Agnes and her husband, Bill, now have three bands of 1,000 sheep each. All three children climbed on horses as soon as they could and by the time Myrn Jean was six and Aggie four, they were riding alone. When the baby, Andy, was six months old he was riding along in the saddle with his mother. Myrn said that as Andy reached the teen-age years, he liked the pickup better and rode but little after that. In 1960, both Aggie and Myrn Jean, then eighteen and twenty, were riding with the Ada County Posse-Ettes with Aggie as Queen.

The three children inherited the land, buildings and animals when Myrn died. Aggie is executor of the estate. Like her mother and grandmother Little before her, she works wherever she is needed, at home or in the field and on the range.

After returning to the family home, Myrn wanted peacocks to strut about the place in all their beauty. Many of the glorious birds can be seen along the water road out of Moffat, Scotland, from the old Little home to the schoolhouse where Andy and his siblings learned. There are so many pea fowl that a sign reading "CAUTION PEACOCKS" is set at the side of the road. Myrn said that Andy had written a provider of peacocks at one time to order a pair. He was so incensed that he cancelled the order when they wrote back, "You must mean a cock and a pea hen, if you want a pair, and not two peacocks."

In many ways like his father, Drew bought a grader for the road-building projects on his ranches. He came along one day while a man he had hired was grading a new road. Drew watched for a bit and didn't like what he saw. Even though he had never driven a grader, he hoisted himself up to the seat and finished the job.

Another large piece of equipment he learned to handle was a huge, wooden water-wagon. It was used to haul water to the sheep when the springs went dry.

Drew was as competent in public life as he was in private. Along with the love of his family and a good reputation among his friends, Drew was elected president of the Payette Forest Wool Growers Association.

Robert Sproat Little
1914–1935

Both Andy and Adis had received—and taken—some difficult times in their lives. They were strong people, born and raised in the vital earthiness of Scotland. But nothing could have prepared them for the hard blow of losing their second son, Robert, whose death came from an automobile accident. They had seen death in their immediate families before they built a family of their own. It was a terrible blow to lose Bobby, likely, the hardest they had to bear.

Robert was the shortest, and the stockiest, member of the family. He was five foot and three inches, muscular and walked with a rolling gait, just as his father. Roy Murray said, "When you saw Robert walking toward you, there was no doubt that here was a son of Andy Little."

His parents believed that a heart flare-up which he had as a youngster contributed to his short stature. When small and not too well, the entire family rallied around Robert and took splendid care of him. As a result he developed into a sturdy boy and young man. All of the Little children did well in school and teachers said that Robert had the brightest mind of the five.

Roy Murray said, "Robert was not only sharp, but he was outgoing. He liked people and had many friends." Myrn remembered him as jovial and liking to tell jokes and play pranks. "He went lots of places with Drew and me, and we always had fun."

Both Drew and David enjoyed the horses and riding. The more

Robert Little was a student at the University of Idaho when this was taken in 1935, the year he lost his life in a truck accident enroute to the Long Valley headquarters sheep camp.

spirited the horse, the better. In fact, Drew was said to be "a genuine cowboy" in that he enjoyed breaking wild horses to ride. Robert was more entranced with cars and drove a good deal for his father. In many ways, he was beginning to replace George Smith who had driven for Andy for years.

Agnes had married Docky Bettis and was living away. Jessie was a graduate of the University of Idaho and running the office. Drew was on his own, as well as doing supervising work for Andy. David was the youngest. So, Andy and his second son had been spending lots of time together and had grown close. Bob was industrious and looking forward to helping his father in the ever-growing sheep operations. He would have completed his studies at the University the following year.

Bill Guthrie and Bob were good friends and graduated together from Emmett high school in 1932, and were often in the home of each other. That fall Bob went on to the University of Idaho while Bill spent a year doing mapping in Gem County to earn funding for school. "It didn't faze our friendship a bit that I wasn't able to go on to the university with him," Bill said, "he always came to see me as soon as he came home to the valley. We remained good friends."

John McMurray liked Bob and said, "He was a goer, but he was just a kid yet. So, he didn't always think things through." An example of that is a story told by Joe Acuff, now of Coeur d'Alene and whose family then was also in the sheep business in southern Idaho. Joe was a close friend and classmate of Bob at the University of Idaho.

"We were driving back to Moscow after a holiday at our homes in the south and just as we got to Cascade, we heard a thump, thump, thump and drove on into the little town and discovered we had a flat tire. We both jumped out, changed the tire in a hurry and got back in the car. Something had happened to the machine. The engine would run, even race, but the car just wouldn't budge. We thought it must be in the gear shift. After a few minutes of listening to the engine roar, we got out and learned we had left the jack under the wheel!"

During the summer of 1935, when Robert was twenty and

tending camp for Andy, he left Emmett on a Monday evening about seven o'clock with a truckload of provisions for the Long Valley headquarters sheep camp where his parents were stopping. He was never to arrive. The truck had turned over the grade about six miles from Hank Goul's camp on the Payette River, plunging downward for 100 feet into the rocky canyon, pinning the young man under the wreckage.

Robert was barely alive the next morning when the Gouls and their son, Cecil, driving to Smith's Ferry, noticed a truck track breaking the shoulder of the road. They stopped immediately and looked over the edge, saw the big truck which was bottom-up among the rough rocks. Hank Goul scrambled down and found Bob, whom he knew well, lying on top of the bottom of the truck bed and wedged in between metal crossbars. Bob was crushed and bleeding and nearing death. Hank got water from the river to press to the boy's parched lips, but he was too weak to swallow. Mrs. Goul was attempting to flag a passing car and Cecil had raced for the nearest telephone.

Soon a number of drivers had stopped and assisted Hank in removing Bob from the wreckage and carried him up the side of the canyon and placed him in the Goul car. In the meantime the parents had been reached and were on their way to their son.

Dr. O.F. Swindell had been called and left the Boise airport in a plane flown by Lionel Kay. About the same time the Goul car and the Littles were arriving at the little Cascade airstrip. Bob was met by a physician with the Civilian Conservation Corps and readied for the flight to Boise aboard a plane that had been arranged for by the Littles' close friend, Ben Rice, and other forestry service men. Bob King was the pilot.

The two planes passed in the air. The Littles flew with their son. An ambulance met them at the Boise airport and they rushed to the hospital. About 4:30 that afternoon Bob died from his injuries, including a skull fracture, severe bruises and exposure. He never regained consciousness.

It is conjectured that Bob may have turned out for another car and lost control of the heavy truck on the curve. No one knew.

In the custom of the Scots, funeral services were held at the family home, this time in the front yard with a large number of relatives and friends joining the family in paying tribute to Bob.

It was said that both Andy and Adis grieved terribly the loss of their son, and, at times, it seemed they couldn't overcome the grief. Andy was determined not to show his feelings, but Adis seemed to age several years overnight.

David Little

At commencement exercises at Moscow in May, 1989, David was presented an honorary Doctor of Natural Resources degree from the College of Agriculture. He had received his Bachelor's degree in Education which proved a fine accompaniment to his hands-on knowledge of the livestock industry as he acquired his own livestock and land operations. The citation accompanying the honorary degree listed outstanding services to his community, his state and to his university.

David, the last of Andy and Adis' children, was born January 31, 1918. His wife, Geraldine Laidlaw, was born on April 9, 1919. Their children and grandchildren are Jim, born August 27, 1943; his wife, Jan, born September 16, 1945; and their three daughters, Gretchen, born September 5, 1968; Rochelle, born May 17, 1972; and Dinah, born March 16, 1975.

Daughter Judy Woodie was born October 6, 1946, and her husband, Ron Woodie, was born May 2, 1942. Judy has two sons by a previous marriage. They are, David Judy, born July 23, 1965, and Steven Judy, born September 4, 1969. Brad Little was born February 15, 1954, and his wife, Teresa Soulen Little, born July 16, 1954. Their sons are Adam, born November 1, 1979, and David, born December 28, 1982.

It is with great affection in his voice that David still speaks of Claude Lewis and G.H. "Old Mud" Miller, who worked and cooked on the home ranch. "They darned near raised Drew and me. Mud always had a pot of savory beans on the stove and I can still remember the wonderful smell of those beans and his homemade white bread, lavishly spread with butter. I liked beans and bread and butter better than anything else when I was four. I'd scramble out of the house and run all the way to the cookhouse to eat Mud's beans."

This photo is of the youngest Little, David, while a student at the University of Idaho. Inset is his wife, Gerry Laidlaw Little, in the late 1980s.

Mud nicknamed David "Bean Eater," a name which he bore proudly for a long time. Both Mud and Claude Lewis took Drew and David under their wings and both boys enjoyed being with them. "Claude endeared himself to us by saying what good boys we were, while saying that Agnes and Jessie were 'brats'," David laughingly remembers.

At age ten, David rode his horse the twenty-three miles to the Butte Ranch. He started very early in the morning and hurried the horse right along. About mid-morning he stopped and asked a fellow, "I'm heading for the Butte Ranch, do you think I'll make it before dark?" The laconic answer was, "At the rate you're going, you'll be there before noon."

On one of David's rides he was up on Squaw Butte, during a spring storm in the early thirties. Sheep had just been sheared on the Van Deusen, and a herder was taking them from there to the Butte. Caught in the deadly wind-driven rain and snow, there were 2000 frozen ewes scattered up and down the creeks. David and the herders trailed 2000 bum lambs back to the surviving ewes.

Mud Miller was more than a cook for Andy. He was also what is now called a trouble-shooter. The Van Deusens had 25,000 to 30,000 sheep and the Littles about 60,000 at the same time. A terrible jealousy arose between the Van Deusen and Little crews. After Andy bought the Van Deusen ranch, former employees there created much difficulty because of that jealousy. Andy sent his bachelor cook Mud, who was also a 'tough old sonovagun,' according to David, out to shape things up on the Van Deusen. He was always successful because he carried authority in his voice, and a .44–caliber pistol in his hip holster.

David recalls a Japanese cook who established somewhat of a record as a sheepherder's gourmet. Although Japanese, he gained the name "China Louie" from someone who knew only that he was an Oriental. He could make *sake* from the company rice and sugar and amazed the boys with his swimming prowess. "He could swim like a fish, and we all liked to go with him when he swam in the canal. He cooked at the Butte ranch and our home for several years. You had to be on the select list to be invited to one of his meals."

Andy also enjoyed the cooks and often ate at the cookhouse near the Little home that became a kind of headquarters for the ranches and the herders. Minnie Whipple often presided over the kitchen at the headquarters cookhouse. Her daughter, Edith, helped her mother. Edith married Ed Florence, also a Scot, who drove truck, delivering supplies to the ranches and sheep camps, and on occasion was a driver for Andy. Edith later married Willard Foreman.

Another fondly-remembered cook was Emma Rice, wife of Oscar, who ran the commissary at the Van Deusen. There were eighteen camptenders packing out of the Van Deusen at one time. They would pick up beans, rice, canned corn and peas, dried apples, apricots and prunes, coffee, etc. Bacon was a good staple because, if cured correctly, it would keep for a long time. There was another such storeroom at the Aikman and also at the McCann, although that was not used as much.

During the haying season at the Van Deusen, Oscar butchered every night. Emma had at least fifty men to cook for and she cooked two mutton a day. Under Andy's instructions, Oscar never butchered a hog until it weighed 300 pounds or more. There would be from 50 to 100 hogs butchered just to feed the camps. It was from these that David's mother built a reputation for the best headcheese in the entire Boise valley.

In later years, Jess Breshears lived next door to David. An old homesteader, Bud Twilegar, once asked Jess if he had any bacon. Jess said, "Yes." Bud said, "If you put half a slab of bacon in that culvert up there, you'll find a jug of wine." Jess went on to say, "I did and it was."

David recalled the labor difficulties that came in the early thirties as the Depression hit with full force. The Amalgamated Butchers and Meat Cutters Union organized and the shearers struck for a raise from six to eight cents a head. A shearing corral was burned to the ground at Jessie and Bob Naylor's outfit on the Aikman ranch. The tracks of the car leading to the corral matched those of a vehicle owned by the person suspected, but the case was not pursued. The Littles were told that they did not have enough hard evidence to convict.

"We hired people we trusted," David said, "and we kept close watch ourselves. I remember riding horseback and finding a guard standing at our gate. Sometimes we would ride thirty to forty miles in one day."

"Dad would go from place to place covering his property to see how things were going. First it was by horseback, later by buggy and still later by car," David said. Andy enjoyed visiting the ranches, but he felt he was accomplishing more when he was irrigating, mending fences, or burning weeds and sagebrush. Gerry said, "David is just like him in that regard."

"No grass can grow where sagebrush is," David explained, "so we carried on a continuing burning program. Every time we came to sagebrush on our land, we burned it. We never had a fire of any size, but burned the old snags and dead trees along with the sage. I remember riding all one night and using up an entire box of wooden matches, but didn't get over ten acres burned. Dad once sent me out in his 1929 Buick to burn the brush along Willow Creek."

David was also like his father in regard to being asked how many head of livestock he owned. Gerry told of David being unhappy with a minister who was a dinner guest and asked how many sheep David owned. "Well," David said, "asking a man how many sheep he has, is like asking him how much money he has in the bank." Gerry said, "Now that we have cattle, I'm afraid to ask the minister back for fear he will ask David how many cows he has."

An Idaho legislator for fourteen years and chairman of the Senate finance committee and co-chairman of the powerful Joint Committee on Appropriations for much of that time, David says he has the unusual distinction of never having moved more than one-quarter mile in his entire life. His home is very near the headquarters ranch.

He is now in partnership with, while in the process of turning operations over to his sons, Jim and Brad Little, and daughter, Judy Woodie,. All three own hundreds of head of cattle. They operate under the Little Cattle Company. They specialize in purebred Hereford stock and are considered among the best livestock operators in the state. In addition, Brad and Jim are administrators of

Jessie's estate, since she asked that her business be kept intact and active for fifteen years after her death.

David is progressive in his range management, which he considers is in its infancy. "We still have much to learn. My feeling is that the approaches we have taken in the past have led to more conflict than is necessary. While I have no problems with the Bureau of Land Management, I feel there are better ways for the multiple uses of public land resources. We need to put more practicality and less theory into resource management."

He is a man who puts his money where his mouth is, giving a section of land to the University of Idaho College of Agriculture for range management research and setting up an $80,000 foundation to promote that research which he is convinced will have significant long-range benefits for cattle, sheep, and forestry products.

David's feeling that range management is in its infancy is shared by son, Brad, who is optimistic about the future of the sheep industry. "It will likely be a short duration, high intensity business. The best range management will be for the flocks to graze in small areas, be on the range a shorter length of time, then get off and allow the range to rest. We can produce a totally finished product in less space.

"In Long Valley, for instance, there are deep soils with lots of moisture, where the sheep could graze two or three times a year. This is Mother Nature's way of grazing. The ungulates, antelope, deer and elk, buffalo, came and grazed a short time and move on. We can duplicate that now with the high intensity-short period grazing.

"With the farm flocks, lots of fences are put in and they are moved every few days, ranging on land from 20 to 200,000 acres."

Brad is chairman of the board of trustees of the Public Lands Foundation for Renewable Resources. He continues, "Out of the 1,250 sheep owners who are following the wool incentive programs only about 100 are using public lands and they are also large land owners in their own right. They also own about sixty percent of the sheep. I'm confident that there will be sheep on the public lands for years to come. The U.S. Forest Service is actually looking for sheep to use as a range management tool. They reduce the brush so that new trees can grow. The alternative is to use hand labor, which is very expensive, or chemicals, which has become extremely controversial. Grazing sheep is the solution.

"The Forest Service isn't alone in feeling this way. Boise Cascade Corporation wants every acre of their land grazed and fertilized by the sheep. They use them in managing their treelands, too. In Idaho, the meat packers tell us that we produce the best lean lamb there is. Nutritionally, Idaho lamb cannot be beat. The big sheep bands are gone, not for biological reasons, but for political reasons. The market will eventually come back.

"Sure, some of the owners take sheep to Arizona and California in the winter. But they get no grain that way. Our lambs are fed grain for twenty days in February before they go out onto the green grass."

David learned well many of the simple but important lessons from workers on the Little ranches. He recalled Alex Brooks, just one of the many blacksmiths hired by his father. "We had blacksmiths employed at all times. They repaired wagon tires that had worn out, or reset those that came off the wheels. They sharpened the plowshares, shaped horseshoes and repaired most of the machinery. I recall showing one of them a broken piece of farm machinery and asked if he could fix it. His answer was a direct 'It's made of iron, isn't it?' End of conversation. I picked it up the next day.

"Dad's crews knew that fenceposts all had to be set at the same height. So when old Jess Currier was running some fence across part of the Upper Bench ranch and he hit some hard ground, he just tacked the posts to the tight wire, cut off the tops on a level, and left the posts standing on top of the ground."

David recalls, "Dad came along to inspect the job and found chunks of posts lying around. He had the crew take out that half-mile of fence, dig into that hard ground and do it right."

It is Idaho's good fortune that the Little children and grandchildren learned well the lessons which father and grandfather Andrew James Bell Little taught. They have also become proficient in adapting to new ideas and methods in American agriculture. With the third generation growing rapidly, it is assured that there will always be Littles around with enough ambition, intelligence, and ingenuity to keep on forging ahead when the times are tough and others are leaving the land for what they perceive as an easier life in urban areas.

C H A P T E R   S E V E N T E E N

THE KING IS DEAD

THE YEARS ROLLED BY. SPRING AND LAMBING. SUMMER AND SHEARING. Autumn and shipping. Winter and repairing. The strong Scots heart that had worked so hard inside that hardy body began to fail. During the late 1930s and in early 1940, Andy had suffered a series of heart attacks.

One early morning in late November of 1940, Andy came out of the big house to see how "things lay." It was a cold day, a bitter wind, and a hint of snow. He was not feeling well again, but he hesitated to report this to Adis. She was strong, but she was aging, too, and each one of his attacks took its toll on her.

Andy had never been patient with illness. He simply ignored it and kept going. Several months earlier, while attending a meeting in the Owyhee Hotel, he suffered a severe heart attack. He was put to bed in a room there and insisted that he be taken home to Emmett, rather than to the hospital. In this case, his word was not heeded and he was taken to St. Luke's hospital in Boise, where he began to recuperate.

Adis and their sons and daughters decided it would be good for the two of them to join Docky and Agnes Bettis, who were wintering in Santa Barbara, California. It was while they were wintering there that he had another attack.

In the iron hospital bed, Andy now found breathing harder. He closed his eyes and it is not difficult to imagine that he saw a twenty-four year old Scots lad with his two Border Collies hiking along Willow Creek toward what was to become his home. He knew he was nearing home now.

Outside his door, doctors consulted with Mrs. Little and Agnes. Andy stirred and then lay still. The doctor rushed in and reached

This photo was taken from the oil portrait of Andrew Little which hung in the famous Saddle and Sirloin Club in the headquarters of the Union Stockyard of Chicago. The club was the meeting place for the most powerful stockmen and meat processors in America. Andy was chosen for the portrait because he was considered by his peers to be among America's great success stories in the livestock business. The club closed in 1977 after the Union stockyards closed. The portrait now hangs with the Saddle and Sirloin Club's collection in the Agricultural Hall of Fame in Louisville, Kentucky. Well-known portrait artist Othmer Hoffler did the painting.

for his hand. There was no pulse. Andy had died quietly. Adis said to her daughter-namesake, for Adis is the Scots name for Agnes, "We will go home now and take Dad with us. Let the others know."

Jessie, David, Drew, and Myrn drove from Emmett to meet Adis and the Bettises at the Spanish-style station overlooking the city of Boise. They had brought Andy back to the valley he had come to love in the state that he and Adis had a large part in building. Then they all waited at the back of the train for the casket to be removed and placed in a hearse to be taken to Emmett.

The last of his many journeys would take him back to the beautiful Emmett valley, the remains of a man who had more than fulfilled his dreams. All that he had done was now in the past, but not to be forgotten. Years later, long after Drew's own death, Myrn said of Drew, "He never did get over Andy's death."

The body of Andy was taken to the home ranch and it was said that "truckloads of flowers filled the home." Many bouquets and sprays carried the Scotch plaid ribbons of his native land. And many were the friends stopping in front of the hall fireplace where the body of Andy lay. They were taking a final look and paying respects to their old friend, neighbor, associate, and acquaintance. Just as he did not live alone, Andy did not leave alone.

The minister from the Presbyterian church which Adis had helped to organize and build conducted the service from the big and handsome home Andy had built for his family. He had said this home "would last forever," because of the strength that was built into it by a man who had an inner strength built into him. Burial was in the Riverside cemetery on the bench overlooking Emmett Valley and the hills beyond.

Pallbearers included longtime friends Boise Riggs, Roy Murray, and Ed Florence of Emmett; Donald MacPherson and Arthur Caine of Boise; and Ben Rice of Ogden, Utah. Rice had been the forester for the U.S. Forest Service on the Payette National Forest and headquartered in Emmett. Little sheep by the thousands roamed on and through the Payette for many years. Honorary pallbearers included: a row-crop farmer and friend from Parma, E.G. Johnson; Frank Connor of Chicago; Guy Mains of Boise; E.K. Hayes, pioneer Emmett resident; James Laidlaw of Boise, father of Geraldine

Laidlaw who would become Mrs. David Little; Clyde Bacon of Twin Falls; Roscoe Rich of Burley; Worth Lee of Mountain Home; E.J. Frawley and C.C. Anderson of Boise; M.M. "Milt" Rants of Emmett; and former Idaho Governor H.C. Baldridge of Parma.

The front page of the *Idaho Daily Statesman* on February 21, 1949 (the day following the death), with a large picture of Andy, carried the headline: IDAHO SHEEP KING DIES IN CALIFORNIA HOSPITAL. The sub-heading was *Andrew Little Built Livestock Empire After Purchasing First Band in 1894.*

The news story went on:

> Andrew Little of Emmett, Sheep King of Idaho and possibly of the United States, died Thursday at 7 p.m. at a hospital in Santa Barbara, Calif. Mr. Little, 70 years of age, suffered a heart attack two years ago but recovered and was active until last November, when he again became ill. He was taken to Santa Barbara on January 22 and remained there until his death. With him were Mrs. Little and a son and daughter-in-law, Mr. and Mrs. Lawrence Bettis of Gannett, Idaho.
>
> His career was that of a youth who knew and loved sheep, saw possibilities of raising them in Idaho and succeeded in building the largest single sheep business in the nation. At one time he owned over 100,000 sheep which he ranged from Boise Valley north to the Salmon River. At the time of his death he owned twenty-seven irrigated ranches with more than 6,000 acres in cultivation, and approximately 60,000 sheep.
>
> He was born in Moffat, Scotland, December 19, 1870. He came to Idaho in 1894 and walked the twenty-two miles from Caldwell to the ranch of the late Robert Aikman. At the time of his death he owned the Aikman ranch. He built a sheep empire. His first band of 1200 ewes was purchased in 1894. Then he acquired 40 acres of scriptland in 1895 and from that beginning he built, in 46 years, his sheep empire.
>
> At his peak in 1929 his sheep produced approximately one-million pounds of wool. The exact size of his holdings was never made public. "I don't talk about those things," he once observed to a newspaperman.

Along with this leading story, the *Statesman* had front-page items reporting that the Nazis were "enjoying" reading messages from the United States insulting Adolf Hitler; that the national income had hit an eleven year high of $73 billion; of Japanese troop movements (in little more than nine months hence the Japanese were to bomb Pearl Harbor, thrusting the United States into the South Pacific war); and an item that would have been roundly supported by Andy: United States Senators Henry Dworshak, Republican, and D. Worth Clark, Democrat, were urging the dismissal of a bill which would cause the deportation of Basques without visas from the states of Idaho, Nevada, and California. Andy's death was the biggest story of the day in Idaho, followed by the others.

Other news items on the death of Andy acclaimed him as, "One of the best-known livestock men in the nation and possibly the biggest individual sheepowner in the United States."

In a follow-up story, the *Statesman* said that it was in Andrew Little's ability to handle labor (the men who worked for him) that his great strength lay:

> He was exacting in his methods, kept his men busy twelve months out of the year, and after they became familiar with it, they liked his system and stayed with him for many years. Many men now in the Little outfits have served faithfully for more than 20 years and others from five to 20. He was described by his friends and business associates as broad-gauged, very systematic and humane.
>
> He had been signally honored by having his portrait painted and hung in the Saddle and Sirloin Club of Chicago, the only Idahoan and one of the few in the entire West to receive such recognition.
>
> In addition to his widow, two sons and two daughters, Andy was survived by one grandson, Harry, the son of Agnes and Docky Bettis.

Andy's good friend, S.W. McClure, wrote an article for the *National Wool Grower* magazine on March, 1941, telling of the death and life of Andy. Included in his writing were statements going even deeper into the type of personality and managerial abilities of Andy. McClure wrote:

> Although for many years Mr. Little owned more sheep than any other operator in the Northwest, his importance to Idaho was not measured by his sheep, land or other holdings. For 30 years he has been a leader in Idaho affairs. He had developed and perfected large properties in his section and knew their operations to the smallest details. He possessed a keen mind and was endowed with physical energy that was the marvel of all who knew him. His place in Idaho looms large. He was a developer and a builder whose work was never finished, and never would have been. He worked for the pure compelling interest he took in all his affairs. His charities were legion and known only to himself, unless discovered by accident, which many of them were. Those who had worked with or for him were always taken care of in adversity.
>
> When he was leaving for California a month ago, a friend who saw him off said, "Now, Andy, go on down there and forget about your sheep and business in Idaho." Andy replied, "I would as soon be dead as to forget them." That was his spirit. For him the flowers and orange blossoms and green hills of California meant nothing. Its large cities and towering buildings were not the tools with which he worked. His place was here in the Northwest, among its hills and forests and ranges. Here in his own country he leaves an empire built and fashioned by his own hands and mind. Had he been in the steel business, he would have been a Carnegie; had he been a railroad builder he would have been Jim Hill; had he been a military man, he would have been a Grant. Andrew Little, like the men here mentioned, was endowed with that "something" that America's developers all have possessed.

Although Andy was gone, his sheep continued to be of the best. In the same issue of the *National Wool Grower* with his obituary, was an item on the Denver Wool Show ending just two days before his death. The Reserve Champion fleece, fine grade, competition was won by the Andrew Little flock. In the class for fine wool, Andy's flocks took first and fifth prizes. And first prize in the low quarter-blood grade went to his sheep.

It could be that S.W. McClure had visited with one or more of a quartet of Andy's best friends who got together with his youngest son, David, several days after his death and visited about his successes and failures. Roscoe Rich, Clyde Bacon, Art Caine, and Alex Campbell, along with David Little, came to the summation that Andy's managerial abilities were of an amazing degree; that he was a visionary and knew when to buy property that would evaluate over the years.

Rich said, "If Andy had died in 1928, before the crash, he'd have been considered one of the best ranchers in the entire world, rather than just in the United States."

"Yes," Bacon added, "it depends a lot upon when a man dies as to how he is remembered."

Banker Alex Campbell said, "I remember when Andy was having so much financial trouble in 1937 and '38. The reason the bank didn't foreclose on his loan was that no one knew as much about ranching as he did and we figured we were in much better shape just leaving things as they were until he could work it out."

Andy Little's portrait hung in the famous Saddle and Sirloin Club. Situated in the Union Stockyards of Chicago, the club was a meeting place for the most powerful stockmen and meat processors in America. The club's gallery of oil portraits honored the contributors to the livestock industry, and included his portrait by Othmar Hoffler. Since the club closed in 1977, after the Union Stockyards were closed, that painting now hangs with the Saddle and Sirloin Club collection, in the Agricultural Hall of Fame in Louisville, Kentucky.

When he died, Andy willed everything to his two sons and two daughters, with a life estate in the home ranch to their mother. Under Idaho law, Adis automatically inherited one-half interest in the entire estate, so the sons and daughters each inherited one-eighth. Jessie, Drew and David later purchased the one-half from their mother. Agnes took her one-eighth and she and Docky sold the property she inherited to Walter Cranston and others. The children gave Adis the notes which were left and paid annually on them. A good businesswoman in her own right, she accumulated funds and did some investing.

Upon the death of their mother, Jessie, Drew and David inherited the notes they had given her. Agnes Bettis took one-eighth of that estate. This included several ranches, including the ones at Norwood, Enrick, Browner, and Workman. The latter three have since been sold by Agnes' son, Harry Bettis, who has retained the Norwood ranch as his home place. This would have pleased Harry's mother who was keen to keep at least one of the ranches owned by her father, and the one preferred was the Norwood. Later, Harry also purchased the Grover Miller ranch in the area.

David gift-deeded three acres of the Haw Creek ranch, which he inherited and is now run by his daughter, Judy, and her husband, Ron Woodie, to Elmer Bowman, who had been a faithful and hard-working foreman. Elmer had always wanted to buy a small lot on the Haw where he wanted to build. Elmer maintains western ways and expressions of speech. A visitor one day admired his two Border Collies which were helping him herd a band of cattle to the feedlot for branding. Elmer grinned, nodded his head toward one and said, "This one here is part 'kyotee'."

Jessie's inheritance included various lands up and down the Big Willow Creek. As David has done, Jessie gifted acres of land to various employees who could then build their homes. Neither talked about these generosities, but when heard about through other sources, would confirm that they had done so.

Board for board, the old Van Deusen ranchhouse, where so many events in the lives of the Littles took place, was finally torn down. David moved a smaller house onto the ranch for the headquarters there. Bullard and Johnson were the original owners of the ranch, before Andy purchased it from Van Deusen. Horses and mules with the JB brand were still roaming the hillsides when the purchase was made.

The Butte ranch was listed as Drew's property and is now managed by his and Myrn's daughter, Agnes Little Brailsford. Myrn also had the Bissell Creek ranch in a beautiful setting off Squaw Butte. The area was framed with the Bissell Creek hills on the west side and the Butte Hills on the east.

Reprise

It grows close on, as westerners say, to fifty years since the death of Andrew James Bell Little. Very few of the big sheep spreads, and many of the cattle ranches, are gone. On occasion, and usually at Eastertime, the meat sections of America's grocery stores carry legs of lamb from New Zealand and Australia, and rarely from Idaho. Yet the name of Idaho's largest sheep rancher comes up often in conversations. No one could employ 600 men at one time as successfully as did Andy and not be remembered by most of them. Or by their children and grandchildren who have heard many stories about Idaho's Sheep King.

Andy's prominence in national and state livestock and agricultural associations and the expanse of his activities made him friends in every state.

Many of today's ranchers have received college and university degrees in the various fields of agriculture and still talk of the productive fashion in which Andy operated his twenty-seven irrigated ranches through well-planned crop rotation, plus fertilizer from the sheep which fed on the crops making each operation a self-sustaining "factory."

Ranchers speak mainly of how Andy's ranches raised the feed crops, mostly hay and grain, to feed the flocks when they were off the range during the winter months, and how they also had gardens and fruit trees for home and ranch consumption. Each ranch with its own equipment and horses negated any reason for moving from ranch to ranch for the many jobs to be done. Supplies for the ranches as well as for the sheep were purchased at wholesale and distributed from the commissary on the Main street of Emmett, where the office for the entire operation was also located.

Everyone seems to agree that Andy was born to be a sheepman. He was a sheepman who was always dealing in the future, concerned with improving the strain of his sheep and horses, the abilities of his ranches to flourish. That concern represented an involvement in something larger than himself, and is today seen in the activities of his children, their children and grandchildren. Andy and Adis live on.

An oft-quoted epigram has it that in America families go "from shirtsleeves to shirtsleeves in three generations." The type of apparel used to be quoted as being "overalls," but since overalls became blue jeans, worn by everyone from laborer to the wealthiest of the socialites, "shirtsleeves" became the operative word. The rationale is that the first working generation makes the money. The second generation squanders it, and the third generation has to start all over. As we come to the end of this story on Andy Little, we agree with the late U.S. Senator Len Jordan that, "Andy was a strong sire."

We now know that he had an unusually strong mate in Adis and that in addition to the splendid building of sheep bands, camps, ranches and homes, he trained herders, tenders, bosses, as well as sons and daughters. Brad Little may very well joke with his father and say, "Forget about me, Dad, when you are writing your will, when you get down to that rusty old scythe." But he has not forgotten the work lessons he learned from his Dad. They have been passed on to Brad, who is now passing those same lessons on to his young sons, Adam and David. Judy is doing the same with her children as is Jim with his. The Sheep King will not be forgotten.

THE LITTLE FAMILY TREE

- Andrew Little
  Married 1867
  Janet Dalgleish
  - ANDREW JAMES BELL LITTLE
    Married Agnes Sproat 1903
    - Agnes McMillan Little
      Married Laurence Moore Bettis
      - Harry Little Bettis
        Married Carol MacGregor
        - Laura Bettis
        - Catherine Bettis
        - Janelle Bettis
    - Jessie Little
      Married Robert Naylor
    - Andrew "Drew" Little
      Married Myrn Henley
      - Myrn Jean Little
        Married Glen Gosse
      - Agnes L. Little
        Married William Brailsford
      - Andrew H. Little
        Married Christine Breshears
    - Robert James Little
      (1914-1935)
    - David Little
      Married Geraldine Laidlaw
      - James A. Little
        Married Jan Debolt
        - Gretchen Little
        - Rochelle Little
        - Dinah Little
      - Judith Ann Little
        Married Ron Woodie
        - David Judy
        - Steven Judy
      - Bradley J. Little
        Married Teresa Soulen
        - Adam Little
        - David Little